Women, Microfin
the State in Neo-li

This book discusses women-oriented microfinance i
India and their articulation vis-à-vis state developmenta
contemporary neo-liberal capitalism. It examines how thes
tives encourage economically disadvantaged rural women to
claims upon state-provided microcredit and connect with mult
state institutions and agencies, thereby reshaping their gendere
identities. The author shows how Self-Help Group (SHG)-based microfinance institutions mobilise agency and create channels of empowerment for women as well as making them responsible for alleviating poverty for themselves and their families. The book also brings out the importance of factoring in women's dissenting voices when they negotiate developmental projects at the grassroots level.

Rich in empirical data, this volume will be useful to scholars and researchers of development studies, gender studies, economics, especially microeconomics, politics, public policy and governance.

K. Kalpana is Assistant Professor in the Department of Humanities and Social Sciences, Indian Institute of Technology (IIT) Madras, India. Her research interests include gender, poverty, women's labour and microcredit. She has extensive experience in organising rural women's self-help groups and leading community health initiatives in Tamil Nadu. In 2013, she received the Young Faculty Recognition Award from IIT Madras for excellence in teaching and research. She is currently a National Executive Committee member of the Indian Association of Women's Studies (IAWS).

Contents

Tables

Preface

This book is about India's women-oriented microfinance and its articulation vis-à-vis state developmentalism and global capitalism in its current neo-liberal phase. Perhaps the best-known development intervention in the world today, microfinance has been celebrated as an instrument to alleviate poverty and empower women, the sought-after participants of microfinance projects worldwide. The United Nations declaration of the year 2005 as the International Year of Microcredit and the award of the Nobel Peace Prize for 2006 to Muhammad Yunus and the Grameen Bank of Bangladesh reflect the entrenchment of microfinance in the world of international development. The global rise of microfinance has been accompanied by great urgency on the part of microfinance lenders (whether commercial banks or microfinance institutions) to capture markets for microfinance services that are seen as lying untapped at the 'bottom of the pyramid'. Once regarded as asset-less portfolio risks to banks, there has been a dramatic re-visioning of the poor as markets of diligent savers and disciplined borrowers of micro-loans. The perception of the poor as nascent markets is the starting point of this book, while the imperative to constitute them as fully efficient market actors informs its central concerns.

Powerful commercial and governmental actors are invested in the poor acquiring certain subjectivities, capacities and skills, in being, for instance, resource-optimising entrepreneurs who manage a range of income-generating activities that contribute to the survival of their households. Given this backdrop, the key questions this book asks are the following: How does the Indian state use microfinance to inculcate entrepreneurial subjectivities on the part of women from economically marginalised households and communities? How are poor women responsibilised for the 'self-care' of themselves, their households and communities in an emergent neoliberal India? How do the women, in turn, experience and negotiate the entrepreneurial impulse of state-mediated microfinance initiatives? How do they respond to microfinance projects that make available low-cost credit from public sector banks and expect that the women earn their 'right' to it by fashioning themselves as creditworthy and market-worthy actors in particular ways?

My interest in microfinance was kindled when I started working in October 1997 with women's microfinance self-help groups (SHGs) in Tamil Nadu. SHGs are informal grassroots groups that save small amounts of cash, make loans to group members and seek bank loans through linkage schemes promoted by the Indian state since the early 1990s. I was drawn to the organisation that I worked with primarily because it envisioned SHGs as a way to create self-sustaining organisations that mobilise rural women towards gender-transformative change. The same year (1997), a global Microcredit Summit held in Washington, D.C., resolved to reach microcredit to the women members of a hundred million of the world's poorest households by the year 2005 so that they may set up micro-enterprises. Evidently, many societal actors were turning to microfinance for various reasons, motivated by diverse impulses.

In 2002, when I began my doctoral research on microfinance in India, the Grameen Bank of Bangladesh announced the inauguration of Grameen-II. In doing so, it sought to respond to research studies that critiqued the monopoly control by the bank headquarters of the terms of savings and loans offered to poor women, the women's inability to negotiate any of these and the propensity of microfinance lenders (both the Grameen Bank and others modelled on it) to place their own institutional interests above those of the poor borrowers they served. Not surprisingly then, the alternative model of microfinance delivery to the poor that the SHGs embodied shaped my enquiry, as I began to study and write about SHGs. Being owned, managed and controlled by the end users of microfinance, the SHGs appeared to permit their members, the women of rural poor households, to take decisions and act in a relatively decentralised manner. On the other hand, decentralised decision-making also meant that class, caste and gender-based social power hierarchies could and did (as I found) mediate the functioning of SHGs as grassroots financial entities.

As important as the social context is the institutional setting that shapes the particular forms that a development intervention takes.

The SHGs had brought women into direct interfaces with nationalised banks, the rural development apparatus of the Indian state at district, sub-district and village levels and a host of other governmental actors, paving the way for claims-making by the women vis-à-vis state actors. At the same time, it was evident that the grassroots collectives of women had to sustain highly unequal 'partnerships' with more powerful institutions in their quest for state-mediated resources. While my writing over the years on SHG-based microfinance has reflected these concerns and issues, this book ties them together and brings them into conversation with each other. What does it mean for the women members of SHGs that the state is an institutional actor of significance in the terrain of microfinance in India? How do issues of caste, class and gender power relations among women play out in a user-managed microfinance programme? What other forms of mobilisation and claims-making (besides microcredit) do SHGs make possible for the women they bring together? I situate these and other related questions this book raises in the light of the intertwining of neo-liberalism and development policymaking since the 1990s and the particular trajectories that neo-liberalism has taken in India.

This book draws, in part, on the primary research in rural Tamil Nadu that I carried out as part of my doctoral research undertaken at the Madras Institute of Development Studies (MIDS), Chennai. I gratefully acknowledge the financial support provided by the Jawaharlal Nehru Scholarship for Doctoral Studies (for 2004–5) offered by the Jawaharlal Nehru Memorial Fund and the Malcolm and Elizabeth Adiseshiah Doctoral Fellowship (for 2006) offered by the MIDS. I thank Prof. K. Nagaraj (MIDS) and Prof. Mick Moore of the Institute of Development Studies (IDS), United Kingdom, for having facilitated a visiting fellowship that enabled me to spend two months of research time at the IDS (March–April 2007). I have carried out fresh research for this book and written its many drafts while teaching at IIT Madras. I am deeply grateful for faculty research grants of IITM such as the New Faculty Seed Grant and the Cumulative Professional Development Assistance that enabled me to buy books, meet other research-related requirements and enabled the book-writing process.

Acknowledgements

I was introduced to SHGs through my work as activist-organiser of the Tamil Nadu Science Forum and the MALAR federation of SHGs in Kanyakumari district, a programme committed to building rural women's leadership capacities. Friends in the People's Science Movement whose life and work have been a source of inspiration are T. Sundararaman, Johnsily Bai, Thomas Franco and R. Ramanujam. During my PhD research, I was extremely fortunate to have as supervisor Prof. Padmini Swaminathan, who remains to this day a valuable mentor and dear friend. I am indebted to her for having pushed me to make serious efforts to publish my work and to state my research questions with clarity and lucidity, and for the unstinting support she extended through the ups and downs that punctuated the period of my doctoral studies.

The NGOs and the women's SHGs that have been part of my field study in Tamil Nadu remain unnamed so that I may protect the confidentiality of the information they shared with me. I wish to express my deepest gratitude to them for having generously shared their time and experiences with me. I salute the fighting spirit of the SHG leaders and members that I met in the course of my fieldwork, and I hope this book does some justice to the many stories of grit, resistance, subversion and perseverance they shared with me – narratives of their struggles to 'fit' state projects to the exigencies of their livelihoods and household circumstances. I have greatly benefited from invitations to present my work at conferences and seminars as well as critical feedback and enthusiastic support from those who have empathetically engaged with my research on SHGs and microfinance over the years. Here I thank Isabelle Guerin, Mick Moore, K. Nagaraj, Nithya Rao, John Harriss, Mangala Subramaniam, Uma Chakravarti, V. Geetha, Lakshmi Lingam, Ashwani

Saith, Tara Nair, Nalini Visvanathan, Judith Heyer, Andrew Wyatt and Carole Spary, among others.

I remain deeply grateful to IIT Madras and my colleagues in the Department of Humanities and Social Sciences for providing an environment that encouraged my academic work. I wish to place on record my sincere thanks to the publishing committee at Routledge and the anonymous reviewer of this book for their insightful comments and suggestions that helped me fine-tune and greatly strengthen the work. I also thank V. Geetha for her very useful suggestions on how I might make the Introduction more readable. Over the last several years of my life, many friendships, new and old, have sustained my spirits and helped me come to terms with my mother's illness and my role as caregiver in her life. I express deep love and gratitude to Suchi, Ajantha, Chandru, Bharathi, Geetha, Revathi, Nithya, Srilatha and Swarnalatha. My husband Balaji has always been a rock to lean on. I thank him for his love and his presence in my life and for putting up with the many ways in which I exasperate him! My father Karunakaran's pride in me has kept me going, and his patient and tender care of my mother has freed my time and energies for writing and research. I owe him much. My mother's passionate engagement in political and public life has profoundly shaped my world view over the years and made me what I am. I know she would have been proud of this book and would have read every page of it, if she could. This book is a very small tribute to my mother, Mythily Sivaraman, and the extraordinary life she has lived.

Abbreviations

AIADMK	All India Anna Dravida Munnetra Kazhagam
AIDWA	All India Democratic Women's Association
APDPIP	Andhra Pradesh District Poverty Initiatives Project
APMAS	Andhra Pradesh Mahila Abhivruddhi Samiti
APRPRP	Andhra Pradesh Rural Poverty Reduction Project
BDO	Block Development Office
BRLP	Bihar Rural Livelihoods Project
CGAP	Consultative Group to Assist the Poorest
CMLF	Community Managed Loan Funds
DMK	Dravida Munnetra Kazhagam
DRDA	District Rural Development Agency
DWCRA	Development of Women and Children in Rural Areas
GOI	Government of India
GOTN	Government of Tamil Nadu
ICDS	Integrated Child Development Services
IFAD	International Fund for Agricultural Development
IKP	Indira Kranthi Patham
IMF	International Monetary Fund
IMY	Indira Mahila Yojana
INGO	international non-governmental organisation
IRDP	Integrated Rural Development Programme
JLG	Joint Liability Group
MaThi	Mahalir Thittam
MFI	microfinance institution
MORD	Ministry of Rural Development
NABARD	National Bank for Agriculture and Rural Development
NBFC	non-banking financial company
NRLM	National Rural Livelihoods Mission

OBC	other backward classes
PLF	Panchayat-Level Federation
PVP	Pudhu Vaazhvu Project
RBI	Reserve Bank of India
RMK	Rashtriya Mahila Kosh
RWO	rural welfare officer
SAP	structural adjustment programme
SC	scheduled caste
SERP	Society for Elimination of Rural Poverty
SGSY	SwarnJayanti Gram Swarozgar Yojana
SHG	self-help group
SIDBI	Small Industries Development Bank of India
SRLM	State Rural Livelihoods Mission
ST	scheduled tribe
TASMAC	Tamil Nadu State Marketing Corporation Limited
TDP	Telugu Desam Party
TNCDW	Tamil Nadu Corporation for Development of Women Ltd
TRIPTI	Targeted Rural Interventions for Poverty Termination and Infrastructure
UN	United Nations
VPRC	Village Poverty Reduction Committee
WDR	World Development Report

Introduction

The paradox of SHG-banking

Microfinance and neo-liberal governmentalities

'Your victory is mine and I hope you will treat my success as yours,' thundered Dr J. Jayalalithaa, the then chief minister of the South Indian state of Tamil Nadu and the head of the All India Anna Dravida Munnetra Kazhagam (AIADMK) during a meeting in Chennai, the state capital, on 26 August 2005 (*The Hindu* 2005). She was addressing a state-level meeting of the women members of self-help groups (SHGs) or microcredit-centred groups functioning under the aegis of the state government's official scheme for SHG promotion, the *Mahalir Thittam* scheme. SHGs are residence-based groups that save and lend small amounts of cash to peer group members and apply for bank credit through SHG-targeted lending schemes that have grown in India since the early 1990s. Dr J. Jayalalithaa's speech exemplifies her dramatic personification of the visible successes of the SHG phenomenon in the state of Tamil Nadu. Her attempt to seek political capital from the state government's promotion of Mahalir Thittam may be understood in terms of the en masse participation of women from low-income and land-poor households in the SHGs that have emerged as a pro-poor, pro-women development intervention that no government (state or central) in India can ignore with impunity today.

In India, the steadily rising incorporation of women within economic development-related planning and policy implementation has come full circle in recent times, dramatically reversing their former exclusion (1950s to the end of the 1970s) from statist developmental projects. While the recognition of women as economic beings by policy planners found place, for the first time, in the document of the Sixth Five-Year Plan (1980–85), India's principal programme for promoting the self-employment-oriented economic activities of the poor targeted 40% of its financial assistance to women from households below the official poverty line by the turn of the century (*RBI* 2011a). Arguably, the most visible mainstreaming of women within economic development–related interventions has taken place through the SHG phenomenon. By the end of March 2014, over 7.43 million SHGs (of which 84% were women's SHGs) maintained savings worth nearly Rs 99 billion with the banking sector in India. Of these SHGs, over 4.2 million SHGs (of which 81% were women's groups) had borrowed loans outstanding from banks worth Rs 429 billion through subsidised and non-subsidised schemes (NABARD 2014). The SHG phenomenon has been described by the National Bank for Agriculture and Rural Development (NABARD), the prime institution promoting agriculture and rural financing in India, as the world's largest microcredit initiative.

Through the institutional mediation of SHGs, women of working poor households and communities are directly interfacing with state institutions (including banks and the rural development administration), seeking to realise entitlements to valued developmental resources perhaps in larger numbers than ever before in post-independence India. If women are making claims upon state-mediated resources, it appears that the Indian state, for its part, expects much from the SHGs and their women members. Indeed, many hopes ride on the back of the SHG phenomenon. As India hurtles towards neo-liberal globalisation, it is hoped that the SHGs will impart a pro-poor character to India's experience of market-oriented reforms by addressing concerns of 'inclusive growth' and institutionalising the participation of the poor in processes of economic growth. These expectations are reflected, for instance, in a special lecture delivered in June 2007 by Jairam Ramesh, the then minister for commerce and industry, who described women's SHGs as 'institutions of participation' that would take India along the path of 'glocalisation' so that economic growth is rendered 'broad-based', 'equitable' and 'sustainable' (*Outlook* 2007). Along similar lines, India's National Rural Livelihoods Mission (NRLM) envisions SHG networks as institutional 'platforms of the poor' that enable them to build up their human, financial and social resources and access rights, entitlements and livelihood opportunities (GOI n.d. 1).

In this book, I ask what it means for women of rural poor households to be wooed as the central actors of poverty-targeted development initiatives during the period that India has transited from a developmental to an emergent capitalist state (Vasavi and Kingfisher 2003) or a period marked by the hegemony of corporate capital alongside the ongoing dispossession of marginalised classes and communities through processes of primitive accumulation (Chatterjee 2008a). How are women's subjectivities and identities shaped and constituted in keeping with the imperatives of an emergent neo-liberal India via SHG-based microfinance, the Indian variant of the global microfinance/credit[1] phenomenon? A transnational development intervention, microfinance programmes encourage neighbourhood-based peer groups to make regular savings, rotate their micro-capital as loans among group members and draw upon or 'leverage' the resources of commercial banks and other formal financial institutions, ensuring thereby the 'financial inclusion' of low-income households and communities (Pagura and Kirsten 2006). Microfinance has come to be globally celebrated for attempting to address the twin developmental concerns of poverty alleviation (by financing small business initiatives and micro-enterprises of the poor) and female empowerment by extending micro-loans to the women of low-income households in the hope that their access to a valued resource might enhance their status vis-à-vis their male kin, besides increasing their autonomy (Mayoux 1998; Morduch 2000).

My personal entry into the world of Indian microfinance was through my work, which began in the mid- to late 1990s, as an activist-organiser of an NGO-promoted statewide federation of SHGs in the South Indian state of Tamil Nadu. When tracking microcredit stories in the Tamil and English media, I was struck by how any 'human interest' story about the struggles and economic achievements of 'women in poverty' usually reported the micro-successes of the women members of SHGs storming bank bastions, securing bank loans en masse at 'loan *melas*'[2] and using credit-financed small businesses to transform into 'micro-entrepreneurs'. My growing unease with these easy certitudes and uncomplicated narratives led to a more critical engagement with the SHG phenomenon in the 2000s, as part of my doctoral research. However, I soon came to realise that women's microfinance-centred SHGs had come to stay and that that they would only become more (not less) important to an India en route to market liberalisation. Likewise, the women members of the SHG federations I worked with resigned themselves to the inevitability of engaging state institutions in the pursuit of bank loans, investing formidable energies in this task.

Somewhat paradoxically, the emergence and growth of SHGs in the 1990s and the 2000s have meant that women's claims to state-mediated resources have been encouraged and endorsed by the highest echelons of policymaking in India during the era of neo-liberal economic reforms and financial liberalisation. As many scholars concur, this is an era that has witnessed the steady erosion of the policy agenda of 'social banking' (of the 1970s and the 1980s) and its commitment to financing 'weaker sections' of the population (Ramachandran and Swaminathan 2002). It would appear therefore that women of rural poor households are knocking on the doors of public sector banks and other governmental bureaucracies seeking to claim entitlements when the idea of state intervention in favour of financing the weaker sections has come under attack.

In this book, I tease out this apparent paradox by asking what the implications are for women to make claims upon state developmental resources, to seek and secure financial inclusion in the era of neo-liberal economic restructuring. In other words, if women are invited to forge links with commercial banks, I ask what they have *to do* and *to be* to earn their entitlement to bank credit in an emergent neo-liberal India. In raising this question, this book seeks to take forward an understanding of how women's subjectivities and citizenship are recast through newly emergent 'technologies of rule' (Rose 1999) that mobilise and foreground their agency in tackling household poverty and livelihood security, responsibilising women in poverty for the 'self-care' (Lemke 2001) of themselves and their families in India, post-structural adjustment programmes (SAPs).

The rationale for the book: making 'markets' of the poor

The intertwining of microfinance programmes with neo-liberal agendas of development policymaking constitutes the thematic backdrop of this book. Microfinance programmes have won powerful adherents and supporters that include international financial institutions (e.g. the World Bank and the International Monetary Fund [IMF]), the international development industry (including UN agencies), national governments, commercial banks and other for-profit lending institutions for having dramatically expanded the 'frontier of formal finance' by moving it 'down market' or towards 'small farmers, micro-entrepreneurs, small and medium enterprises, the very poor and those in remote areas' (Von Pischke 2003: 6–7).

In so doing, microfinance programmes are seen as contributing to 'rural financial deepening' or an expansion in financial transactions in rural areas, the outreach of a wide range of services to broader clienteles and the offer of new contract terms and conditions (Gonzalez-Vega 2003). The 'microfinance revolution' has been described by an influential votary of commercial microfinance as the 'large scale, *profitable* provision of microfinance services . . . by *sustainable* financial institutions to economically active poor people' (Robinson 2001: 10, emphasis mine). This 'revolution' may be understood in the light of what Immanuel Wallerstein (2004: 2) describes as capital's imperative to seek profit, to endlessly accumulate itself, in the process generating 'a need for constant technological change, a constant expansion of frontiers – geographical, psychological, intellectual, scientific'.

Novel transactional technologies that involve innovations in lending and repayment methodologies have set microfinance apart from an older generation of rural credit programmes. Some of these innovations include the peer pressure mechanisms inherent to group-based lending that deliver on-time repayment, the close-to-market rates of interest that many programmes charge and the significant reduction in the transaction costs incurred and efforts and labour expended by lending institutions in disbursing loans, monitoring loan use or inducing/enforcing loan repayment relative to individual-targeted lending; these costs are, in turn, displaced onto jointly liable peer groups of borrowers (Johnson and Rogaly 1997: 38–51; Wenner 1995). Formerly regarded as asset-less risks to bank portfolios, rural poor communities have come to be perceived, not just as 'bankable' and 'credit-worthy', but a vast *market* of savers and borrowers with immense potential and *consumers* of financial services (including micro-loans and insurance products) waiting to be tapped at the 'bottom of the pyramid' (Prahalad 2005). As a former chief executive officer of a prominent commercial bank in India put it, working with agencies such as specialised microfinance lenders or microfinance institutions (MFIs) is a strategy for the bank towards 'leveraging the rural economy' in order to 'break into the top league of global banks' (Knowledge@Wharton 2006).

The global ascendance of microfinance signals an enormous commercial and governmental investment in the quotidian disciplining and responsibilising of its programme participants, in keeping with the imperatives of capital accumulation. As is well known by now, this disciplining is gendered involving as it does women from land-poor and low-income households who are the overwhelming constituency of microfinance projects worldwide.[3] Given this investment in transforming the poor (and poor women in particular) into markets of prudent savers and disciplined borrowers of micro-loans, this book aims to explore how microfinance projects, in specific institutional and regional contexts, seek to train and equip women to operate efficiently in the new markets for microfinance opened up by peer group-based lending technologies.

What this book is about

In this book, I explore how rural women strive to constitute themselves as 'rational economic' actors through their participation in the SHGs populating the Indian microfinance landscape. Residence-based groups that range from 12 to 20 members each, SHGs encourage their members to make regular savings, which are rotated as intra-group loans to borrowers in need. Shortly after its formation, an SHG opens a bank account in a proximate commercial bank as a safe deposit for members' savings and as the first step in establishing a relationship with the formal banking sector. The group leaders, who are women selected from within the group, assume responsibility for maintaining group accounts, liaising with banks and other government departments.

SHGs are grassroots collectives that own the capital they generate and take collective decisions with respect to the terms of lending, interest rates, repayment duration and the disciplinary mechanisms that ensure loan repayment. These user-managed and member-owned SHGs vest control over the micro-capital they generate with their primary constituency – women of rural poor households, rather than an external agent. SHGs thus typify the 'promoter' model (Rutherford 2000) of microfinance that involves promoter agencies (development NGOs or others), who enable the poor through training and other support, to set up credit systems that are *owned, controlled and managed* by the poor. For these reasons, SHGs have been described as 'Community-Managed Loan Funds' (Murray and Rosenberg 2006) and as 'micro-banks' (Harper 2002a) or grassroots entities that function as financial organisations in their own right.

In an organisational context wherein the end users of microfinance own the capital they generate and self-manage their grassroots collectives, I aim to show how the 'self-regulating capacities' and 'self-steering mechanisms' (Miller and Rose 1990) of SHG members are shaped and directed so that the women emerge as rational and responsible savers and borrowers who choose optimal ways and means to accumulate and grow their micro-capital, rotate it in a risk-free manner, ensure/enforce disciplined repayment, efficiently manage their micro-banks and fashion themselves as female entrepreneurs striving for the commercial success of group-owned income-generation activities financed through central government sponsored anti-poverty schemes. The book explores in detail the precise mechanisms by which SHG-based microfinance serves as a governmental strategy to cultivate appropriate subjectivities of women savers and borrowers, the material consequences of this for the women concerned and the 'dissenting counter-conducts' engendered by the 'conduct of conduct' of women SHG members. In this book, I draw on the scholarship on neo-liberal rationalities of rule that exhort governed populations to ceaselessly work on themselves, to manifest an 'active citizenship' and 'capitalise the self' in ways by which 'each individual is enlisted as an ally of economic success' (Rose 1999: 162) in order to demonstrate how the gendered citizenship of women in poverty is being recast in India.

The innovative approach of the book derives from my understanding of SHG-based microfinance as an emergent regulatory technology of neo-liberal governmentality in India that strives to 'implant the ways of *calculating* and *managing* that will make economic actors think, reckon and behave as competitive, profit-seeking agents' (Rose 1999: 65, emphasis mine). This approach illuminates the processual dynamics by which SHGs inculcate the entrepreneurial subjectivities deemed necessary (by policymakers) for women of rural poor households to optimally manage productive resources (of micro-capital) in contexts of scarcity and poverty. Through this approach, I aim to show how SHG-based microfinance operates as part of newly emerging technologies of rule or 'technologies of freedom' that 'govern at a distance' (Miller and Rose 1990) by acting upon the 'autonomous' choices and actions of independent entities, seeking thereby to align their conduct with broader socio-political objectives.

If microfinance seeks to constitute the 'rational economic woman' (Rankin 2001) who embodies market rationalities, I ask how this transformation is both *wrought* and *contested* through SHG-based microfinance. I ask also if *all* women are equally able to constitute themselves as 'market-worthy' and 'credit-worthy' subjects, and in answering this, I show how the social relations of gender, caste and class shape the experience and meaning of SHG participation and access to microfinance for rural women. This book takes cognisance of how the central role of state institutions and personnel in the promotion and the financing of SHGs in India marks a departure from globally dominant microfinance paradigms that advocate a 'leading role' for the private sector in microfinance provision (CGAP 2004). I examine therefore the question of how the legacy of state developmental initiatives executed in the pre-SHGs era (such as credit-based self-employment schemes) shapes the financial linkages between public sector bureaucracies and poor women fostered as part of microfinance promotion in India.

This book addresses contemporary debates at the heart of microfinance and those that extend beyond it as well. In contextualising the emergence and meteoric rise of the SHG phenomenon in the past two decades in India, I engage debates on the 'situated' policy histories and 'path dependencies' (Harriss 2011) that have shaped the particular trajectories of neo-liberalism in India (Sharma 2010). I use the case of SHG-banking and the incorporation of SHGs within anti-poverty programmes to critically examine Partha Chatterjee's (2008a) contention that welfarist policies have endured and expanded since the 1990s in order to 'reverse the effects of primitive accumulation' and his interlocutors' counter-claim that the welfare state, far from extending itself, is in 'retreat' mode instead (Shah 2008). I discuss also the implications (for women) of the ubiquitous presence of state institutions in the SHG sector, addressing thereby a long-standing feminist interest in the question of how women's struggles 'in and against the state' (Rai 2008) play out in the terrain opened up by statist developmental projects in India and elsewhere. The book also offers glimpses of other claims upon the state (besides microcredit) advanced by the women members of SHGs. In doing this, I engage with the question that Corbridge *et al.* (2011) pose: what forms of politics and what forms of citizenship claims are open to different groups of the poor or the 'denizens' of 'political society' (Chatterjee 2004) in post-reform India?

In order to fully address the range of questions this book raises, I discuss and analyse key policy documents of NABARD and the Reserve Bank of India (RBI) that have shaped the broad contours of the SHG-centred microfinance terrain in India, besides drawing on primary field research that I conducted in select villages in the South Indian state of Tamil Nadu. I also draw upon existing writing on the SHG phenomenon from other Indian states in order to supplement my ethnographic fieldwork in Tamil Nadu and to provide a sense of how some of the dynamics that I discuss play out at an all-India level.

Theorising microfinance under neo-liberal capitalism: self-regulating markets and safety nets

> The poor themselves can create a poverty-free world. . . . Credit can create self-employment instantaneously. Why wait for others to create a job for you?
>
> (Yunus 2005)

Globally, microfinance-centred development interventions are perceived as instruments that help keep the peace between social classes by preventing the immiserisation of the world's poor. Mohammad Yunus, the celebrity patron of microfinance, and the bank that he founded, the Grameen Bank of Bangladesh, were jointly awarded the Nobel Peace Prize in 2006 since 'lasting peace cannot be achieved unless large population groups find ways in which to break out of poverty' and for demonstrating that 'microcredit is one such means' by which this is likely to happen (Nobelprize.org). As articulated by Yunus among others (reflected here in the quote at the start of this section), dominant microfinance imaginaries valorise entrepreneurial individuals as responsible agents of their own economic well-being who take the action required (such as initiating income-generating activities and small businesses) to end their economic backwardness. The re-visioning of the poor through microfinance discourses has taken place even as budget-constrained governments implementing neo-liberal economic reforms renege on welfarist commitments to provide access to social services and livelihood opportunities for economically marginalised citizenry (Mayoux 2002; Rankin 2001).

Analysts note that the massive expansion of microfinance-based development interventions occurred in the 1990s – a period marked by the articulation of a 'poverty agenda' by development actors such as the World Bank and the United Nations Development Program in response to the resurgence of poverty and income inequalities associated with neo-liberal economic restructuring projects initiated in the previous decade (Weber 2002). Microfinance was promoted (in several parts of Africa for instance) as the grassroots dimension or the human face of economic liberalisation policies and an ideal self-help strategy that would enable the poor to (use their micro-loans) to secure services such as education, health, water and sanitation in the wake of increased unemployment and the rising costs of basic amenities (Mayoux 2002).

Seeking to locate microcredit in the historical context of crisis management in capitalist societies towards the turn of the 20th century, Weber (2002) uses Karl Polanyi's (1957) thesis of the 'double movement' to argue that the neo-liberal policy reforms, which may be seen as representing the tendency of capitalism to dis-embed the economy from society by permitting the free market to self-regulate in the provision of public goods (the 'first movement'), have provoked popular resistance at local levels in several countries undergoing structural reforms (the 'dialectical counter-process' or the 'second movement'). In this context, the 'strategic embedding' (Weber 2002) of microcredit in the global political economy of poverty reduction serves a dual function. On the one hand, it advances the goals of the first movement (by extending trade in financial services at the grassroots), whereas on the other, it acts as a 'political safety net' by financing and promoting private entrepreneurship, thereby absorbing surplus labour in informal sectors and mitigating income insecurity. To Weber (2002), the case of microcredit is paradigmatic of certain policy initiatives associated with the Post-Washington Consensus that dampen and contain resistance at local levels to the unfettered operation of markets, thereby disciplining the politics of the second movement.

In a somewhat similar argument, Fernando (2006) points to the twin crises of capitalism that microfinance addresses, namely the crisis of *accumulation* or the barriers to the expansion of surplus value due to the rising costs of production and resources and that of *legitimation* or the social and political crises generated by the ongoing accumulation that limits capitalist expansion. While governmental policies that aim to resolve one crisis usually undermine the efficacy of the other, microfinance and its associated vocabularies of self-reliance and self-sufficiency provide legitimacy for the withdrawal of the state from development, even as they create conditions conducive for capitalist expansion. The compatibilities between microfinance-based development interventions and economies undergoing neo-liberal reform are further explored by Karides (2010), who argues that state welfare or social assistance to low-income populations in the Caribbean region has increasingly taken the form of support to petty market operations during the period of the SAPs. In effect, two historic and distinct strategies aiming to overcome the crisis of capitalism, namely governmental transfer to the poor and informal sector self-employment, have been fused into the single form of micro-enterprise development, perceived as a safety net under globalisation and vigorously promoted during the SAPs (ibid.).

While Weber (2002) and Karides (2010) underscore the relief that microfinance programmes offer to populations, impacted adversely by neo-liberal economic restructuring, others have argued that microfinance itself may be seen as a financial object capable of generating and sustaining forms of profit and capital accumulation (Aitken 2010). Aitken situates his discussion of microfinance in the organisational context of specialised financial services providers or MFIs that charge their borrowers interest rates that are high (so as to attract international investors) and, in effect, significantly higher than the rates at which other clientele borrow from the formal financial sector. While I broadly draw on these frameworks to understand the strategic embedding (Weber 2002) of microfinance in the gendered political economy of anti-poverty initiatives in India post-SAPs, I also take into account vibrant and ongoing debates on the question of state withdrawal in a post-colonial context or the abdication of the Indian state's responsibilities towards the welfare and survival needs of the poor (Chatterjee 2008a). In so doing, I foreground the specific policy contexts and institutional legacies that have shaped the contours of SHG-based microfinance in India.

Situating microfinance in India

> Why is the state running SHGs in India? This is not the business of the state. The state should be running banks and making them finance the poor.
>
> (A delegate speaking at a seminar on the 'Future of Microcredit' held at the World Social Forum, 16–21 January 2004, Mumbai)

Microcredit programmes for women in India have evolved in a policy context shaped by the legacy of social banking or the mobilisation of commercial banks in the cause of affirmative action, social engineering and wealth redistribution (Pulley 1989). As part of bank nationalisation in 1969, commercial banks were directed to finance weaker sections and establish branches in semi-urban and rural areas in order to extend banking services to unbanked sections of the population. However, despite the proliferation of bank branches in the rural countryside and the setting of targets for lending to designated priority groups, the banking sector fared poorly in financing the landless poor, the socially oppressed castes and women of rural poor households (Kabeer and Murthy 1996; Swaminathan 1991). Consequently, in the early 1990s, the central bank of the country, the RBI, and the NABARD initiated and promoted a direct linkage (non-subsidised) scheme, wherein women's SHGs were encouraged to seek and secure bank loans, in order to supplement their groups' loanable resources (*RBI* 2009: 2–4).

The NABARD-pioneered idea of linking residence-based peer groups comprising women of rural poor households to nationalised commercial banks has, therefore, emerged in response to dual realities – the impressive presence of bank branches in rural and small towns across the country and the simultaneous poor track record of banks in lending to the poor. Analysts of the Indian microfinance sector identify the presence of the public sector formal lending institutions, the nationalised commercial banks in particular, as a distinctive marker that sets apart the Indian experience of microfinance from that of several other developing countries, notably India's neighbour Bangladesh (Harper 2002a). 'Inclusive banking' initiatives apart, commercial banks were also required to make subsidy-bearing loans to SHGs as part of a central government sponsored anti-poverty scheme – the SwarnJayanti Gram Swarozgar Yojana (SGSY) introduced in April 1999 (*RBI* 2011a). The SGSY used the SHGs to deliver subsidy-bearing financial assistance targeted to disadvantaged population groups and prescribed particular end-uses for loans such as the initiation of small business or micro-enterprise activity.[4]

Besides financing SHGs through bank linkage and anti-poverty schemes, state institutions that include the rural development administration, public sector banks, diverse departments of state governments and state-promoted Women's Development Corporations vie with each other and with non-state actors (such as development NGOs) to form and promote groups. The presence of the state sector in SHG promotion is ubiquitous enough to convey the impression of trespassing on what some might see as the legitimate domain of civil society, accounting for the displeasure of some NGO activists at the domineering presence of state actors in the microfinance landscape in India.[5] The emergence of SHG-based microfinance as a state-promoted phenomenon in India and its anchoring to statist discourses of poverty alleviation and economic development signal a crucial point of departure from the globally dominant microfinance paradigm, backed by 'industry leaders' such as the Consultative Group to Assist the Poorest (CGAP)[6] and the World Bank. In keeping with the limited functions of the state vis-à-vis markets in neo-liberalism, the former is expected to create a facilitative legal, regulatory and policy environment that explicitly recognises the leading role of the private sector in microfinance provision and serves to 'embed microfinance within financial systems, with private and non-governmental actors taking the lead' (CGAP 2004; see also CGAP 2003: 9–10). In contrast to this, the Indian state has taken upon itself the responsibility of directing the emergence and growth of SHGs as a pan-Indian phenomenon in consonance with the inception of SHG-targeted banking schemes.

The questions that I raise and attempt to answer in this book take cognisance of the departure that the Indian SHG-based microfinance phenomenon represents. As I elaborate in the next section, unravelling the 'paradox' of SHG-banking is both the starting point and the thread that enables me to hold these questions together.

The paradox of SHG-banking: linking economic entitlements and entrepreneurial conduct

Significantly, the enthusiastic promotion of women-targeted microfinance programmes since the early 1990s has coincided with the Indian government's adoption of liberalisation policies consisting of the standard IMF/World Bank policy prescription of short-term stabilisation and medium and long-run structural adjustment measures. India has embraced economic liberalisation to the extent that, as Gupta and Sivaramakrishnan (2011) observe, the relationship between economy and state has been reformulated in wide-ranging ways, besides also transforming India's perception of itself and its place in the world system. In addition to reforms aiming at the international integration of the Indian economy through changes in taxation, trade barriers and investment, a spate of internal changes have facilitated the entry of private operators in core sectors that include health care, education, transport, telecommunications, sanitation and energy (ibid.).

Critical analysts observe that the decade of the 1990s was marked by the steady erosion of social banking, with the Indian state diluting in multiple ways its commitment to financing the credit requirements of backward regions and economically marginalised sections of the population, as a fallout of the financial and banking sector reforms that accompanied the macro-economic reforms (EPW Editorial 2000; Mujumdar 1999; Narayana 2000; Ramachandran and Swaminathan 2002; Shahjahan 1999).[7] And, therefore, it appears ironic that the highest echelons of decision-making in the formal credit sector (i.e. the RBI and NABARD) have opened up institutional spaces for women of poor households to forge links with nationalised banks during the era of financial liberalisation marked by the freeing of the social control of banks, as part of efforts to 'dis-embed the economy from social and political control' (Weber 2002). How might we make sense of the Indian state's proactive intervention to foster rural women's collectives and legitimise their claims to developmental resources despite the erosion of the social banking commitment to replace 'class banking' with 'mass banking'?

In this book, I situate the emergence and meteoric growth of SHG-banking in the 1990s and 2000s in the light of Partha Chatterjee's (2008a) contention that the vast majority of India's poor or its potentially 'dangerous classes' cannot, for moral and political reasons, be left utterly bereft of survival-oriented or welfarist measures during the period that corporate capital has gained hegemonic ascendance. Following from his early work arguing that the post-colonial Indian state derives its legitimacy by steering the programme of economic development and national regeneration, as opposed to the 'alien', 'extractive' colonial state (Chatterjee 1998), Partha Chatterjee (2008a: 62) argues that the ongoing primitive accumulation of capital dispossessing subaltern classes and communities in the 1990s and beyond warrants governmental policies that seek to 'reverse the effects of primitive accumulation' in the political/electoral context of a representative democracy. Endorsing Chatterjee (2008a), Corbridge *et al.* (2011: 4) and Harriss (2011: 128) argue that path dependencies and a strong state tradition in India mediate the trajectories of neo-liberalism in the post-SAPs era, tempering its effects and consequences for different sections of the population.

Gupta and Sharma (2006) likewise observe that the rise of neo-liberal regimes may not always signal the end of welfare, especially in post-colonial countries such as India that never had a strong social state to retreat from, unlike the advanced capitalist countries. They point out that neo-liberal policies and welfare programmes may coexist when the pressures of populist democratic politics necessitate proactive state interventions in favour of sections of the population excluded from the gains of market liberalisation. Problematising the universal welfare-dismantling effects supposedly produced by the advance of neo-liberalism on a global scale, Sharma (2010) draws on Aihwa Ong (2006) to argue that particular, situated policy histories and political projects in diverse country and regional contexts may be 'unevenly articulated' by neo-liberal technologies of governing. Taking my cue from this scholarship, I identify the policy histories and institutional legacies of 'social and developmental banking' in India as a crucial component of the path dependencies in the rural credit sector that are unevenly articulated (Ong 2006: 3) by a transnational development intervention such as microfinance. In the course of this book, I show how this uneven articulation is manifested in the *dual anchoring* of the SHG phenomenon to the (pre-liberalisation) agenda of making available the resources of nationalised banks to those historically denied access as well as the creation of self-regulating markets for microfinance via a grassroots-level 'disciplinary neo-liberalism' (Weber 2002).

While SHG-banking makes it possible for women from unbanked rural households and communities to lay claim to development resources earmarked for them by policies of the Indian state, I argue that this access nevertheless hinges on the women inculcating the appropriate subjectivities by constituting themselves as fiscally disciplined actors – prudent savers and responsible borrowers – in the village-level markets for microfinance that the SHGs have opened up. An SHG that had functioned for a minimum period of six months was eligible to seek a linkage loan provided it built 'financial discipline' and 'credit history' and displayed 'mature financial behaviour' through the rotation of the group's internally generated financial corpus. Rural women were expected to 'imbibe the essentials of financial intermediation' (NABARD 2006) and to provide manifest evidence of their 'creditworthiness' so that commercial banks may finance them through the direct linkage scheme. In order to secure financial assistance through the SGSY scheme, the women members of SHGs were required to display entrepreneurial agency by demonstrating willingness and capacity to initiate enterprise activity, besides cultivating proper financial intermediation skills (as in the case of the linkage scheme).

In terms of Weber's (2002) formulation then, we might understand SHG-based microfinance as advancing the goals of the first movement (Polanyi 1957) by creating and deepening self-regulating markets for microfinance at village levels and inculcating among rural women the skills and capacities required to efficiently inhabit these market spaces. Simultaneously, it seeks to create a political 'safety net' (Karides 2010; Weber 2002) for households in poverty belonging to the potentially dangerous classes (Chatterjee 2008a) through the provision of low-cost bank credit for consumption purposes (via the linkage scheme) and subsidy-bearing credit for financing income-generating activities intended to raise households above the poverty line (via the SGSY scheme). Unravelling the paradox of rural poor women pressing their claims upon public sector banks and other government bureaucracies during the era of neo-liberal economic restructuring requires, therefore, that we centre-stage the processes by which the women's access to economic entitlements is made contingent on their re-fashioning as development subjects who acquire entrepreneurial subjectivities and contribute to rural 'financial deepening' at the grassroots. It requires that we understand how SHG-based microfinance in India strives to make citizenship conditional upon conduct (Rose 1999).

I also make sense of the paradox of banking *with women* in the neo-liberal era in terms of the global and national ascendance of 'efficiency' concerns that have informed gender and development discourses in the last two decades of the 20th century. I show that SHG-banking and the official efforts to mainstream women in anti-poverty programmes (such as the SGSY) resonate with the efficiency paradigm that envisions women as a valuable and (hitherto) underutilised *resource* for development (Razavi 1997; Razavi and Miller 1995) and that this is reflected in the official policy documents of RBI and NABARD which constitute gendered citizenship in consonance with the commercial interests of the banking sector in the post-reforms era. I show therefore that it is hardly incidental that women are the sought-after constituency of microfinance programmes in India.

Microfinance and neo-liberal governmentalities: 'capitalising the self'

Central to this book is Foucault's understanding of government as a way of acting on the actions of individuals, so as to shape, guide, modify or affect the way they conduct themselves; as endeavours to urge and educate one to bridle one's passions, control one's instincts and govern oneself; and as a form of rule wherein political authorities seek to understand what mobilises the entities to be governed and to act upon these forces in order to shape actions, processes and outcomes in desired directions (Rose 1999: 3–4). The book draws upon conceptualisations of neo-liberalism as a positive technique of government that spawns new regulatory technologies whereby the state acts upon diverse and multiple social forces and entities (the financing banks, promoter NGOs and the SHGs as grassroots collectives in this case), *autonomising* and *responsibilising* these, so that they may, in turn, regulate and align the conduct of governed populations with broader socio-political objectives (Burchell 1996; Rose 1999: 174). In seeking to constitute rural women as worthy development subjects who optimally manage productive resources in contexts of scarcity and poverty, SHG-based microfinance may be regarded as one of many technologies of freedom that proliferate in neo-liberal forms of rule and govern at a distance by utilising the freedoms of relatively independent entities and acting on their autonomous choices, decisions and actions (Rose 2000: 323–324).

Constituting citizens as active and responsible entities, neo-liberal rationalities of rule offer them involvement in action to resolve issues formerly regarded as the province of authorised governmental agencies (Burchell 1996). In so doing, they autonomise citizens in ways by which the state may divest itself of direct responsibility for and control over their actions and calculations (Rose and Miller 1992). In recent times (both in India and elsewhere), there has been a proliferation of diverse modes of public provisioning, in the sectors of public health, water supply, sanitation, irrigation and so on, that actively solicit and rely on structured forms of 'user participation' at local levels (Joshi and Moore 2004).[8] Microfinance programmes entail user participation in the delivery of financial and banking services in which such participation serves to transfer the costs and efforts of monitoring the actions and financial decision-making of numerous dispersed savers and borrowers onto 'autonomised' and 'responsibilised' community-based peer groups, contributing thereby to the commercial viability of these programmes and the institutional viability of lending agencies.

If the *form* of government under neo-liberalism increasingly relies on 'shaping the power and wills of autonomous entities' (Rose 1996: 56), the *tasks* of government are oriented towards establishing the market as the organising principle underlying state and society and basing decision-making processes in all spheres of life on a market criteria or an assessment of relative costs and benefits (Burchell 1996; Lemke 2001). The 'free, entrepreneurial and competitive conduct of economic-rational individuals' is to be arranged by government (Burchell 1996: 23–24), which must strive to construct a free market by 'establish(ing) the conditions under which the "laws of supply and demand" can make themselves real, to implant the ways of calculating and managing that will make economic actors think, reckon and behave as competitive, profit-seeking agents' (Rose 1999: 65). All social actors are required to adopt 'models of action that are based on the idea of an (economic) enterprise' (Burchell 1996: 27). They are required to conduct their own lives as a kind of enterprise through a constant economic *capitalisation of the self* that involves investing in the 'management, presentation, promotion and enhancement of their own economic capital as a capacity of their selves and as a life-long project' (Rose 1999: 161–164).

Elaborating on the unceasing activity that 'capitalisation of the self' entails and the active citizenship it demands, Rose (1999: 162) describes an emergent government of unemployment in advanced capitalist economies undergoing neo-liberal restructuring. He argues that the re-casting of the unemployed as 'job-seekers' implies that they are expected to ceaselessly train, skill and re-skill, to improve their employability and to incessantly engage in the active search for employment, leading both to personal employment and to macro-economic health. In analogous fashion, I posit that the representation of the poor as the 'financially excluded' requires that they organise themselves into small peer groups, learn and practice responsibility to one's self and one's peer group members, acquire skills in 'financial intermediation', ceaselessly work on and build their capital generation and loan repayment capacities and improve their perceived creditworthiness in order to secure financial linkages with formal financial institutions. Microfinance programmes enable the financially excluded to capitalise the self so that they may enjoy financial inclusion, even as their responsible fiscal behaviour contributes to the financial health of MFIs, microfinance NGOs and commercial banks in ways by which 'each individual is solicited as a potential ally of economic success' (Rose 1999: 162).

Becoming micro-banks: transformations wrought and contested

In this book, I aim to capture the processual dynamics by which this transformation of the self is both wrought and contested. I show how SHGs come to be autonomised and constituted as micro-banks (Harper 2002a) when their women members capitalise the self by fashioning themselves as prudent savers who assiduously generate micro-capital, risk-averse investors (each loan sanctioned to a group member may be regarded as an investment of group capital), disciplined borrowers, vigilant enforcers of disciplined repayment, effective monitors of group accounting practices and efficient managers of micro-banks. As the regulatory technology of an emergent neo-liberal governmentality in India that seeks to 'make economic actors think, reckon and behave as competitive, profit-seeking agents', I argue that SHG-based microfinance deploys the techniques of accountability (both self and peer) and practices of evaluation (self and peer) to steer women politically at a distance, thus making for a regulated autonomy (Rose 1996).[9]

I show how the weekly neighbourhood-based SHG meetings are 'contact points' between techniques of discipline and technologies of the self or spaces of interaction marked by 'complementarity and conflicts between techniques which assure coercion and processes through which the self is constructed or modified by himself' (Foucault 1993 in Lemke 2001: 204). As Cruikshank (1999: 21) observes, the subject, in the Foucaultian sense, is one who is simultaneously under the control of another and the author of her own actions. The agents who seek to shape, guide, mould and 'conduct the conduct' of women savers and borrowers so that they acquire the appropriate capacities and self-identities are the entities who promote SHGs. Promoter organisations are required to provide social intermediation services that include the formation of groups, supervision, training in accounts maintenance, periodic financial auditing and troubleshooting as well as facilitating bank linkages of the SHGs they promote (Harper 2002a). In addition to promoter agencies, I include the commercial banks that finance SHGs and the rural development bureaucracy (the District Rural Development Agency at district levels and the Block Development Office [BDO] at sub-district levels) that is charged with implementing anti-poverty schemes targeted at women's SHGs, as the principal actors who regulate and direct the financial decision-making of rural women and their emergence as micro-entrepreneurs.

In this book, I am concerned with showing how the policy idea of SHG-banking or financial intermediation through all-women's grassroots collectives has come to acquire a hegemonic sway in the rural development and banking sector in India. In order to do so, I draw upon David Mosse's (2004) seminal work on how development projects sustain themselves as coherent policy ideas or 'authoritative interpretations' by having their central goals *translated* in ways that make possible the recruitment of a range of supporting actors who come to be invested in the interpretive premises of the project. The book illustrates the processes of 'translation' (Miller and Rose 1990; Mosse 2004) that align the key objectives or policy goals of the 'centres of authority', namely the RBI, NABARD and the Ministry of Rural Development, with the personal projects, 'the aspirations, judgements and ambitions' (Rose 1999: 48) of prominent actors in the world of SHG-based microfinance, including commercial banks, the rural development administration and development NGOs.

While I use the policy documents of RBI and NABARD to show how the 'centres of calculation' govern at a distance by autonomising and responsibilising women's SHGs towards certain ends, I also draw upon ethnographic field study to demonstrate that the central goals of SHG-financing (through both subsidy and direct linkage schemes) are constantly translated into the multiple, conflicting and diverse 'practical interests' (Mosse 2004) of state and non-state personnel and project implementers at lower levels who engage in direct interfaces with the SHGs and their members. These include branch-level bankers, BDO staffers and the employees of promoter NGOs. I show how these actors seek to 'enterprise' themselves in ways that suggest that their compulsions, priorities and needs are not always perfectly aligned with those prescribed by the highest levels of policymakers.

Microfinance projects may envisage and seek to constitute entrepreneurial, responsibilised subjects who act in ways consistent with the neo-liberal agendas of establishing and deepening self-regulating markets at grassroots levels. And yet, as has been well established, and especially by feminist research that maps the engagement of women with/in development organisations and interventions, development projects do not completely manage or manipulate the behaviour and life worlds of their subjects who may appropriate instrumentalist policy packages to serve ends unanticipated by policy planners (Jackson 1997). Bringing to bear the analytical lens of governmentality to their ethnographic research on microfinance in diverse settings, Rankin (2001) and Karim (2011) contend that the constitution of women borrowers as 'self-maximising' entrepreneurs' who function efficiently and sustainably in the market domain may be thwarted in a variety of ways. Dominant sociocultural practices and the ideologies of female seclusion inhibit the access of the women microfinance clients to market spaces culturally defined as male in the *Newar* community of rural Nepal (Rankin 2001). While microfinance NGOs in Bangladesh privilege the principles of competition, entrepreneurship and profit-oriented behaviour, rural women are unable to freely act in keeping with market rationalities on account of their embedding in kinship networks and community ties (Karim 2011). In this book, I centre-stage the question of how women *actively* resist, defy and subvert the transformations of the self that SHG-based microfinance attempts to induce, even as I show that these attempts are not entirely without success either.

Indian microfinance and the complexities of gender, class and caste

SHGs have been perceived by Indian planners as a means to reach institutional credit to women from low-income households through bank linkage schemes. Owing to overwhelming female participation, SHGs have also been perceived as a strategic component of government programmes explicitly articulating empowerment goals,[10] besides poverty-related concerns. Hence, the literature on Indian SHGs (with some of it being directly undertaken by NABARD or commissioned by NABARD) has, by and large, prioritised similar concerns and assessed outcomes such as the social empowerment effects of women's participation in SHGs (Fernandez 2002; Holvoet 2005; Parthasarathy 2005), the poverty-alleviation impacts of micro-loans borrowed or micro-enterprises financed by microfinance lenders (Puhazhendi and Badatya 2002; Puhazhendi and Jayaraman 1999; Swain and Wallentin 2009), or has examined programmes along both dimensions (Anand 2002; Deininger and Liu 2013; EDA 2005; EDA and APMAS 2006; Garikipati 2008; Kabeer 2005; Murthy *et al.* 2005).

Studies that have probed the gender-transformative or redistributive potential of microfinance by locating it with respect to the internal contradictions of gender, caste and class in Indian rural society are fewer. Nonetheless, they raise important questions. Drawing on data from the South Indian state of Andhra Pradesh, Rao (2008) argues that SHGs may worsen caste and class inequalities between women participants when the poor administrative support for these programmes, implemented in the face of reduced state spending and budget cuts, requires that rural women expend their own energies and resources. Pattenden's (2010) study of SHGs in Karnataka points out that microfinance may shore up social power hierarchies when dominant classes maximise benefits from programmes that do not redistribute power and resources in rural society, failing therefore to transform the material or political position of the labouring class poor. Guerin, Kumar and Agier (2013) draw on field data from Tamil Nadu to show how the women members of SHGs (group leaders in particular) may seek and express power over other women in their microcredit groups, their kinship and neighbourhood groups so that for women, the exercise of agency may require some degree of power over other women.

There is a need to explore further how the social relations of gender, class and caste shape the experience of SHG participation and access to microfinance for rural poor women. In this book, I ask what the material costs to women are of striving to fashion their selves in particular ways and of how women's gendered life circumstances and their identities as members of (dominant and oppressed) caste groups and of specific households marked by uneven resource endowments mediate their emergence as market-worthy and credit-worthy subjects. How might the new subject identities that SHGs seek to cultivate interact with, draw upon or even erode the identifications, solidarities and tensions engendered by the social hierarchies of gender, caste and class? As I show in the book, the systemic inequities and power asymmetries that inform community dynamics and inflect 'community-driven', 'participatory' and 'bottom-up' development interventions in multiple and complex ways (Cooke and Kothari 2001; Guijt and Shah 1999) acquire particular salience with respect to SHG-based microfinance. This may be attributed to the organisational structuring of SHGs, which devolves considerable decisional authority upon community members, or the end users of microfinance with respect to the critical dimensions of group functioning.

While much of the literature on SHGs has sought to examine the social and economic outcomes or the impacts they produce upon the lives of microfinance users (as discussed earlier), a smaller part of it has studied the operation of varied self-help promotion institutions and their interactions with the SHGs they promote. These studies have done so primarily from the viewpoint of ascertaining the financial and institutional viability of SHGs as grassroots financial organisations and the potential contribution of promoter agencies towards this end (CGAP 2007; Harper 2002b; Tankha 2002). In this book, I seek to outline the contested nature of the relationships between the SHGs and the diverse (state and non-state) actors that conduct the conduct of their women members and the broader political economy within which they play out. Taking a close lens to these conflicted relationships also allows me to engage with some of the concerns that feminist scholars have raised with respect to 'systematic subversion' of the struggle dimensions of women's mobilisation through the instrumentalism of statist developmental projects and interventions (Chakravarti 2008).

Engaging 'the state'

The emergence of women as subjects of Indian development planning since the 1980s has provoked feminist researchers and scholars of gender studies to problematise and critically interrogate state developmentalism that incorporates women through diverse programmes espousing the goals of women's social empowerment and/or economic development. Economic development programmes launched by the state, in particular, are regarded as posing (to the women's groups that partner with the state) the threat of cooption by statist agendas and a drifting away from the political goals of women's collective organising (Poonacha 1996). In the 1990s and the 2000s, the visible mobilisation of rural women through SHGs, often federated at block or district levels through the intervention of NGOs or state agencies, had raised concerns regarding the vulnerability of SHGs to manipulation by a wide range of interest groups including government officials. A study of government-sponsored SHG programmes in 3 states and NGO-run programmes in 16 states points to the absence of 'empowering learning processes' that may help women counteract the punitive, repayment-oriented 'logic of microcredit' (Dwivedi 2007). Drawing on the case of Kudumbashree, the anti-poverty programme of Kerala that includes microfinance and micro-enterprise promotion as key components, Devika and Thampi (2007) observe that it has installed the image of the woman engaging in income-generating work and contributing to her family's monetary well-being at the heart of the domestic feminine ideal in Kerala, without, however, challenging or damaging prevailing gender norms.

Batliwala and Dhanraj (2007) draw attention to the instrumentalism inherent in state-promoted initiatives (such as SHGs) that absorb women's energies in loan repayment, even as they sustain a depoliticised local activism that does not threaten power structures, cultivating instead carefully nurtured vote banks for political parties at the state level. Kalpana (2008) argues that the women members of SHGs who seek bank credit are rendered vulnerable to the institutional imperatives of commercial banks and the systemic corruption and political compulsions of local development bureaucracies. In this book, I echo some of these concerns, especially those that pertain to the asymmetrical relations of power and authority that suffuse the SHGs' terms of engagement with diverse state actors. These issues acquire particular resonance in the case of state-promoted microfinance given that the state bodies and agencies implementing credit-based livelihood promotion schemes (that predate the era of SHG-banking) have often been corrupt, anti-poor and gender insensitive in their modes of functioning (Dreze 1990; Kabeer and Murthy 1996; Mayoux 1989).

Even as I outline the challenges, risks and opportunities that emerge when informal, community-based groups of women attempt to secure their entitlements from banks and the rural development bureaucracy, I pay heed to post-structuralist theorists who remind us that the state being too diverse, contradictory and divided to be evoked as an entity might be perceived instead as 'erratic' and 'disconnected' (Pringle and Watson 1992: 63) or as a 'network of power relations' existing in cooperation and in tension, with sufficient attention paid to the 'fluidity' and 'dispersal' of power within the state (Rai 2008: 50). And, therefore, the state institutions, personnel and actors who populate this book act in ways that repudiate the idea of the state as an undifferentiated whole or a monolithic entity but function instead as a 'multilayered and conflictual ensemble' (Gupta and Sharma 2006: 291), which is marked by institutional and organisational dispersion. In the book, I show how the women members of SHGs recognise and make strategic use of the fluidity and dispersal of power within the state, even as they represent the state to each other in ways that enable them to successfully press their claims upon state-mediated resources. Through a close ethnographic account of how SHG-banking re-configures women's subjectivities in its efforts to make them the bearers of a regulated autonomy (Rose 1999), I show that women do not enter the arena of microcredit-centred developmental interventions as pre-constituted subjects (Mohanty 1991; Sharma 2010), but are produced as certain kinds of development actors in and through their negotiations with each other (intra-group interactions) and with external institutions (extra-group interactions).

I also engage Partha Chatterjee's (2004: 38) account of how the members of political society or those who are only 'tenuously', 'ambiguously' and 'contextually' rights-bearing citizens as imagined by the constitution encounter the state in their pursuit of survival-oriented resources, services and amenities. He argues that the poor in 'many parts of the developing world' engage in the outright violation of rules or commit acts of illegality in order to access public services and amenities to which they cannot claim legal access. In their interfaces with state bureaucracies, I show that the SHG women deploy similar strategies to stake and sustain successful claims to entitlements, *even when they do enjoy legitimate access to resources*. I show why this is necessary and what the costs to women are of the relentless strategies they forge to wrest resources from the state. Finally, I offer glimpses of other claims (besides microcredit) that the women advance through the SHGs' institutional networking with state institutions and ask what insights this offers us on how women's struggles in and against the state (Rai 2008: 56) play out in the terrain of SHG-based microfinance.

A summary and a way forward

The starting point of this book is the enormous governmental and commercial investment there is (both in India and globally) in fostering entrepreneurial subjectivities on the part of the poor and transforming them into markets of diligent savers and disciplined borrowers of microfinance, in keeping with the ascendance of neo-liberal development rationalities and paradigms. The primary concern of this book is to explore how this transformation plays out – how it is both wrought and contested – in the specific institutional and programme context of SHG-based microfinance, the Indian variant of the global microfinance phenomenon. I begin by pointing to a paradox in the heart of the Indian SHG-based microfinance scenario and laying out the central question that animates this book. The origin and growth of SHGs during the period of neo-liberal economic and banking sector reforms (the 1990s and 2000s) have meant that rural women from low-income households have sought to realise their credit-related entitlements from state institutions at the same time that an older policy commitment to financing weaker sections of the population has steadily eroded. How might we make sense of the Indian state's official support to rural women's claims to bank credit, despite the dismantling of the social banking agenda during this period?

In this book, I tease out the implications of this seeming paradox, even as I attempt to situate the paradox in the light of the particular trajectories of neo-liberalism in India and the path dependencies (Corbridge *et al.* 2011; Harriss 2011) that have shaped it. I show how the policy histories of social banking have anchored the SHG phenomenon to both a (pre-liberalisation) agenda of making available the resources of nationalised banks to those denied access and the creation of self-regulating markets for microfinance at village levels. The RBI and the NABARD have encouraged women of rural poor households to seek and secure access to bank credit, even as this access hinges on their self-fashioning as rational economic actors who display adequate skills in the management of their micro-banks, 'imbibe the essentials of financial intermediation' (NABARD 2006) and provide evidence of their creditworthiness in order to secure bank credit. The women's access to subsidy-bearing loan schemes (such as SGSY) is contingent on their willingness to display entrepreneurial agency, as these schemes mandate the management of self-employment-based income-generation activities.

I argue therefore that the liberalising state has solicited, mobilised and harnessed women's participation in economic development and anti-poverty projects as part of safety nets (Weber 2002) that aim to assist the survival struggles of land- and resource-poor households and communities or the potentially dangerous classes (Chatterjee 2008a) of India. Simultaneously, it seeks to bring the women members of SHGs in line with mainstream financial practices and constitute themselves as disciplined neo-liberal subjects who fashion their aspirations, reform their conduct and act in appropriate ways, earning thereby their entitlement to state-provided resources. While I situate my analysis of microfinance with respect to India's experience of neo-liberal economic reforms, I draw on Foucaultian scholars of governmentality who conceive of neo-liberalism as a positive technique of government that spawns new regulatory techniques seeking to govern economic life. By acting upon diverse and multiple social forces and entities (the financing banks, promoter NGOs and the SHGs as grassroots collectives), the state autonomises and responsibilises these, so that they may, in turn, steer the conduct of governed populations in desired directions (Rose 1999).

In this book, I show how SHGs come to be autonomised and constituted as micro-banks (Harper 2002a) through the techniques of accountability (self and peer) and practices of evaluation (self and peer) that steer women politically at a distance, thus making for a regulated autonomy (Rose 1996). However, development projects do not completely manage or manipulate the behaviour and life worlds of their subjects, and unintended and contradictory outcome may well ensue when rural women, the intended instruments of this process, strike back to subvert and re-define project goals and objectives (Jackson 1997; Mosse 2004). While the women members of SHGs strive to grow their capital, manage their micro-banks and access bank credit, as the bearers of a regulated autonomy, *they simultaneously endeavour in multiple ways to expand the scope of this autonomy*, both as collectives vis-à-vis the promoter and financing agencies they interact with and as individual members vis-à-vis the SHG collectives they belong to, as I show in the following chapters of the book. In order to do this, I draw upon both the secondary literature on SHG-based microfinance in India and my own ethnographic fieldwork in the state of Tamil Nadu.

My fieldwork in Tamil Nadu, in particular, explores the 'conduct of conduct' of SHG women and their (self)-constitution as micro-banks through close observation of the routine weekly meetings of SHGs in which the women made autonomous decisions regarding their financial transactions. It is important to note that the SHGs take group-level decisions with regard to (a) the *generation* of capital (through member savings and interest rates on group loans), (b) its *distribution* among group members (as intra-group loans), (c) the *repayment* of group and bank-sourced capital, (d) the *eviction* or 'weeding out' of 'high-risk' members who are unable to keep up with the repayment deadlines and fiscal disciplining expected of all group members and (e) the *management/governance* of the micro-banks and the sharing of the responsibilities, risks and labour involved therein. This warranted, therefore, close attention to *group dynamics* using the lens of inter-member negotiations, on the one hand, and negotiations between SHGs and a range of promoter and financing agencies, on the other. Although group dynamics have been the essence of joint liability microfinance schemes, studies on microfinance in most parts of the world, as Marr (2003) observes, have tended to focus on the end-uses of credit, neglecting group dynamics and the complex impacts that they give rise to. For the purposes of this book, I show how a focus on group dynamics is also important from the viewpoint of deepening our analysis of how the social power hierarchies of gender, class and caste mediate the quotidian functioning of SHGs. In this book, I explore how the diverse social positioning of women informs both intra-group dynamics and extra-group relationships (or those between SHGs and promoter and financing agencies) and consequently the making of SHGs as micro-banks.

Organisation of the book

In Chapter 1, I trace the ascendance of SHG-based microfinance within national development strategies with a view to uncovering the particular forms a 'win–win' discourse (that corresponds to global win–win claims in microfinance) has taken here. I uncover the processes of translation (Miller and Rose 1990; Mosse 2004) at work that account for the remarkable growth of SHG-banking from its origin as NABARD's pilot project in the early 1990s to its metamorphosis into a 'microfinance movement' (NABARD 2005: 38) in the country. I show how the RBI, NABARD and the Ministry of Rural Development have harnessed the key concerns of the efficiency, 'anti-poverty' and 'economic empowerment' frameworks in order to enlist the participation of powerful institutional actors (commercial banks, the rural development administration, State Women's Development Corporations and development NGOs) in growing the SHG phenomenon in India. I also outline the political-economic compulsions that facilitated the growth of women's microfinance SHGs in the Indian states, highlighting the investment of various state governments in promoting microfinance projects. I discuss how the principal promoter agencies (namely government departments, NGOs and the banking sector) were recruited to undertake SHG promotion both nationwide and in the administrative block (in Tamil Nadu) in which I carried out fieldwork. I conclude with a description of the field site and discussion of the methodology that informed my ethnographic fieldwork in Tamil Nadu.

In Chapter 2, I show how SHGs strive to instil the appropriate skills, capacities and self-reliant subjectivities so that their women members may function as prudent, fiscally disciplined and resource-optimising agents in harsh economic terrains. I do so by tracing the calculations, judgements and actions that govern the financial transactions of the SHGs with regard to (a) the *generation* of capital, (b) its quick *turnover* and (c) its timely *repayment*. Drawing on both my fieldwork in Tamil Nadu and the secondary literature from other states, I show how SHGs are incited by promoter and financing agencies to constitute themselves as 'calculable spaces' or a 'complex of incessant calculations' (Rose 1999: 152) that adopt a financial rationality oriented towards maximising productivity, eliminating waste and choosing between competing priorities on the basis of a cost–benefit calculus. I discuss how the SHGs conflicted with promoter agencies that envisioned disciplined financial intermediation in ways that did not always resonate with the women's views on the matter. I show also how the SHG women's decisions and actions were motivated by diverse concerns that did not conform to a financial rationality in all contexts.

In Chapter 3, I pursue further the question of how women produce themselves as rational economic actors and constitute their collectives as micro-banks. In this chapter, I explore the group-level practices and dynamics that govern (a) the *distribution* of the group's corpus through internal loans to women members and (b) its *preservation* via termination of the membership of women whose fiscal indiscipline is perceived as a threat to the financial viability of the group. Such action may either be an act of 'choice' on the part of a member (dropout) or be expulsion by co-members (push-out). I show how the SHGs constituted themselves as calculable spaces (Rose 1999: 152) by provoking each member to self-evaluate the risk she was likely to pose the collective, even as the group incessantly and collectively assessed and deliberated upon the creditworthiness of its members. My fieldwork as well as studies from other parts of India shows that the economic status of the households of SHG women and their gendered life cycle–related social status mediate their access to the groups' resources. Nonetheless, the 'consensus' regarding what constitutes prudent or risk-averse practices of resource distribution within SHGs is fragile and always subject to dispute and contestation.

In Chapter 4, I discuss the financial management or the governance of SHGs by exploring how the collectives share the costs, efforts and labour involved in managing their quotidian affairs. I discuss the motivations and ambitions of group leaders who, I argue, are autonomised and responsibilised to a greater extent than group members as well as the consequences that flow from the uneven distribution of both the 'privileges' and the 'burdens' of SHG management. Although vested with ensuring the waste-free, leakage-free rotation of group finances, the group leaders did not always embrace a financial rationality aimed at maximising productivity. Instead, their calculations, judgements and priorities were influenced by their acute sense of the 'unfair' expectation that they toil without reward. In Chapters 3 and 4, I show that weekly SHG meetings were sites of contestation wherein the women positioned themselves and each other in multiple ways – for instance, as 'leaders' who bring to bear a 'collective' judgement upon all when evaluating the creditworthiness of loan seekers or as 'women of no means' who draw attention to the webs of power that pervade SHG operations and limit their credit entitlements. I show that the women constantly strove to refute a positioning that did not serve their interests and to fashion instead a counter-positioning of the self that expanded their spaces of manoeuvre within their SHGs.

In Chapter 5, I discuss how rural women's access to bank loans did not depend only on disciplined financial behaviour or the smooth functioning and successful management of their micro-banks, as expected by policymakers. I show how the 'imperfect translation' (Mosse 2004) of the policy idea of SHG-banking into the intentions and ambitions of the collaborating agencies, their institutional interests and organisational cultures produced multiple unintended consequences, with autonomised bank officials steering women's decisions and actions in ways that were not anticipated by policy mandates. I complicate the discursive construction of gendered citizenship (of women as the desired clientele of group-based lending) by the centres of calculation (the RBI and the NABARD) by showing how *branch-level* bank personnel address and position the rural women members of SHGs. I show how the women, in turn, counter-position themselves as certain kinds of development actors, even as they appeal to and position (particular) bank officials in ways that bolster their claims to state developmental resources. I discuss how the social policy and institutional contexts that frame the bank–SHG relationships generate multiple flash points of tension and conflicts, covert or manifest.

In Chapter 6, I discuss how state policy steers the rural women members of SHGs towards managing self-employment-based income-generating enterprises and women's negotiations with the entrepreneurial impulse of these initiatives. I do this by mapping the women's responses to SGSY scheme, which used SHGs to extend subsidy-bearing bank loans to rural poor households in order to finance income-generating economic activities. I show how the women's calculations, decisions and actions, which were hardly in consonance with the formal goals and objectives of the scheme, constituted the SGSY as 'policy (that) primarily functions to . . . legitimise rather than to orientate practice' (Mosse 2004). This makes it necessary to ask how the authoritative interpretations that underpin (SGSY) policy are socially produced and sustained by its 'interpretive communities'. Sustaining SGSY policy on the field required the unceasing translation of its policy goals into the practical interests of its participant organisations such as commercial banks, the BDO, promoter NGOs, group leaders and group members. Despite the costs, the stress and the risks associated with the SGSY scheme, the women valued it owing to their success in instrumentally appropriating the financial assistance it offered and redirecting it to meet a diverse range of end-uses in keeping with the particular requirements of their households.

In Chapter 7, I build further on the arguments in Chapters 5 and 6 in order to flesh out better the ways in which the rural women members of SHGs experienced and perceived the state. I show how women's multiple and conflicting perceptions of the state and their variegated encounters with diverse state agents enabled them to fashion strategies of resistance, of subversion and of appeal and to work the dissonance among multiple state agents to their advantage. I draw upon Partha Chatterjee's (2004) account of the mobilisational strategies of political society when it seeks access to state-mediated resources to which it lacks legal entitlements. I do so in order to identify points of congruence between these and the modes of engagement that the SHGs displayed during their interfaces with diverse state personnel and actors. Drawing on both my fieldwork and reports on SHGs from other Indian states, I show how the women members of SHGs strategically invoked the dense network of ties they cultivated with state actors, not only to wrest development resources from state institutions but also to contest the oppressive practices and inequitable relations of gender and caste, striving thereby to democratise political society.

In the concluding chapter, I suggest that SHG-based microfinance, as a neo-liberal technology of government, strives to produce the effect that Chatterjee (2012) describes as a 'steady widening and deepening of the web of governmental power in India'. And yet, while it seeks to govern at a distance by making the women members of SHGs the bearers of a regulated autonomy (Rose 1996), this book has shown that the women endeavoured in multiple ways to expand the scope of this autonomy, both as collectives vis-à-vis the promoter and financing agencies they interacted with and as individual members vis-à-vis the SHG collectives they belonged to. And thus, the question of how SHGs govern is incompletely understood without appreciating the simultaneous resistance and challenge to (some elements of) neo-liberal governmentalities posed by the women. I discuss the effects of SHG-based microfinance in terms of its efficacy as an instrument in the 'reversal of primitive accumulation' and the considerable gap between policy *intention* and actual *outcomes* in this respect. I also discuss the expectation that it will function as a *political* safety net that dampens or contains resistance at local levels to the unfettered operation of markets (Weber 2002). I discuss some of the key challenges and issues that the Indian microfinance sector has faced over the last decade (2005–15), including the rise of commercial microfinance and its implications for SHGs, the debates on the cost of credit (interest rates) and the terms of lending to the poor, demands by civil society actors such as organised women's groups in favour of state regulation of the sector and recent initiatives by NABARD ('SHG-2') to invigorate SHG-banking.

Towards the end, I briefly discuss the Indian state's current and ongoing anti-poverty initiatives at the level of both the central government (the NRLM) and several state governments (World Bank–financed rural poverty and empowerment projects in several states), the centrality of SHGs to these initiatives and the questions they raise.

Notes

1 It is generally accepted that 'microcredit' or small loans for income-generation or consumption purposes are but one component of a wider array of 'microfinance' services that include savings, insurance, money transfer and other related financial services. In the book, I prefer to use the term 'microfinance' owing to the reliance on group-generated savings in the SHG model of lending to the poor.

2 Loan *melas* are public gatherings at which multiple loans are simultaneously disbursed to a large number of borrowers.
3 Based on data gathered from 3,098 microfinance programmes worldwide, the Microcredit Summit Campaign Report (2015) finds that women constituted 83% (94.4 million) of the poorest clients (114.3 million) reached, as of the end of December 2013. The Summit Campaign's goal was to reach 175 million of the world's poorest families, especially the women of these families, with microfinance by 2015 (Microcredit Summit Campaign n.d.).
4 The SGSY has since been restructured as the National Rural Livelihoods Mission (NRLM), discussed in some detail in the concluding chapter of the book.
5 This is reflected in the comment at the start of this section.
6 The CGAP was established in 1995 as a multi-donor consortium by founding members that included the World Bank, with the mandate to provide financial and technical assistance to microfinance programmes worldwide. Housed at the World Bank, the CGAP is currently a partnership of 34 organisations that aim to advance 'financial inclusion' (CGAP n.d.).
7 There was a marked decline in the share of rural to total bank branches and rural to total bank credit from March 1990 to September 2004. Lending to small borrowers and informal sectors had declined considerably from March 1990 to March 2003. The falling share of credit to agriculture and small-scale industries within the 'priority sector' during the same period and the RBI's re-definition of the priority sector in the 1990s in ways that incorporated profit-oriented sub-sectors signalled an overall scaling down of institutional finance for marginalised sections of the rural population (EPWRF 2005).
8 Frameworks such as 'institutionalised co-production' (Joshi and Moore 2004) seek to capture the emergence of myriad organisational entities, involving regular interaction between state agencies and organised citizen groups. These hybrid organisations aim to deliver public services such as sanitation, water supply and health care in a cost-effective manner, to a large number of dispersed households inhabiting complex and variable environments (ibid.).
9 Rose (1996: 56–57) uses the term 'regulated autonomy' to describe entities (service provider organisations in advanced capitalist countries in the specific case he discusses) that are allowed a certain measure of decisional autonomy for their actions and yet continue to be steered politically 'at a distance' through techniques that aim to hold them accountable such as audits, performance measures, contracts and the setting of targets.
10 An example is the central government–sponsored *Swayamsidha* scheme which was launched to mark the Women's Empowerment Year (2001) and included the formation of women's SHGs as a pivotal component (GOI 2001a).

Chapter 1[1]

The ascendance of SHG-based microfinance

'Win–win' in India

Globally, microfinance appeals to a diverse range of developmental and commercial actors through the 'win–win' hypothesis (Mayoux 1998; Morduch 2000), which posits that group-based lending programmes address the developmental concerns of poverty alleviation by financing livelihoods of the poor and the empowerment of women (by channelling a valued productive resource to poor households through their female members), besides offering the prospect of commercial viability and even profitability for the lending agency or the financial service provider. The win–win claims that underpin the microfinance edifice have brought development donor agencies, non-governmental organisations (NGOs), microfinance institutions (MFIs), commercial banks and informal peer groups of the poor into consonant action with each other even as development actors persuade individual savers and borrowers to adopt modes of responsible financial behaviour that meet the viability-related goals of lending agencies.

In this chapter, I trace the ascendance of self-help group (SHG)-based microfinance within national development strategies with a view to uncovering the particular forms that a corresponding win–win discourse has taken in India. I show how the win–win hypothesis may be understood as a case of successful 'translation' (Miller and Rose 1990: 10) – the process by which one actor comes to count on a particular way of thinking or acting from another by convincing the other to construe their problems or goals as intrinsically linked, their interests consonant and 'their fate as in some way bound up with one another'. The adoption of shared vocabularies, theories and explanatory frameworks links various 'centres of authority' to the personal projects or the 'aspirations, judgements and ambitions' of multiple scattered entities, thereby enabling the former to govern their dispersed subjects at a distance (Miller and Rose 1990; Rose 1999: 48). In this chapter, I trace the processes of translation whereby the centres of calculation (Reserve Bank of India [RBI], National Bank for Agriculture and Rural Development [NABARD] and the Ministry of Rural Development) have aligned the goals of SHG promotion and financing (via subsidised and direct linkage schemes) with the 'personal projects' of institutions that include commercial banks, the rural development administration and promoter NGOs. These actors are, in turn, made responsible for the formation and successful functioning of women's self-managed collectives and their credit linkage to formal financial institutions.

In order to elaborate the precise ways in which this alignment of goals takes place, I also draw on David Mosse's (2004) argument that development projects seek to maintain themselves as coherent policy ideas by stabilising the interpretation of events or establishing 'authoritative interpretations' and having their central goals *translated* in ways that make possible the recruitment of 'interpretive communities' or a range of supporting actors who come to be invested in the interpretive premises that underpin the project. By uncovering the processes of translation (Miller and Rose 1990; Mosse 2004) at work, I contextualise the remarkable growth of SHG-based microfinance from its inception as NABARD's experimental pilot project in the early 1990s to its emergence, within the span of a decade, as the agent *par excellence* for (a) financial intermediation between banks and a dispersed rural population, (b) the cost-effective delivery of poverty-alleviation schemes to the poor and (c) mainstreaming women within economic development programmes from which they had been long excluded.

This chapter also outlines the political-economic compulsions and the institutional infrastructure that facilitated the growth of women's microfinance SHGs in the Indian states, drawing attention to various state governments' investment in and ownership of what NABARD (2005: 38) describes as the 'microfinance movement' in the country. Subsequently, I show how the key institutional actors involved in SHG promotion, namely., government agencies, civil society actors such as development NGOs and nationalised banks, have been motivated to undertake the demanding tasks of SHG promotion both at the national level and in the specific context of the administrative block in Tamil Nadu – the site of my ethnographic fieldwork.

Situated policy context of SHG-banking: competitive banks and complementary social measures

In the early 1990s, the Indian government embraced 'root and branch' liberalisation of the Indian economy in contrast to the 'reforms by stealth' that marked the 1980s (Byres 1998: 4). Mooij and Dev (2002) argue that policy planners' preoccupation with growth as the prime concern of economic policy in the 1990s was accompanied by the pragmatic acceptance that the poor were likely to suffer the consequences of fiscal austerity and falling public expenditure in the short run. Poverty-alleviation measures were perceived as a compensatory mechanism that would contain the inevitable fallout of the economic reforms; this was reflected in the macro-economic policy framework of the Eighth Five-Year Plan (1990–95), which outlined stabilisation and structural adjustment measures as well as complementary social measures (Van Stuijvenberg 1996). During this period, reforms in the Indian banking sector were also undertaken, as a component of the overall financial sector and economic policy reforms, following the recommendations of the first Narasimham Committee on Financial System set up in August 1991. Critics note that the reforms strongly emphasised improvement of the allocative and financial efficiency of the banking sector, with performance evaluation criteria of the banks shifting towards profitability and portfolio quality above other indices (Kohli 1997).

Projects of inclusive banking have thus taken shape in a policy context marked, on the one hand, by the banking sector's pursuit of institutional viability in a competitive and deregulated environment and, on the other, by the need to direct public planning towards complementing the unfettered market mechanism. Besides, as briefly mentioned in the Introduction, the legacy of social banking had bred both expectations and disappointments in its wake. Some of the key measures of the social and development banking era that were pursued vigorously until the end of the 1980s included the en masse expansion of bank branches in semi-urban and rural areas (following the nationalisation of 14 major commercial banks in 1969), the directed flow of bank credit to state-designated priority sectors,[2] interest rate capping in order to lower the cost of credit through the Differential Rate of Interest scheme targeted at the eligible poor and the creation of a separate structure of regional rural banks (RRBs) in 1972 to cater exclusively to 'weaker sections'. And yet these initiatives did not guarantee the credit entitlements of small and marginal cultivator households, nor did they reduce the costs borne by the poor seeking to deal with the formal financial sector (Bhende 1986; Sarap 1991). The land-based lending policies of banks, the non-eligibility of the movable securities the poor possessed and the rigid distinction maintained by banks between production and consumption needs, with the latter being delegitimised, foreclosed the access of the landless and land-poor sections to bank credit (Swaminathan 1991).

Despite a policy thrust that mandated rural financing, the effective disenfranchisement of substantial sections of the rural poor (by the banking sector) on account of their non-ownership of property and the absence of stable incomes and reliable livelihoods speaks of the 'tenuous' and 'ambiguous' sense in which the inhabitants of 'political society' (Chatterjee 2004) are rights-bearing citizens as imagined by the constitution. The NABARD Taskforce on Microfinance attributes the failure of commercial banks in financing large sections of the rural poor to the high transaction costs of doing business with a geographically dispersed population, the 'urban orientation' of field staff and the perception of the bank as an 'alien institution' inaccessible to the poor (NABARD 1999: 1.7.2). NABARD's interest in the SHG-bank linkage programme derived from its participation in the mid- to late 1980s in the Asia Pacific Rural and Agricultural Credit Association, set up by the United Nation's Food and Agricultural Organisation to promote innovation in rural finance. The association transmitted key elements of the (then) 'new thinking' on rural finance, promoted by the World Bank and UN agencies, that advocated the promotion of financial linkages between formal financial institutions and the informal sector (Dasgupta 2001).

SHG-banking, which began as a pilot project linking 500 SHGs to commercial banks in 1991–92, was modelled on a three-year experimental project between the NGO MYRADA and NABARD in the late 1980s. In the project, MYRADA promoted women's SHGs that were financed by NABARD. Mainstreamed as part of routine banking business in 1996,[3] SHG-banking offered non-collateralised credit, which the poor (organised into SHGs) could use for any purpose, including household consumption. The quantum of credit was linked to the volume of group savings (in a ratio of 4:1) and provided in a relatively de-bureaucratised manner. The bank could directly make a loan to an SHG (which had functioned for a minimum period of six months) or to a promoter NGO/MFI which would on-lend to the SHGs it promoted. Having built 'financial discipline' and 'credit history' and displayed 'mature financial behaviour' through the rotation of 'their own hard-earned money' or 'warm money', the SHGs were permitted and encouraged to secure 'cold (outside) money' from the bank (NABARD 2006: 2).

Aligning 'the fate' of SHGs and banks: constructing consonant interests

The SHG-bank linkage scheme is striking for the extent of operational autonomy that it has allowed commercial banks in order to foster their participation in the scheme. The banks that financed SHGs were permitted to make 'deviations' with respect to the conventional viability norms that governed bank lending such as margin requirements, the scale of finance, unit costs and security 'where deemed necessary'. The bank was allowed to decide upon and prescribe simple documentation that it judged an SHG capable of providing. The repayment period on the linkage loan was to be decided by the bank after negotiation with the SHG. The NABARD exhorted banks to delegate adequate powers to branch-level managers to undertake 'autonomous' decision-making for the purpose of this scheme, where they did not have such powers usually (NABARD 1992, 1996). In 1999, the RBI deregulated interest rates on all loans made by banks to MFIs and NGOs. In 2000, banks were encouraged to formulate their own model or choose any conduit/intermediary for extending microcredit. Correspondingly, all microcredit extended by banks to individual borrowers, whether directly or through an intermediary, was designated as priority sector lending (*RBI* 2000). These measures further enhanced the operational autonomy of banks, seeking thereby to incentivise bank lending to SHGs as well as other actors in the emerging microfinance sector in the country.

While the RBI and the NABARD vigorously promoted SHG-banking (through measures such as incorporating SHG lending within priority sector lending and NABARD's refinance of bank loans to SHGs), they did not set annual targets or quotas mandating the volume of credit flow from banks to SHGs through the linkage scheme. It might be posited, therefore, that the operational autonomy allowed to banks was intended to steer them *of their own volition* towards SHG financing, a project that was discursively constituted in ways that established a clear departure from the erstwhile 'poverty lending' associated with the social banking era. In other words, the banks were to be freed of operational constraints, to be *autonomised* in ways by which the state may divest itself of direct responsibility for their actions and calculations (Rose and Miller 1992) so that they would 'choose' SHG-banking. The operational principles of SHG-banking, in turn, resonated with the efficiency considerations of recovery performance, institutional viability and transaction costs reduction. These concerns had grown increasingly salient since the inception of the banking sector reforms (Ramachandran and Swaminathan 2002). As a former governor of the RBI put it, the SHG-bank linkage programme evolved in a macro-policy environment dominated by the concerns of revitalising Rural Financial Institutions (RFIs) damaged by the 'twin problems of non-viability and poor recovery performance' (*RBI* 1997: 70).

The policy documents of RBI and NABARD advocating the SHG-bank linkage project and the public speeches of their officials have unequivocally voiced these concerns, seeking validation for the 'policy idea' (Mosse 2004) of SHG-banking by anchoring it firmly to the dilemmas and predicaments of a key 'supporting actor' – the financing banks. In particular, they underscore the 'user participation' advantages that SHGs offer banks by freeing them from direct responsibility for the financial decision-making of numerous individual savers and borrowers, who will be governed instead by their own autonomised and responsibilised grassroots collectives. The first NABARD circular on the linkage scheme outlines the potential of SHGs to enable 'externalisation of a part of the work items of the credit cycle, . . . a reduction in the formal paper work involved and a consequent reduction in the transaction costs' (NABARD 1992).

A NABARD handbook on SHG-banking for branch-level bankers identifies the banks' benefits as being the cost-saving advantages ('only one account is needed for 20 members'), the transfer of appraisal and monitoring costs from the bank to the group ('the moral authority of group members . . . means supervision of effective utilisation and repayment'), the anticipated increase in the deposit base as 'SHG financing will become big business over a period of time' and the prospective increase in the 'social base' of the bank in the rural areas by earning 'social recognition' and 'commanding the good will of the people' (NABARD n.d. 1). The NABARD

Task Force on Microfinance anticipates that an impending transformation of SHG members into 'micro-entrepreneurs' and their 'eventual graduation into bank customers' providing an 'ever-increasing volume of business for banks' will ensure that SHG linkage emerges as one of the more important means to secure the long-term sustainability of RFIs such as RRBs (NABARD 1999).

The inception of the linkage scheme is thus co-terminus with the valorising of the SHG and its constituency as ideal bank clientele and customers. SHG-banking is discursively constituted as a profitable avenue that enables beleaguered bankers[4] to adhere to the commercial principles of banking even as they fulfil the developmental mandates of a welfare state. We see therefore that the RBI and the NABARD have attempted to shape SHG-banking in keeping with some of the constitutive principles of financial liberalisation. However, the SHG-based microfinance landscape in India has also been shaped by the agenda of the Ministry of Rural Development and the competing pulls of delivering subsidy-bearing poverty-alleviation schemes to targeted poor households.

The SGSY: re-assertion of poverty lending?

In April 1999, the central government introduced a nationally implemented poverty-alleviation programme, namely the SwarnJayanti Gram Swarozgar Yojana (SGSY), that used SHGs as organisational channels to deliver financial assistance to targeted beneficiaries below the official poverty line in order to set up self-employment activities and thereby cross the poverty line. In contrast to the direct linkage scheme, the SGSY tied the use of the loans to the financing of enterprise activity, contained a subsidy component and specified 'below poverty line' status for loan recipients. The amount of capital disbursed as loan finance was not linked to the quantum of women's savings (as in the case of the linkage scheme) but was determined instead by the financial requirements of the enterprise activity proposed by the SHG. Being a targeted intervention (unlike the linkage scheme), the SGSY aimed to cover 30% of families living below the official poverty line in an administrative block within a five-year period. It mandated sub-quotas for the scheduled castes (SCs) and scheduled tribes (STs) (50% of beneficiaries), women (40%) and the disabled (3%) and prescribed that at least 50% of the SHGs formed under the scheme in an administrative block be women's SHGs (GOI n.d. 2).

Not surprisingly perhaps, the SGSY provoked the ire of microfinance practitioners and analysts for its violation of the 'essential' features of microfinance. Commentators on the microfinance sector expressed their disappointment that the SGSY reflected the continuing 'obsession of the Indian planning environment with old style socialist thinking despite ten years of economic reforms' (Sinha 2000). The SGSY was believed to pose the long-term risk of corrupting a more sustainable microfinance system by introducing subsidies and generating the expectation of loan waivers (Malhotra 2000). The non-linkage between group-generated savings and the quantum of the bank loan disbursed through the scheme was held to violate a 'fundamental' tenet of microfinance, namely that the group savings must bear a necessary relationship to the volume of credit circulated (Harper 2002a; Malhotra 2000). Observing that the 'autonomy', 'flexibility' and 'spontaneity' of the SHG system were the determining factors of its success, a NABARD-commissioned study emphasises that it 'should not' and 'cannot' be utilised as an instrument to implement government schemes (Kropp and Suran 2002: 26). How then do we understand the incorporation of SHGs within the SGSY scheme despite its repudiation of the essential features of the microfinance paradigm? What do we make of the insertion of a subsidy-bearing scheme within a microfinance programme that was intended to jettison 'government spoon-feeding' (Kropp and Suran 2002: 26) and cultivate 'self-reliant' subjectivities instead?

We turn again to the 'path dependencies' (Harriss 2011) of the rural credit sector in India and their 'uneven articulation' (Ong 2006) by a neo-liberal technology of governing such as microfinance. The SGSY sought to incorporate the SHGs within a developmental legacy of centrally sponsored anti-poverty schemes implemented by the rural development administration and inaugurated during the period of the Sixth Five-Year Plan (1980–85). As part of the Revised 20 Point Programme associated with the then prime minister Indira Gandhi, the Sixth Five-Year Plan launched wage and self-employment boosting programmes such as the Integrated Rural Development Programme (IRDP) in order to directly attack poverty and destitution (Mathur 1996). Introduced nationwide in 1980–81, the IRDP offered credit-cum-subsidy assistance to targeted poor individuals to finance the acquisition of income-earning assets, undertake self-employment activities and thereby cross the income-poverty line (Kabeer and Murthy 1996). The growth of the

SHG phenomenon in the 1990s and its loan repayment successes in particular highlighted design flaws in the IRDP. The Hashim Committee, set up by the Planning Commission in 1997 to review the performance of all wage and self-employment programmes, identified the absence of social intermediation or the processes whereby the poor were encouraged to form groups, accumulate savings and practice credit discipline, as a key contributor to the shortcomings of the IRDP (GOI 2001b).

The Hashim Committee recommended that the multiple existing self-employment programmes be consolidated into a single comprehensive scheme that targeted *groups* of beneficiaries, substituting the earlier focus on the individual beneficiary. An outcome of the Hashim Committee recommendations, the SGSY typified 'poverty-lending' initiatives, even as it sought to capitalise on the commercial successes of the NABARD's SHG-banking project. In designating the rural development administration as the primary agency in charge of scheme implementation, the SGSY drew the rural development administration to the institutional arena of SHG formation and promotion, 'recruiting' personnel of the District Rural Development Agency (DRDA) and the Block Development Office (BDO) for these tasks countrywide. It is instructive to note the striking contrast between the IRDP, which showed dismal rates of coverage of women borrowers,[5] and the SGSY, in which women constituted 66% of total beneficiaries by 2007–8, a little less than ten years after the scheme was launched (GOI 2009). The mainstreaming of women within the SGSY scheme signals both the successful targeting of women's SHGs by the scheme and the wide-ranging acceptance of women's presence within anti-poverty and development-oriented statist projects by the turn of the 21st century.

Mainstreaming women in development: from the margins to the centre

The recognition of women as economic beings by India's policy planners was reflected, for the first time, in a separate chapter on 'Women and Development' in the Sixth Plan (1980–85) document. The growing visibility of Indian women's movements in the 1970s, the emergence of women's studies scholarship that highlighted women's invisible labour in the unorganised sectors of the economy and the sustained criticism of the welfarist bias of an older generation of community development programmes (1950s to the end of the 1960s) forced Indian development planners to rethink the gendered social roles conventionally attributed to women and inscribed within planning for development (Agnihotri and Mazumdar 1995; Seth 2001). Consequently, economic development and income-generation projects that acknowledged and sought to support women's identities as workers and producers began to gain currency in the 1980s (Seth 2001; World Bank 1991).

Two important reports published in the 1980s sought to further the Indian state's commitment to securing women's equitable access to development resources. Both reports identified institutional credit as an important component of a comprehensive support package. Following the recommendations of the National Perspective Plan for Women 1988–2000, state governments established Women's Development Corporations (WDCs), with the mandate of identifying women entrepreneurs, assisting them with marketing linkages, credit from banks and financial institutions and training in technical skills and financial management (World Bank 1991). Besides the establishment of state-level WDCs, a national body – the Rashtriya Mahila Kosh (RMK) or the National Credit Fund for Women – was set up in 1993 with the objective of financing the enterprise and livelihood-related activities of women informal sector workers (Mishra 2000). The RMK was created in response to the recommendations of the National Commission for Self-Employed Women and Women in the Informal Sector or the Shramshakti (1988) report, which drew attention to the vulnerable working conditions of women of the working poor in India.

Feminist scholars note that the ascendance of neo-liberal ideologies in India since the 1990s has also played a part in facilitating development programmes that draw women into market-based production and enhance their ability to support their households (Vasavi and Kingfisher 2003), besides giving rise to agency discourses that foreground women's managerial and entrepreneurial skills and their contribution as micro-entrepreneurs and managers of household poverty (John 1996). Globally as well, the valorising of the economic agency of 'women in poverty' has proceeded apace with the advance of neo-liberalism since the 1980s. Women came to be constituted as a valuable and (hitherto) underutilised *resource for development* whose participation potentially enhances efficacy and helps attain desired outcomes on a range of interventions, aiming to raise family incomes, guarantee food security, reduce fertility or protect the environment (Jackson 1996; Razavi and Miller 1995).

The emergence of women as the 'missing link' (Razavi 1997) in low-cost poverty-alleviation strategies has, in turn, reflected both 'anti-poverty' and efficiency concerns.[6] Women's claim to productive resources (such as microcredit) was legitimised on the grounds of both their greater *need* or material deprivation (following concerns regarding the feminisation of poverty) and the *economic sense* of directing scarce resources to women who contributed more (relative to men) to household survival and the well-being of children[7] (Razavi 1997; Razavi and Miller 1995).

In the case of microfinance, the efficiency rationale for lending to women also drew strength from the accumulating evidence of women's response to the (loan) repayment imperative of programmes. The gendered constraints on women's mobility and their embedding in local neighbourhood and community ties increase the costs of defaulting on micro-loans. Besides, women's 'positional vulnerability' (Rahman 1999) renders them susceptible to public shaming by microfinance project staff. These factors reinforce each other, contributing to disciplined repayment. As microfinance researchers Cheston and Kuhn (2002: 11) observe, the programmes that serve men are more likely to use extensive monitoring procedures and require collateral to reduce default risk, while programmes targeting women can take the inexpensive route of tapping social guarantees and informal mechanisms including 'client capacity for self-monitoring and cooperation'. A growing perception of the multiple social and developmental gains of 'investing in women' has thus paved the way for mainstreaming women within economic development and anti-poverty programmes (both in India and elsewhere) in the last two decades of the 20th century.

Feminisation of microfinance in India: repayment and empowerment concerns

The feminisation of SHG-based microfinance in India conforms closely to the global scenario. It is important to note that the SHG-bank linkage programme was conceived and initiated after the notion of women as disciplined borrowers had gained the status of a development truism, following the proliferation of women-targeted programmes in neighbouring Bangladesh during the 1980s. Not surprisingly, financial policymakers in India have enthusiastically welcomed the overwhelming female participation in SHGs. A former director of the Department of Economic Analysis and

Policy, RBI, observed that women were encouraged to form SHGs due to their 'trustworthy', 'sincere' and 'committed' natures, their 'excellent' repayment record and their willingness to use peer pressure to ensure timely repayment (Dadhich 2001). A NABARD-commissioned study attributed the preponderance of women's groups in the linkage programme to their supposed 'homogeneity', 'greater group solidarity' and women's 'willing acceptance' of peer pressure. On the other hand, men have 'heated discussions' and find it difficult to make decisions on fund allocation among members, lowering the chances of sustainability of men's groups (Kropp and Suran 2002). The Housing Development Finance Corporation, which targeted a range of microfinance services to peer groups of borrowers, included the participation of women as one of the critical conditions for the commercial success of microfinance programmes, besides other criteria, including market rates of interest and loan recovery based on social intermediation (Tiwari and Fahad n.d.).

If the instrumental advantages of lending to women have mobilised the formal financial sector to participate in inclusive banking projects, a different set of programme objectives have appealed to other governmental actors. Given their overwhelming female membership, SHGs have been positioned as a strategic component of government schemes explicitly articulating empowerment goals, besides poverty-related concerns. A centrally sponsored scheme such as the *Indira Mahila Yojana* (IMY) is a case in point. Launched by the Ministry of Women and Child Development in 1995–96, the IMY promoted the formation of small savings groups of women in the *anganwadi* area of 238 administrative blocks in the country. Aiming to provide women an organisational structure to come together and access state and central government schemes, the IMY prioritised the objective of empowering women to demand their rights from family, community and government; increase their control over material, political and social resources; and enhance their awareness, improve their skills and raise issues of common concern through mobilisation and networking (GOI 2001a).

The discussion thus far suggests that SHG-based microfinance has garnered enormous support from diverse and powerful interest groups and institutional actors. We see that the win–win formula in the Indian context is premised on the claims that SHG-based lending (a) enables commercial banks to meet their priority sector lending requirements and fulfil the social goals of banking; (b) reduces transaction costs, delivers high repayment rates and addresses the viability concerns of commercial banks and RRBs; (c) addresses poverty-related concerns of the Indian state and policy planners by serving as an effective organisational channel to deliver institutional credit to economically marginalised households; and (d) offers the possibility of attaching empowerment rhetoric to programmes that claim to support group-based social mobilisation processes. By extending financial support to women's livelihood activities, SHG-based microfinance foregrounds women as the central actors and agents of economic development in consonance with currently dominant development imaginaries. As I have shown, the goals of SHG-banking have been translated (Miller and Rose 1990; Mosse 2004) in ways that appeal to an array of institutional supporters, including commercial banks, the rural development administration (the DRDA/BDO structure), development NGOs and State Women's Development Corporations, by harnessing the key concerns of the efficiency, the anti-poverty and women's (social and economic) empowerment frameworks. In the following section, I provide a brief account of the political and institutional configurations that sustained the growth of the SHG phenomenon across the country.

SHG growth in the states: political compulsions and diverse institutional configurations

NABARD (2005: 38) observes that the SHG-bank linkage programme has passed through three phases of pilot testing (1992–95), mainstreaming (1996–98) and expansion (1998 onwards) to assume the form of a 'microfinance movement' in the country. However, the movement has displayed pronounced regional variations and unevenness in its growth, especially in the early years. The two southern states of Tamil Nadu and Andhra Pradesh assumed an early lead and accounted for 44% of all credit-linked SHGs and 64% of total bank loans disbursed in the linkage scheme by the end of March 2005, close to a decade after the banking sector had incorporated SHG-banking as part of routine bank activity. In the same period, all four southern states accounted for 59% of the total number of credit-linked SHGs (NABARD 2005: 41). Seeking to redress these regional disparities, NABARD initiated efforts in 2001 to intensify SHG-banking in 13 targeted 'priority states' comprising 70% of the rural poor population. Consequently, the momentum of the linkage programme gathered steam in the *non*-southern states, with the number of credit-linked SHGs in these states increasing from 29% in March 2001 to 48% by March 2007 (NABARD 2007: 42).

SHG-banking is currently a nationwide phenomenon, even if the early lead has favoured South India, with its states accounting for 54% of all SHGs with outstanding bank loans in 2012 and 2013 (Nair and Tankha 2014: 9). While women's SHGs have originated as part of an innovative bank linkage programme promoted by NABARD, their phenomenal growth in many parts of India may be attributed to official patronage and ownership of the SHG phenomenon by state governments. In Andhra Pradesh, early support for women's microcredit emerged in response to the recognition of rural women as a significant electoral constituency following women's en masse participation in the anti-liquor movement that rocked the state in the early 1990s. While the imposition of prohibition on state-sponsored liquor in 1994 was a recognition of women's political mobilisation, its repeal two years later by the regional party in power (the Telugu Desam) made it necessary for the state government to placate its rural female support base and compensate for letting women down by targeting them as the prime beneficiaries of its development projects (Rao 2008). Smriti Rao (2008) argues that the state government's enthusiastic endorsement of microcredit for rural women has accompanied its turn to policies of economic liberalisation in the region from the mid-1990s, paving the way for what she describes as 'reforms with a female face'.

In Tamil Nadu, the *political* investment of the state in SHG promotion is no less urgent. In the 2000s, successive state governments headed by two dominant political parties (the Dravida Munnetra Kazhagam [DMK] and the All India Anna Dravida Munnetra Kazhagam [AIADMK]) have competitively staked claim to ownership of the SHG programme. Budget speeches delivered during the term of the AIADMK (2001–6) date the launch of the SHG scheme to 1992 when Dr J. Jayalalithaa was chief minister.[8] During the election campaign that preceded the state assembly elections of 2006, the DMK chief Dr M. Karunanidhi vehemently refuted the AIADMK's 'canard' that his party would wind up the SHG programme should it return to power, reminding the electorate that the SHGs were, after all, started during the DMK's regime in 1989 (Murari 2006). The NGOs I interviewed during my fieldwork (2005–6) spoke of the assiduous efforts of the then chief minister Dr Jayalalithaa to convey the message that her stewardship of the state as a *woman* chief minister was the primary reason for the official support to women's SHGs. Not surprisingly then, when the DMK came to power after the state assembly elections of April 2006, the governor's address to the first sitting of the new assembly contained a reference to the SHG programme. In his address, the governor assured the Tamil people that the DMK government had always acted as a 'catalyst' for the effective functioning of SHGs and would make 'all-out efforts' to 'nurture' and 'strengthen' the movement in the state (GOTN 2006). The reference to SHGs was evidently intended to dispel the possible public association of a popular development scheme with the leader of a rival political party.

While shared political impulses may have motivated state governments to seek close association with the SHG programme, the institutional configurations that underpin the SHG landscape have varied from one state to another. Some programmes have consciously integrated SHGs within the panchayat[9] structure right from their inception (Kerala's Kudumbashree), whereas others have relied on a network of NGOs to form SHGs creating panchayat-level federations at a later period (Tamil Nadu's Mahalir Thittam). State government efforts to promote SHG-banking have also received financial and technical support from multilateral and bilateral aid donors for women-targeted microfinance projects, aiming to facilitate the social and economic empowerment of rural women. For instance, the support provided by the United Nation's International Fund for Agricultural Development (IFAD) was critical to kick-starting the SHG programme in Tamil Nadu (IFAD n.d.). On the other hand, the impetus for the woman's savings movement in Andhra Pradesh (*Poduppulakshmi*) emerged from the Total Literacy Campaign and the anti-arrack movement (in Nellore district) in the early 1990s with an active role for the district development administration in promoting the groups (Ramachandran 1996).

Subsequently, the SHG programme in Andhra Pradesh attracted donor agency support through the United Nations Development Program (UNDP)-sponsored South Asia Poverty Alleviation Programme implemented in three drought-prone districts from 1995 to 2000. Seeking to build on the UNDP's initiative, the government of Andhra Pradesh launched the District Poverty Initiatives Programme (popularly called *Velugu*) with World Bank support in June 2000. The Velugu project aimed to develop 'self-reliant' and 'self-managed' community-based organisations of the poor that included SHGs at the lowest (hamlet) level (World Bank 2015).

In Kerala, the women-centred Kudumbashree programme, aiming to eradicate absolute poverty through community action, was initiated in collaboration with NABARD in 1998. In keeping with Kerala's greater engagement with democratic decentralisation and people's planning initiatives, Kudumbashree operates through a three-tier federated structure involving neighbourhood groups (NHGs) at the basic tier, area development societies at the ward level and community development societies at the panchayat/municipality/corporation level. Doubling up as thrift and credit societies, the NHGs conduct weekly meetings, maintain accounts and seek bank credit through linkage and subsidy-bearing loan schemes (Anand 2002).

In states such as Tamil Nadu, state–NGO partnerships have played a significant role in expanding the scale and reach of the SHG phenomenon in the rural countryside. Financially supported by IFAD, the Tamil Nadu Corporation for Development of Women (TNCDW), an undertaking of the government of Tamil Nadu,[10] supervised the formation and bank linkage of women's SHGs through a network of local NGOs in five districts of Tamil Nadu from 1990 to 1998 (IFAD n.d.). In Maharashtra as well, women's SHGs were created as part of the Maharashtra Rural Credit Programme (MRCP), implemented by the State Women's Development Corporation through NGO partners and financially supported by IFAD. Under the aegis of the MRCP, over 5,000 SHGs were created in 12 districts of Maharashtra between 1994 and 2002 (Tankha 2012: 111). Besides the WDCs, the Women and Child Development (WCD) departments of state governments have sought to expand the base of women's SHG programmes in rural areas. For instance, Mission Shakti, launched by the WCD department of the government of Odisha in 2001, has used the staff of the Integrated Child Development Services (ICDS)[11] centres, which the department administers to form and supervise SHGs (Tankha 2012: 113).

The formation and expansion of SHG networks in the rural countryside require the investment of considerable reserves of time, labour and energies by institutions and individuals willing to assume the responsibilities of SHG promotion. A prominent institutional backer of microfinance, NABARD has provided financial and training support to development NGOs, specialised MFIs, the branches of commercial, cooperative and regional rural banks, farmers' clubs/associations and even interested individuals so that they may form and nurture SHGs and enable their credit linkage to banks (NABARD 2013: 26). In the following sections, I provide a brief outline of the institutional context of SHG promotion across the country, showing how the three principal actors, namely government agencies/departments, development NGOs and the banking sector (Harper 2002b), have emerged as SHG promoter agencies, nationally and in the specific instance of the administrative block in Tamil Nadu in which I conducted my field study.

Recruiting NGOs and banks in the neo-liberal era

The endeavours of the RBI and NABARD to enlist the NGO sector for the promotion of microfinance may be situated in the context of what Kudva (2005: 246) describes as the growing efforts of the central and state governments, since the 1990s, to pursue collaborative partnerships with NGOs in order that they may enhance the efficacy of developmental projects at the grassroots and function as implementers of government programmes to 'tight specifications'. Since the advent of SHG-banking, the central government has used its powers to shape and mould the non-state sector by steering it towards microcredit-based developmental action. The participation of NGOs in SHG promotion was actively welcomed by NABARD at the inception of the SHG-bank linkage project in 1991–92 (NABARD 1992). In order to motivate NGOs to promote SHGs and ensure their credit linkage to commercial banks, the promoter agency was offered remuneration for each SHG credit-linked under the direct linkage scheme and subsequently the SGSY scheme (Harper 2002b). In the microfinance sector, state agencies hope to harness the grassroots contacts and outreach of NGOs or what a former chief of the RBI describes as the 'trust', 'commitment', 'flexibility' and 'empathy' assumed to mark their dealings with rural poor communities (*RBI* 1997). Senior officials of the RBI have affirmed the great value of NGO intermediaries, particularly when their role extends beyond reaching credit to the poor and includes monitoring the effective use and recovery of loans.[12]

The preceding discussion suggests that the recruitment (Mosse 2004) of NGOs was perceived as critical to the *cost-effective* promotion of the microfinance phenomenon in the country. NABARD has also recruited the voluntary sector for financial intermediation, by popularising the on-lending model by which NGOs borrow in bulk from commercial banks, microfinance wholesalers or international sources and on-lend to the SHGs they promote. By the end of March 2006, 6% of the SHGs credit-linked to banks were promoted by NGOs and other formal agencies that on-lent bank funds to the groups and played the dual role of social and financial intermediation (NABARD 2006: 7). The question of whether NGOs ought to take up financial intermediation has provoked contentious debate within the microfinance sector. Microfinance analysts have pointed to the high interest rates charged by NGOs and MFIs that lend to the poor (Kropp and Suran 2002) and the minefield of legal and regulatory issues involved when the NGOs engaging in financial intermediation are formally registered as non-profit entities (Fernandez 2000).[13] For these and other reasons, some of the older and well-established NGOs engaging in SHG promotion such as the DHAN Foundation, PRADAN and MYRADA[14] have consciously chosen not to be financial intermediaries themselves. They have focused instead on creating secondary- or higher-level federations of SHGs that provide support services, including accounting/auditing assistance, troubleshooting, lobbying government, marketing, storage and input supply (in case the groups engage in enterprises) and legal services to their member SHGs.[15]

While NABARD and RBI have successfully enlisted banks to finance SHGs given the considerable cost-saving advantages vis-à-vis individual-targeted lending, the banks have been more wary of doubling up as SHG promoters. A study of different types of SHG promoters in the states of Uttar Pradesh, Odisha and Karnataka found that half the bank managers interviewed were apprehensive of taking on SHG promotion due to the anticipated work burden on staff and the high transaction costs involved (Harper 2002b). By the end of March 2006, SHGs formed, promoted and financed by banks accounted for 20% of all credit linked SHGs. The bulk of credit-linked SHGs (74%) were promoted by NGOs, government or other formal agencies and financed by banks (NABARD 2006: 7), indicating that banks have, by and large, left SHG promotion to other actors. The literature suggests that the decisions and choices of banks to enter (or not) the field of SHG promotion have been diverse and where banks have undertaken SHG promotion, their performance as promoters has varied considerably. While a bank such as the District Central Cooperative Bank of Bidar (Karnataka) took a much-acclaimed 'national lead' by directly promoting 7,000 SHGs (Harper 2002b), not all promoter banks have been equally conscientious. For instance, an RRB in Kalahandi district (Orissa), visited as part of an EDA and APMAS (2006) study of SHGs undertaken in four states, was found to be an absentee promoter. When the bank staff accompanied the research team to meet an SHG ostensibly promoted by the bank, the group members did not recognise the staff, nor could they recall the name of the promoter bank (ibid.).

Contours of SHG promotion in Thillai block (Tamil Nadu)

The ethnographic study in Tamil Nadu was carried out in two phases between August 2004 and April 2006 as part of the doctoral dissertation of this researcher. The first phase included interviews with 12 NGOs active in SHG promotion in six districts of Tamil Nadu. The second phase consisted of intensive fieldwork over a period of 14 months (February 2005–April 2006) involving 27 SHGs in 3 villages in a district of northern Tamil Nadu.[16] The primary institutional types of SHG promoters, namely development NGOs, government departments/agencies and commercial banks (Harper 2002b), were active in the administrative block (code name: *Thillai*) in which the three villages were located. The most prominent SHG promoters in Thillai block were (a) an international NGO, (b) a grassroots NGO that was the designated partner of the state government's official scheme for SHG promotion (Mahalir Thittam) and (c) and the Block Development Office.

The principal official arrangement for SHG promotion in Tamil Nadu has taken the form of Mahalir Thittam, a project of partnership between the TNCDW and NGOs. Launched by the state government in 1997–98 in all the districts, Mahalir Thittam succeeded the IFAD-sponsored women's microcredit programme operational in five districts. Under Mahalir Thittam, the TNCDW identifies and trains a statewide network of NGO partners and provides financial and technical assistance. The NGO partners are, in turn, assigned the responsibility of forming, training and supervising SHGs. Under the scheme, 441,311 SHGs were formed in the rural and urban areas of Tamil Nadu enlisting 6.9 million women members by the end of March 2010 through a partnership with 469 NGOs (GOTN 2010: 138–144). The TNCDW has endeavoured to identify and enlist a sufficient number of NGO partners *willing* and *able* to undertake SHG promotion in the districts. The case of Thillai block discussed here reflects the challenges that the TNCDW has faced in its quest for suitable NGO partners.

In Thillai block, the district collector (head of the rural development administration) was approached by officials of the TNCDW in 2000, to help identify a suitable NGO partner for the Mahalir Thittam scheme. The collector, in turn, sought the assistance of the Mahalir Thittam partner NGO in the adjoining administrative block. The director of the partner NGO used his network of friends and contacts to identify three locally based social workers in Thillai block, who underwent the training provided by Mahalir Thittam to facilitate the formation of SHGs. Financial assistance from Mahalir Thittam was routed to the 'sub-NGOs' in Thillai block through the 'main NGO'[17] based in the neighbouring block. This arrangement ran into trouble when a local newspaper carried reports of the sub-NGOs making extortionate demands upon the SHGs they had formed. It was alleged that the head of a sub-NGO had demanded cash and gifts of household furniture from the SHGs in order to set up a new household after his marriage! Eventually, one of the three sub-NGOs, which was relatively unscathed by charges of corruption, secured the position of the official partner NGO of Mahalir Thittam for Thillai block in 2003. As this account suggests, the TNCDW's strategies of recruitment have taken myriad forms at field levels, often appealing to what Mosse (2004) identifies as the 'practical interests' of the NGO actors in question. In this case, the financial support provided by Mahalir Thittam was indispensable for the partner NGO to execute the programme and even for its continued organisational survival.[18]

If the Mahalir Thittam partner NGO in Thillai was resource-poor, this was clearly not the case with its competitor, the local branch of an established international non-governmental organisation (INGO). The INGO was drawn to the promotion of SHGs as part of the global endorsement of microfinance and the Indian state's validation of SHG promotion as legitimate, desirable development activity towards which the energies of the voluntary sector might be directed. Drawn to Thillai block by the prevalence of bonded labour (including that of children) in the beedi-rolling, match and brick kiln industries, the INGO's primary objectives were the elimination of child labour and rehabilitation of former child labourers, rather than the formation of SHGs per se. The INGO secured the release of children bonded in the beedi industry, made their mothers the members of the newly formed SHGs and offered them subsidised financial assistance to buy milch cattle and goats. Besides SHG promotion, the INGO supplied free or subsidised education material to schoolgoing children; organised children's clubs, adolescent clubs and health camps; and sponsored preschool *balwadis* in the absence of government balwadis. The INGO was widely perceived as a benevolent purveyor of largesse that brought village communities resources unmatched by other SHG promoter agencies in Thillai block.

Interestingly, the SHG landscape in Thillai block, and in Tamil Nadu more generally, was marked not only by competition between state-partner and non-partner NGOs but also by competition within the state sector. The introduction of the SGSY scheme in April 1999 by the central government had led to a phase of conflict in Tamil Nadu (in the early 2000s) between the Department of Rural Development charged with implementation of the SGSY scheme targeting SHGs and the Social Welfare Department (in whose administrative control the TNCDW was then placed), with both staking claim to being the primary agency for promoting SHGs on behalf of the state.[19] In many parts of the state, the SHGs formed by the DRDA/BDO structure either became dysfunctional on account of poor institutional support or were taken over by Mahalir Thittam. However, pockets of BDO-promoted SHGs continued to remain active. In Thillai block, during the period of my fieldwork, the Mahalir Thittam partner NGO perceived the Block Development Office as its principal rival. The BDO used its field-level functionaries (rural welfare officers) and its links to local panchayat presidents to form SHGs that it zealously protected from being poached by the Mahalir Thittam partner NGO.

Besides the BDO, INGO and the MaThi partner NGO, the branches of nationalised commercial banks also undertook SHG promotion on an *ad hoc* basis in Thillai block. In Nalloor, one of the three study villages in Thillai block, the bank's entry into SHG promotion was sudden and unforeseen by both the bank and the SHGs. The SHG landscape in Nalloor village was marked by volatility and flux during the three-year period that the sub-NGOs attempted to form and foster SHGs. Having been abandoned by the NGO that had formed the groups and devoid of assistance in maintaining group accounts,[20] the nine SHGs active in the village contacted a second locally based NGO. This relationship also did not work out. The NGO demanded a bribe of Rs 500 from each SHG to pay the BDO for processing a loan through the SGSY scheme. When an SHG offered to pay officials of the BDO directly, the NGO was furious. On one occasion, the NGO ordered all the SHGs to bring their account books for auditing, which was reportedly performed by 'two young people who looked like college students'. Although the SHGs paid for this service, they were not informed of the outcome of the audit and did not receive a receipt for the payment.

The SHGs in Nalloor were particularly angered by the NGO's 'order' that they pay for the celebration of the International Women's Day in March 2003 and by the shoddy arrangements made by the NGO at the event. An SHG member described it thus:

> The NGO made us pay Rs.160 per SHG for the March 8th celebration. More than 1000 women had gathered at the event. There was only one drum of water. No glasses. And a single tent that did not provide enough cover for all. Most women were sitting on the mud. Imagine how much money the NGO must have made from the 70 or more SHGs that were gathered.

When interacting with the manager of the local bank branch in which the SHGs had savings bank accounts, the women complained frequently about the NGO, leading the bank manager to offer his assistance in overseeing group accounts. On the suggestion of the bank manager, all the nine SHGs in Nalloor decided to host a function to mark the International Women's Day in the village in 2004, rather than the block headquarters as suggested by the NGO. This assertion of independence decisively severed the ties of the SHGs with the NGO and marked the moment they became bank-promoted SHGs. By pleading their case as the helpless victims of unscrupulous and duplicitous NGOs, the women appealed to the financing bank. In this instance, the bank assumed the mantle of promoter (and protector) well after the groups were formed and functional and sought primarily to eliminate NGO intermediaries. Given the presence of multiple actors in the microfinance landscape of Thillai, the SHG women often self-identified their groups as 'BDO office' groups, 'bank groups' and 'Mahalir Thittam groups'. The quality of the promotional services offered by different agencies also varied considerably.[21]

The village context: livelihood profiles

The three villages of study in Thillai block were selected on the basis of contrastive livelihood profiles and the presence of SHGs promoted by diverse agencies. The 2001 population census provided data on the occupational profile of villages through the principal categories of 'agriculture', 'household industries' and 'other workers'. An economically backward village, *Karisal* had the highest percentage (36%) of total working population engaged in 'household-based industries' among all the 45 villages in the administrative block of Thillai.[22] The industry in question was the *beedi* or low-cost, hand-rolled cigarette industry. Local informants and officials of the BDO described Karisal village as one of high poverty owing to the concentration of a beedi-dependent, impoverished and overwhelming SC[23] workforce, formerly characterised by the bondage of adults and children. The geographic location of Karisal as interior village also contributed to its economically deprived status. Unlike the two other villages that were located close to a main road linking two major townships (on which buses arrived every 10–15 minutes), the buses that linked Karisal village to the nearest town arrived at fixed hours of the day.

Agriculture accounted for 68% of total working population in *Prakasam* village. Local informants pointed to the absence of non-agricultural (non-farm) livelihood activities in the village, re-emphasising the centrality of agriculture to their livelihoods. *Nalloor* village had the highest percentage of working population (92%) listed as 'other workers' in the administrative block of Thillai. The clustering of leather-based industries in a neighbouring township provided the residents of Nalloor village the prospect of round-the-year employment in shoe companies and leather tanneries as well as home-based 'job work' in the manufacture of footwear. In the villages of Karisal, Prakasam and Nalloor, the women from land-poor households – the principal constituency of the SHGs – performed daily wage labour in agriculture, brick kilns, the construction sector and leather-based industries; domestic work in wealthier households; and subsistence-level self-employment activities.

The two principal caste groups in the three villages were the other backward classes (OBCs) and the SCs. The OBCs in the villages consisted of the *Mudaliars*, *Naidus*, *Gond (Kuruman)*, *Boyd*, *Asaris*, *Kosavars*, *Mandiris* and *Vaaniyars*. Besides the *Parayars* (the numerically dominant SC community in northern Tamil Nadu), Karisal village had a smaller residential settlement comprising the *Arunthathiyars*, who are traditionally ranked lower than Parayars in the caste-based social hierarchy of Tamil Nadu.

Institutional context: SHGs in the study villages and fieldwork methods

All 27 SHGs in the 3 villages were exclusively women's groups, with age ranging from three to seven years.[24] Each SHG, as soon as it was formed, had opened a savings bank account with a nearest bank branch. The number of members per SHG ranged from 16 to 20. Of the 27 SHGs, barring two groups, all the others were composed exclusively of the SCs or the OBCs. It is not uncommon for SHGs in rural Tamil Nadu to have exclusive members of the SCs or the OBCs given that the two caste groups usually live in segregated fashion in separate hamlets. Table 1.1 shows the distribution of 27 SHGs by village, caste and promoter agency.

The fieldwork consisted primarily of participant observation of the weekly SHG meetings as well as semi-structured, open-ended and wide-ranging interviews conducted over several sessions with SHG leaders and members. In order to observe the SHGs' multiple negotiations (initiated and led by group leaders) with banks, the BDO and NGOs, I routinely accompanied the women on their visits to NGO-organised meetings held to facilitate communication between promoter agencies and the SHGs as well as visits to the BDO and the bank to seek details about specific schemes or to urge the officials to act quickly on a particular loan they had applied for. I sought out women who had dropped out or were pushed out from the SHGs, seeking to understand the circumstances that had led to their expulsion. The account books of SHGs and their loan ledgers in particular were a rich source of primary data on the 'credit

Table 1.1 SHGs by village, caste and promoter agency: Karisal, Prakasam and Nalloor

Caste	*Karisal*		*Prakasam*		*Nalloor*	*Total*
	INGO	*BDO*	*Partner NGO*	*BDO*	*Bank*	
Scheduled castes	3	2	5	1	4	15
Other backward classes	3	–	2	–	5	10
Mixed (SC and OBC)	2	–	–	–	–	2
Total	8	2	7	1	9	27

Source: Fieldwork data.

histories' (record of borrowing and repayment) of all members since the formation of the groups. In Karisal and Prakasam villages, I recorded the credit histories of all the (327) women members in the 18 SHGs and sought information on the livelihoods that sustained their households in order to understand the extent of socio-economic disparities among SHG members and the ways in which these impinged on group functioning.[25]

Of 327 (100 OBC and 227 SC) women members in 18 SHGs in Karisal and Prakasam villages, 83% belonged to landless and wage labour–dependent households. Given the overlapping of caste- and class-based hierarchies and deprivation in the Indian social context, it is not surprising that the OBC households relied on small enterprises or 'own-account' enterprises to a greater extent as compared to the SCs. Of 100 women of the OBCs in the 18 SHGs, the households of 18 women (hence 18%) managed own-account enterprises. Among the 227 SC women, the households of no more than 9 women (4%) managed own-account enterprises. Conversely, the reliance on beedi-rolling as principal livelihood was far higher among the SC women's households. A total of 34% (77 of 227) of SC women's households relied on beedi work in stark contrast to 5% (5 of 100) of OBC women's households.

Conclusion

This chapter has described the processes of translation by which the novel policy idea of SHG-banking or financial intermediation through women's self-organised collectives stabilised itself as an authoritative interpretation (Mosse 2004) and gained hegemonic sway over the development sector in India. By harnessing the central concerns of the anti-poverty, efficiency and women's economic empowerment frameworks, an array of influential institutional actors have been enlisted for the project of financing SHGs through direct linkage and subsidy-bearing anti-poverty schemes.

In this chapter, I argued that the development rationality that underpins SHG-banking (via the direct linkage scheme) contrasts in stark ways with the older ethos of social banking with respect to both the *means* and the *ends* of microfinance lending. The *means*, namely no interest concession, no capital subsidies, no grace period of non-repayment, no sectoral targets, no attempt to direct borrowing purpose and the linkage of credit disbursed to the volume of group savings, have set apart SHG-banking from the conventional poverty lending–type programmes of the social banking era (late

1960s to the end of the 1980s). Likewise, the *end* of contributing to the financial sustainability and profitability of the banking system points to the shift in signification that microfinance-type lending to the poor heralds. I have also made explicit the links between the overwhelming female constituency of SHGs and the (global and national) ascendance of the efficiency paradigm within gender and development discourses by showing how the conceptualisation of women as crucial and underutilised *resources* for development underpins SHG-banking.

If the RBI and NABARD have attempted to fashion SHG-banking in conformity with the commercial principles of banking, the Ministry of Rural Development has responded to other priorities and imperatives. It has sought to incorporate SHGs within a policy legacy of central government–sponsored, subsidy-bearing anti-poverty schemes. The SGSY scheme has, in turn, provoked the displeasure of microfinance analysts and practitioners for its signal departure from the essential tenets of microfinance. By foregrounding the divergent and contradictory nature of the 'ambitions' and 'calculations' of the central actors involved in the promotion of the SHG phenomenon in India, I suggest that SHG-based microfinance, like other technologies of rule, is best understood as 'hybrid, heterogeneous [and] traversed by a variety of programmatic aspirations and professional obligations rather than implanted through the monotonous implementation of a hegemonic will to govern' (Rose 1999: 54). The 'centres of calculation' have aspired to construct and align rural women's goal of 'financial inclusion' with the banking sector's objective of profitability, on the one hand, and governmental goals of the entrepreneurial success of women in poverty on the other. In the subsequent chapters, I show the many ways in which these goals are, in part, resisted and even subverted by the women 'subjects' of development.

In my discussion of the spread of SHG-banking targeting rural women in the Indian states, I highlighted the growing political investment of state governments in owning a highly visible development initiative that mobilises large numbers of the rural poor, besides extending survival-oriented assistance to population groups least likely to benefit from market liberalisation and neo-liberal economic reforms gaining momentum during this period (Chatterjee 2008a; Gupta and Sharma 2006). The financial and technical aid provided by bilateral and multilateral agencies to state governments in order to expand the rural base of women's SHGs during the late 1990s and the 2000s reflects the growing global support for the agenda of mainstreaming women in development and building the capacities of women from low-income households and communities to engage in the self-care (Lemke 2001) of themselves and their families. In this chapter, I discussed also how development NGOs and the banking sector were induced and motivated to assume the responsibilities of both SHG promotion and financing. Through financial and other incentives, the RBI and NABARD have steered and directed NGOs nationwide to promote SHGs and even to intermediate financially by on-lending bank credit to SHGs. It is evident that the recruitment (Mosse 2004) of NGOs has been perceived by policymakers as critical to the cost-effective promotion of the microfinance phenomenon in the country.

In the last section of this chapter, I outlined the institutional context of SHG promotion in Thillai block, in particular, and Tamil Nadu, more generally, and the key actors therein. During the period of this field study,[26] they included the Mahalir Thittam partner NGOs, other (non-partner) NGOs, the rural development administration and the banking sector. In Tamil Nadu, the TNCDW has identified, trained and financed NGO partners in order to expand the outreach of SHGs in all the districts of the state. In Thillai block, the BDO and the Mahalir Thittam partner NGO often vied with each other to attract and retain the loyalty of SHGs within their fold. The INGO retained a competitive edge owing to its ability to provide significant material resources valued by rural communities. In some villages (like Nalloor), exploitative NGOs drove the SHG women to seek protection from the financing bank that, in this specific instance, offered it willingly.

Notes

1 A part of the material in Chapter 1 of this book, drawing on my fieldwork in Tamil Nadu, has been discussed in my paper titled 'SHG Intermediation and Women's Agency: A View from Tamil Nadu' published in Tara S. Nair (ed.). 2015. *Microfinance in India: Approaches, Outcomes, Challenges*. India: Routledge.

2 Banks are mandated to direct 40% of net bank credit to 'priority' sectors that include agriculture, micro and small enterprises, education, housing and designated 'weaker sections' such as small and marginal farmers, artisans, village and cottage industries. The scope of the priority sector as well as targets and sub-targets applicable to specific groups has undergone several changes over the years (*RBI* 2013). An account of the re-definition of the priority sector in the post-reforms era is available in Shahjahan (1999).

3 The growth of a pilot project into corporate bank strategy is outlined by Dasgupta (2001) and Kropp and Suran (2002).

4 SHG-banking has been described as a 'cool breeze for sweating bankers' that offers the prospect of social banking with profits (Sheokand 2000).

5 Although the IRDP aimed to include 30% women among total beneficiaries, a mid-term review found that women constituted less than 5% of all beneficiaries and were the priority group most likely to be excluded; this led to the launch of the Development of Women and Children in Rural Areas (DWCRA) in 1982–83 which exclusively targeted women with financial assistance intended to promote income generation (Kabeer and Murthy 1996; World Bank 1991). The IRDP, DWCRA and a host of smaller self-employment-oriented schemes were dissolved and replaced by the SGSY in April 1999.

6 An analytical account of shifting paradigms within gender and development discourses is provided by Kabeer (1995), Moser (1993: 55–79) and Razavi and Miller (1995).

7 A study of three leading microcredit programmes in Bangladesh reported an increase of 18 taka in annual household consumption expenditure for every 100 additional taka borrowed by women, compared to an increase of 11 taka for men (Pitt and Khandker 1998). The study findings are often quoted in the microfinance literature to buttress claims regarding the efficacy of lending to women.

8 See, for instance, the budget speech of the minister of finance and food Mr Ponnaiyan of the AIADMK delivered to the state assembly in 2004–5 (GOTN 2004).

9 The village panchayat, the lowest unit of elected government, is part of the three-tiered Panchayati Raj structure, direct elections to which have been regularly held every five years since the 73rd and 74th Amendments to the Indian Constitution. The origin and history of political decentralisation in India is available in Chaudhuri (2006).

10 The TNCDW was established in 1983 with the twin objectives of socio-economic development and empowerment of women.

11 The ICDS centres address child malnutrition in India by providing health, nutrition and pre-school education services to children between zero and six years. The services are provided through a network of *anganwadi* centres established in rural areas.

12 See, for instance, the speeches of Dr C. Rangarajan, former governor, RBI, reported in the *RBI Bulletin* (1994, 1997).

13 Most development NGOs are registered as non-profits under the Societies Registration Act 1860 or the Indian Trusts Act 1882. During the 2000s, several NGO-MFIs have transformed themselves or converted legally to commercial entities or non-banking financial companies registered under the Companies Act, 1956, so that they may expand the outreach of their microfinance activities by receiving investment or borrowings from outside, offer diversified financial products (including savings and insurance), overcome reliance on donor funding and take the most promising route to financial sustainability (Sriram and Upadhyayula 2004).

14 DHAN Foundation works in Tamil Nadu; MYRADA in Karnataka, Andhra Pradesh and Tamil Nadu; and Pradan in Odisha, West Bengal, Bihar, Jharkhand, Chhattisgarh, Madhya Pradesh and Rajasthan.

15 While they do not directly undertake financial intermediation themselves, MYRADA and DHAN Foundation have created not-for-profit (Section 25) companies that lend to the SHGs they promote in order to meet a large 'unmet demand' from the groups that the bank linkage programme does not fully meet.

16 The names of the administrative block and the three villages of intensive study are code names. Likewise, I refer to the type of promoter agency without revealing the actual names of the specific NGOs or identifying the nationalised bank in question. My aim is to protect the identities of the SHGs and the NGOs so that they do not face adverse consequences (such as the denial of bank loans) for the information they have shared with me. However, all contextual details pertaining to the study villages, the SHGs and their members have been retained.

17 This terminology was used by the NGOs in question in the region of study.

18 Usually the founders of such NGOs had several years of work experience as field staff in larger, funded, well-established NGOs. After quitting their former employers, these individuals seized the opportunity presented by Mahalir Thittam to establish their own NGOs.

19 Personal communication with an official of TNCDW, April 2004.

20 The Mahalir Thittam scheme required an SHG to maintain seven books for the purposes of financial accounting and recording group proceedings. Even NGOs that did not participate in Mahalir Thittam reproduced this accounting protocol as bank officials were familiar with the templates.

21 This is discussed at length in Chapter 4.

22 Data on the working population in each village was sourced from the Primary Census Abstract, Census of India 2001, http://www.censusindia.gov.in/2011-common/census_data_2001.html.

23 The Indian government classifies caste groups as the scheduled castes and the other backward classes in decreasing order of social oppression and deprivation.

24 In the villages of study, I focused on all SHGs that were older than three years of age so that the women might have sufficient experience in SHG participation. The annexure provides SHG-wise data including the name of the group, age of the group at the time of study, its caste composition, its promoter agency and the quantum of bank loans it has secured via the direct linkage and the SGSY schemes.

25 The data on household livelihoods and the credit histories of group members was not obtained for the nine SHGs in Nalloor owing to the constraints of time and resources. However, I carried out all other aspects of the fieldwork, including the interviews with SHG members, leaders and observation of group meetings in Nalloor village.

26 Other actors have entered SHG promotion more recently in Tamil Nadu. These are discussed in the concluding chapter.

Chapter 2

Becoming micro-banks

Generating capital, building discipline

A SHG has an average size of about 15 people from a homogeneous class. . . . They are encouraged to make voluntary thrift on a regular basis. They use this pooled resource to make small interest bearing loans to their members. The process helps them imbibe the essentials of financial intermediation including prioritisation of needs, setting terms and conditions and accounts keeping. This gradually builds financial discipline and credit history for themselves. . . . They also learn to handle resources of a size that is much beyond their individual capacities. The SHG members begin to appreciate that resources are limited and have a cost.

'Self Help Group – A Concept' in *Progress of SHG Bank Linkage in India 2005–6*, NABARD (2006)[1]

'All strategies are available to a woman in trouble except asking the SHG for extra repayment time.'

A member of *Annai Parasakthi* SHG (Mahalir Thittam [MaThi]-SC).[2]

Cultivating autonomy

Microfinance analysts observe that the decisional autonomy that the village-level peer groups enjoy in the SHG model of microfinance is greater than that of their counterparts in the microfinance institution (MFI)-organised Joint Liability Groups or the Grameen bank-styled model of rural banking (Dasgupta 2001; Harper 2002a; Kalpana 2005). In the latter case, also described as the 'provider' model of microfinance provision to distinguish it from the 'promoter' model (Rutherford 2000), peer groups of borrowers save with and borrow from the local branch of the MFI, which owns the funds. The paid employees of the MFI manage bookkeeping and accounting responsibilities and set the terms of financial transactions within the groups. The MFI takes decisions regarding the size of loans, the interest rates, repayment duration and the sequencing of loans among peer group borrowers, in keeping with its broader policy on these issues (Rutherford 2000). In contrast, the SHGs generate their own capital and make group-level decisions regarding the circulation and repayment of their funds among group members prior to seeking bank credit. Acknowledging this, a National Bank for Agriculture and Rural Development (NABARD)-commissioned study observes that SHGs are 'organised, owned, operated and controlled by members, based on solidarity, reciprocity, common interest and resource pooling' (Kropp and Suran 2002: 13). It points out that SHGs display 'capacity for self-governance', make 'autonomous' decisions regarding their savings and group-generated credit and enjoy 'full autonomy' with respect to the use and allocation of bank loans secured through the linkage scheme. The decisional autonomy of the SHGs sets them apart from other microcredit systems such as the Grameen model, making the former a 'unique contribution to microfinance' (Kropp and Suran 2002: 25).

NABARD's manuals on SHG-banking unequivocally clarify that the financial transactions of SHGs must be governed by the terms and conditions selected by the women themselves through autonomous, group-level choices. The NABARD (n.d. 1: 10) handbook for branch-level bank managers emphasises that the SHGs are expected to cultivate savings as a 'regular and continuous habit' and that the 'savings first-credit later' principle is a means to foster 'self-dependence' and 'self-reliance'. SHGs are exhorted to 'supply' capital to meet the 'demand' for low-cost credit that poor households have, with the women deciding for themselves the purpose, the amount of loans, the rate of interest and the schedule of repayment.[3] NABARD (2006) expects that the women's autonomous decisions and actions will enable them to acquire 'financial discipline', imbibe 'the essentials of financial intermediation' and make prudent reasoned decisions 'when resources are limited in relation to demand'. The experience of SHG participation is thus expected to serve the *pedagogic* purpose of instilling the skills and capacities by which women living in poverty learn to optimally manage productive resources in contexts of scarcity and poverty and cultivate the subjectivities deemed necessary for survival in neoliberal economies. The SHGs may therefore be seen as sites wherein autonomous actors who are expected to be free, self-managing and self-actualising with respect to their group transactional practices and the management of their 'micro-banks' learn to responsibly exercise their freedom in appropriate ways (Rose 1999).

In this chapter, drawing on my fieldwork from Tamil Nadu and secondary literature from other parts of the country, I show that the women members of SHGs were expected and encouraged by promoter and financing agencies to be calculative actors who adopt a 'financial rationality' by accurately estimating the relative costs and benefits of selecting particular financial practices rather than others and to exercise their autonomy in responsible ways. I show how the women members of SHGs act on themselves and on each other in their efforts to 'capitalise the self' and constitute their collectives as 'calculable spaces' or a 'complex of incessant calculations' (Rose 1999: 152), which strive to maximise productivity, cut out waste and choose between competing priorities on the basis of a cost–benefit calculus. However, as Miller and Rose (1990) point out, while governmentality is eternally optimistic, realities always escape the theories that inform programmes and the ambitions that underpin them. I show therefore how promoter and financing agencies' conceptualisations of disciplined financial intermediation were often at variance with the expressed needs and concerns of the SHG women, who chose practices that embodied alternative judgements and rationalities. In this chapter, I outline these tensions by discussing the financial transactions of the SHGs with regard to the *generation* of capital (via member savings and interest rates on internal loans), its quick *turnover* and timely *repayment*.

Generating capital: promoter stipulations and livelihood conditions

An ethnographic study of microfinance programmes in five villages of *Koppal* taluk[4] (Karnataka) finds that the amount and regularity of SHGs' savings are determined as much by the rules of promoter NGO as the women's capacity to save (Premchander *et al.* 2009). Likewise, a study of SHGs sponsored by the NGOs MYRADA and Hand in Hand in Karnataka and Tamil Nadu reports that while the groups are free to determine their two key financial variables, namely minimum savings requirements and interest rates on loans, the promoting NGOs do provide general guidelines based on the available evidence of successful groups (Gadenne and Vasudevan 2007). The EDA and APMAS (2006) study of 214 SHGs drawn from the four states of Andhra Pradesh, Karnataka, Orissa and Rajasthan also observes that the decision regarding the groups' savings is usually guided by the promoter agency and accepted by group members at the time of group formation. In my fieldwork villages in Thillai block as well, the principal promoter agencies had issued guidelines regarding the terms of transactions when the SHGs were formed.

All promoters in Thillai block (barring the international non-governmental organisation [INGO] to a certain extent) exhorted women to accumulate their reserves of capital as quickly as possible and to set their quantum of savings and interest rates to meet this objective. While the SHGs heeded promoter instructions regarding appropriate financial practices, they self-assessed and collectively evaluated their capacity to save and to generate capital keeping in mind the livelihood conditions in the village economy and the terms of lending that prevailed in the informal sector. Urged by the Block Development Office (BDO), the Mahalir Thittam NGO and the bank, the SHGs they promoted in the three villages made regular weekly savings of Rs 10 per member (Rs 40–50 each month) and deposited the cash in the bank on a weekly basis. The INGO, which had consciously sought to initiate its developmental activities in economically deprived villages (such as Karisal) in Thillai block, was wary of urging SHGs to accelerate the pace of capital generation. It instructed SHGs to permit their members to make weekly or monthly savings and did not stipulate the minimum savings amount, leaving it to the discretion of the groups instead.

The quantum of savings in the INGO-promoted SHGs in Karisal village (Thillai) varied from group to group, with the variation corresponding to differences of caste and the associated severity of economic deprivation. The predominance of beedi-related livelihoods in the Dalit colony of Karisal village was reflected in the lower quantum of monthly savings among the SHGs therein. The INGO-promoted SHGs comprising women of the scheduled castes and the mixed-caste groups saved Rs 24 and Rs 30 per member on a monthly basis, whereas the SHGs populated by women belonging to the other backward classes (OBCs) in the village saved Rs 50 per member each month. A study of 240 SHGs in eight districts of Andhra Pradesh also points to the link between the caste of the groups (a proxy indicatory for poverty) and the amount of savings their members are able to set aside (APMAS 2007). While regular savings in these SHGs varied from less than Rs 20 up to Rs 100 a month per member, 59% of SHGs with members drawn only from the SCs and 63% with members from the scheduled tribes (STs) saved Rs 30 or less per member on a monthly basis. On the other hand, 62% of SHGs with members drawn from the backward classes or the other caste category saved over Rs 30.

The directives from promoter agencies could sometimes outweigh livelihood-related considerations as I found in the case of the two BDO-promoted SHGs in the Dalit colony of Karisal village. These SHGs, in contrast to the INGO-promoted groups in their hamlet that saved Rs 24 a month, saved Rs 40–50 a month, despite the participation of women from the poorest households in the village. In this case, the rural welfare officer of the BDO, who had formed the groups, had cautioned the women that they would not receive financial support from a benevolent external agent (as would the INGO-promoted groups in the village) and urged them to accelerate their own accumulation of capital in order to compensate. Women's autonomous choices regarding the terms of their financial transactions also came to be shaped by their growing awareness that their decisions affected their chances of securing bank loans. The INGO-promoted SHGs in the SC habitation of Karisal village had set the savings amount per member at Rs 10 per month when their groups were formed and increased it (to Rs 24) after officials of the BDO reprimanded the women for their 'low' savings capacity likely to render them ineligible for bank loans.

The EDA and APMAS (2006) study of sample SHGs drawn from four states also found that the savings amount of SHGs usually changes with time and that a significant factor inducing women to raise the savings amount was the groups' eligibility from the point of view of assessment for bank loans. Over half the 214 SHGs in their study had raised the monthly savings per member from Rs 30 to Rs 50 and a few even to Rs 100 (in the case of 25 SHGs in Karnataka and Rajasthan). As the direct linkage scheme ties the amount of bank loan sanctioned to the volume of group savings (ratio of 4:1), the prospect of larger loans from financing banks acts as a powerful incentive for the women to increase the quantum of savings. However, not all SHGs are able to increase their savings in the expectation of receiving large-sized bank loans. The EDA and APMAS (2006) study found that one-third of the SHGs (including the majority of the groups studied in Andhra Pradesh) saved less than Rs 30 a month and were reluctant to increase the savings amount. While a government-supported federation of SHGs comprising the STs in Orissa insisted that the members save a minimum Rs 30 per month from the point of view of securing bank loans in the future, the promoter NGOs were reported to be uncertain whether (or not) to 'push' the SHG members to increase the quantum of savings (ibid.).

Insofar as interest rates on the group loans are concerned, a study of 34 SHGs in Karnataka and 35 in Tamil Nadu finds that they averaged 22% per annum and were set at least as high (and usually higher) than the interest charged by the bank to SHGs ranging from 9.6% to 12% per year (Gadenne and Vasudevan 2007). The EDA and APMAS (2006) study in four states likewise finds that SHGs generally lend to group members at an average rate of 24% per annum (or 2% per month), with 85% of the sample SHGs lending at this rate or less. In Thillai block as well, the BDO, MaThi and bank-promoted SHGs chose (for the most part)[5] 24% annual rates of diminishing interest, in response to promoter instructions to do so. When choosing interest rates, the frame of reference that guided women's decisions was the rates that prevailed in the informal sector,[6] making 24% rates of interest appear concessional and an acceptable alternative. In keeping with its conscious decision to form SHGs in impoverished hamlets, the INGO instructed the SHGs it promoted to set annual (diminishing) interest rates at 12%. As a result, all the INGO-promoted SHGs in Karisal village chose 12% annual rates of interest in contrast to the 24% rates preferred by the other SHGs in the three villages.

Enforcing repayment and disciplining the self

The available literature on group transactional practices of SHGs reports a great diversity of practices with respect to the repayment of internal loans or those borrowed out of group funds. Micro-level studies of SHGs in Koppal taluk (Karnataka) found that the women preferred 'balloon repayment' or a practice whereby borrowers repaid the interest regularly and the loan principal only when they had money or needed another loan and wanted, therefore, to complete repayment of the current loan (Premchander *et al.* 2009). Likewise, a large-scale study of SHGs in nine blocks of four districts in Assam found that 71 (of a total 109) sample SHGs had no fixed time period to return the loan amount, collected interest regularly and permitted borrowers to repay the principal at their convenience. In contrast, the SHGs I studied in Thillai block set a formal repayment period and expected that loans be fully repaid within this period. As with the interest rates and the savings amount (discussed earlier), the repayment duration of internal loans varied between the INGO-promoted SHGs in Karisal and those promoted by the other agencies in the three villages. In the former SHGs, loans could be repaid between five and seven months, often extending to ten months or even longer. The women affirmed that co-members showed sufficient understanding and granted grace periods of non-repayment (of two to three months) of loan principal during a period of household stress.

On the other hand, the Mahalir Thittam–promoted SHGs in Prakasam village expected that all internal loans be repaid in five equal monthly instalments, *no matter the loan amount*. Among the bank-promoted SHGs in Nalloor village, the loans were repaid on a fortnightly (rather than monthly) basis over a five-month cycle, requiring women to generate cash and meet repayment deadlines at shorter intervals. The fortnightly repayment of principal over five-month cycles made the repayment terms of these groups the most exacting of all 27 SHGs in the three villages. The easy availability of non-farm livelihoods in Nalloor village (especially jobs in the leather industry) had made it possible for the SHGs to adopt and their women to comply with these repayment terms. While the INGO instructed its SHGs to generally adopt a sympathetic attitude towards women facing repayment crises and never resort to strategies involving public humiliation, the other promoter agencies did not issue explicit instructions on the strategies that SHGs might use to enforce repayment.

Seeking to facilitate the quick turnover of their group capital, the Mahalir Thittam and bank-promoted SHGs in Prakasam and Nalloor villages steered their women towards on-time loan repayment through multiple disciplinary strategies. These included increasing the social costs to women of requesting additional repayment time, condoning a delay *only* during circumstances that were declared exceptional, aggressively calling upon women to borrow from the informal lending sector to repay SHG loans and frequently declaring (during group meetings) that the punitive repayment schedules of the informal lending sector were model practices worthy of emulation. In particular, these SHGs strove to cultivate an atmosphere in which women sanctioned and censored each other whenever a borrower sought additional time. In the words of a member of *Annai Janaki* SHG (MaThi-SC), a woman who sought extra time on the grounds of household distress was likely to be taunted by co-members thus, 'The women ask – did you not put out your hand to take the loan when it was given to you? You said nothing of household distress then.' The president of Annai Janaki SHG justified her decision to not grant additional time, however extenuating the circumstances, by drawing on the example of the informal credit sector (The SHG president: 'Will the moneylender allow us extra time? Why should I?').

The bank-promoted SHGs in Nalloor village displayed the least tolerance for delayed loan repayment and allowed a borrower to miss a month of repayment by declaring it an extreme case deserving of exceptional treatment and doing so in a manner that underscored the non-negotiability of the repayment schedules in all other circumstances. *Vetri Magalir* SHG (Bank-OBC) permitted a member to miss a month's instalment since the family's milch cow had died and 'she was poor with small children to feed'. The direct supervision of the SHGs by the financing bank-cum-promoter was at least partly responsible for their relative inflexibility in accommodating a borrower's need for additional time. The bank manager insisted that the reason for missing a month's repayment of an internal loan be written in the Resolution Book of the SHG and shown to him each month. In case the reason was not recorded in the book, the manager summoned the concerned SHG member and directly sought an explanation. Having secured greater credit linkage from banks as compared to the groups in Karisal and Prakasam, the SHGs of Nalloor village simultaneously repaid multiple loans sourced from the bank and the group.[7] The secretary of Vetri Magalir SHG admitted (to me) that the group leaders shouted at women who delayed repayment and ordered them to pledge jewellery or other household assets to repay their loans on time.

While it was common practice for the women members of the SHGs that prioritised the quick turnover of capital to pledge/pawn jewellery and household utensils to repay SHG loans, it was not unknown among the other SHGs in the fieldwork villages in Thillai either. The implications of asset pledging were different for women from poorer vis-à-vis those from relatively better-off households. A member of *Tamarai* SHG (INGO-OBC) pledged gold jewellery to repay a balance (of Rs 2,000) on a loan of Rs 5,000 when she had only a month of repayment time left. She did so in order to immediately apply for a new loan, which would give her ten months of repayment time. All SHGs refused to approve new loans to members unless the existing ones were fully repaid. Intended to ensure continuing high loan access within the SHG, the rationale that underlay asset pledging in such instances differed from the compulsions that marked asset pledging as a distress-induced strategy. The women of poorer households were more likely to account for informal borrowing as a strategy that enabled them to discharge SHG-sourced debt 'with honour' in a context marked by 'uncertain incomes and multiple loans owed to informal lenders and the SHG', as described by a member of *Roja* SHG (MaThi-SC). Having pledged assets 'countless times' to repay SHG loans, she maintained that household economic stress made it impossible for her to repay even a loan of Rs 500 without pledging assets.

If their borrowers delayed repayment, the SHGs were faced with decisions about deploying (or not) public shaming strategies such as collectively showing up at a defaulter's doorstep and demanding repayment. The EDA and APMAS (2006) study of 214 SHGs from four states (Andhra Pradesh, Karnataka, Orissa and Rajasthan) found that irregular repayments were often tolerated, and groups did make adjustments to support a member in difficulty. The extent to which such adjustments took place depended not only on the amount of default but also on the group's plans to apply for an external loan. The repayment cultures of SHGs were shaped both by the group leaders and by the field staff of the promoter agency, and members often compared the role of different group leaders or of a new fieldworker in this regard. A group usually waited for six months to a year in the case of delayed repayment, and some groups took extreme action after this period. Such action included instances of locking a defaulting member out of her house and seizing the key or attaching household assets, until loans were fully repaid. The SHGs assessed their relationship to a member before initiating disciplinary action. They disciplined those they felt able to, sparing group members who belonged to powerful or locally influential families (EDA and APMAS 2006).

The SHGs I studied in Thillai block feared that strategies involving public humiliation of a borrower (and by implication, her household) could backfire by involving men, developing into a community-level conflict and securing the SHG a 'bad image' in the perception of the village public. The SHGs eschewed strategies that involved public shaming and chose those (such as the imposition of fines) that could be executed in relative autonomy of the community at large, in order to avoid public knowledge of and hostility towards their disciplining strategies.

A case of peer harassment?

> It was not uncommon for the repayment enforcement strategies that an SHG pursued to be perceived as distasteful or excessive by another in the same village and sharing the same disciplinary regime. Among the bank-promoted SHGs in Nalloor, *Then-Koodu* (OBC) had acquired the worst reputation for hounding borrowers who delayed repayment. An SHG member (a poorer woman who made her living by vegetable vending) missed monthly payment on a bank loan when her son underwent a throat surgery. She was forced by the SHG to pay a fine of Rs 50 for each day of repayment missed on the bank loan. In addition, she was required to pay a daily fine of Rs 10 for late payment of her internal, SHG sourced loan. When she paid the total fine of Rs 550 for the period of late repayment, she broke down at the SHG meeting. A total fine of Rs 2,000 collected by Then-Koodu SHG over a two-year period was distributed equally among all its members as part of group earnings.

The women members of Mahalir Thittam and bank-promoted SHGs in the study villages in Thillai block described the constant reigning in of household and self-consumption in order to sustain disciplined financial performance, signalling the inculcation of a self that exercises constant vigilance, bridles its hungers and values at all times the preservation of personal honour above bodily survival needs. A member of *Vaigai* SHG (MaThi-SC) reported that poor women like her often had to prioritise loan repayment over food-related expenditure. As she said with some bitterness, 'Even if there is nothing to eat at home, we repay the loan. Is food important? Honour is more important.' She added after a silence, 'No one cares if you eat or starve.' Several women testified that high-cost food including egg, fish, meat and even vegetables were excised from the household diet about 10–15 days prior to the repayment of a monthly loan instalment.

Competing priorities: 'collective' mandate or 'individual' need?

When choosing appropriate financial practices (the savings, interest rates, repayment duration and enforcement strategies), the SHGs in the study villages in Thillai block implicitly evaluated and assessed alternative and competing priorities. Women admitted that the cost of attempting the rapid generation of their resources (through higher savings, higher interest rates, shorter loan cycles, stringent enforcement) was the intensification of household stress. On the other hand, they recognised that the transactional practices that protected borrowers (lower interest, longer cycles and a greater tolerance of delayed repayment) could slow down the pace of capital generation and impede the groups' capacity to meet the frequently recurring loan requirements of women. Central to the constitution of SHGs as micro-banks that generate their own capital was women's recognition, implicit or otherwise, of conflicting interests between the group as a *collective (and lender)* seeking to maximise the SHGs' capital and the *individual member-borrower* whose interests were better served by low-priced credit, a longer repayment cycle or greater flexibility in repayment. In a few cases, the SHGs' choices between these priorities even differed among groups in the same village and promoted by the same agency.

A minority of SHGs in each village of study in Thillai block adopted transactional practices that diverged from the normative practices observed by the other SHGs in the village. For the most part, these differences were motivated by disagreement with the emphasis on rapid capital generation that the promoter agencies had advocated. Two Mahalir Thittam SHGs had 12% annual interest rates in Prakasam village when all the other groups in the village had 24% rates. One of the SHGs had lowered the interest rate (from 24% to 12%) through a case of inter-village social and kinship interaction. The SHG's secretary was counselled to reduce the interest so as to lessen repayment stress by her aunt (SHG leader in another village) who often shared ideas with her niece on SHG-related affairs.

Autonomy for the individual

> Two Mahalir Thittam–promoted SHGs in Prakasam and two bank-promoted SHGs in Nalloor eschewed the practice of strict five-month loan repayment cycles and allowed a more relaxed repayment schedule for internal loans in marked contrast to the other groups in their villages. The varied motivations and needs of individual actors (the SHGs' leaders in particular) also shaped inter-SHG differences with respect to transactional practices. In the case of Roja SHG (MaThi-SC), the SHG president's frequent requirement of loans to finance her daughter's high-cost postgraduate education in Chennai was believed to have motivated the SHGs' willingness to tolerate delayed repayment

> extending to ten months. An SHG member put it thus, 'When the president breaks the rule (of five months) herself, she has to allow us to do so.' In *Bharathi* SHG (bank-SC), there was no 'rule' and the repayment duration was entirely determined by the circumstances of individual borrowers. A loan of Rs 3,000 could be repaid at Rs 300 a month over ten months or Rs 300 a week over ten weeks. When two SHG members repaid their loans in a ten-week cycle and pressured co-members to do the same, the others fought back and vigorously defended their right to determine the duration of their repayment cycle.

In the case of the four SHGs that permitted women to fine-tune their loan repayment schedules in keeping with household and livelihood-related circumstances and requirements, the loan periodicity was not predetermined, but the outcome of negotiation between the individual and the collective. The SHGs that institutionalised flexibility with respect to transactional norms (loan repayment cycles in particular) permitted their members greater autonomy vis-à-vis the collective. This flexibility and decisional autonomy, albeit rare and permitted only by a few SHGs (in my study sample of SHGs), was sought after by women. Where group transactional practices did not institutionalise flexibility, individual members attempted to wrest concessional terms for themselves – a longer repayment duration or even lower interest rates – on an individual, case-by-case basis.

If the SHGs are envisioned as serving a pedagogic function, my field study in Thillai block found that the women learn how to 'prioritise needs' (NABARD 2006) through their autonomous decisions on whether to prioritise the collective's mandate to accelerate the generation of micro-capital or the individual's need to protect herself and her household's resources from excessive strain. SHGs' decisions were not static and could change over time, even as SHG members spoke on behalf of the collective or the individual, with group leaders tending to assume the voice and interests of the collective, more often than not. Not infrequently, a woman's standpoint on her SHGs' priorities shifted depending on her own position within the group. As a borrower with a current loan outstanding, a woman might ask that her group consider the individual's plight with sympathy and disavow practices that worsen repayment-related tensions and disputes within households, usually between the spouses.

Disciplined financial intermediation: who decides?

In Thillai block, all promoter agencies strongly advocated that the SHGs strive towards the uninterrupted supply of capital through regular monthly savings and the efficient rotation of their corpus without a pause. They reminded the SHGs that the interest rates that the banks paid them on a savings bank account (about 4%–6% annual rates) were far lower than the rates they charged each other through intra-group loans (12%–24%). Women were urged to calculate the difference for themselves and then act as profit-seeking, rational economic actors would by retaining no more than the minimum balance in their respective bank accounts. However, the uninterrupted rotation of capital did not happen sometimes for reasons that women had little control over. In Karisal village, the SHGs in the SC habitation (promoted by the BDO and the INGO) reported irregular savings, infrequent group meetings and staggered loan repayment over a three-year period preceding the commencement of my field visits in February 2005. The women attributed this state of affairs to the dismal livelihood scenario in the village – an outcome of the near-drought conditions that had prevailed during four successive years (2002–5) in Tamil Nadu.

While the failure of rains had affected Thillai block as a whole, the meagre incomes yielded by the beedi industry in Karisal village made the availability of alternative sources of wage labour (in agriculture and the non-farm sectors) essential for survival, especially in the SC habitation. A scenario commonly described as 'no rains, no work' had adversely affected group transactional activities and sapped the enthusiasm of the early years of SHG formation in the village, besides producing stagnant cash reserves in the bank accounts of the groups. Livelihood vulnerabilities apart, the literature from other parts of India suggests that other reasons also drove women to retain their group savings without rotation (as loans) among group members. In Jharkhand, women's SHGs retained their savings as group money or 'box money' that would serve as a buffer or backup during emergencies (such as snake bites or accidents) and could be given out as loans when the agricultural season started. To the promoter NGO, the box money signalled idle cash that was not being effectively rotated on account of low demand for loans and could be loaned instead to other SHGs that could use the funds (Premchander *et al.* 2009).

Besides the rotation of cash, loan repayment practices could also be a bone of contention between promoter agencies and SHGs. In Koppal taluk (Karnataka), the promoter NGO found fault with the 'balloon repayment' of internal loans (or the non-payment of monthly loan principal) preferred by the SHGs. When seen through the financial lens preferred by the promoter NGO, it was regarded as creating 'sub-optimal' cash flows. NGO staff expressed great discomfort at women's unwillingness to pressure each other or even discuss loan repayment at group meetings and their refusal to create a repayment system of fixed duration on internal loans (Premchander *et al.* 2009). Referring to similar repayment practices, the APMAS[8] (2009a) report on the status of SHGs in Assam laments that the flexible repayment schedule followed by an overwhelming majority of the 109 sample groups in four districts 'is not a healthy practice according to the experts' and that the SHGs have emulated the informal financial sector in this practice, disregarding the potential risks involved.

My fieldwork in Thillai block also uncovered other instances of irresolvable differences between SHGs and promoters on what constituted disciplined financial intermediation. A form of financial disciplining that all promoters advocated was the charging of penal (or non-diminishing) interest rates in the case of the delayed repayment of loans by borrowers. However, all SHGs chose to charge diminishing interest even during the months that the loan principal was not paid, disregarding the BDO and promoter NGOs' instruction that they charge the full interest.[9] The women's decision to charge diminishing interest reflected their implicit acknowledgement that delayed loan repayment was not wilful, but an outcome of household economic stress, that the SHGs should not exacerbate. Even those SHGs in Thillai block (promoted by Mahalir Thittam and the bank) that prioritised rapid capital accumulation disregarded certain directives from the promoter NGOs and the BDO to cut out waste and strictly adhere to a financial rationality in all dimensions of group operations. A pertinent case in point is the sharing of interest incomes among SHG women.

Why not a bonus?

> The majority of SHGs in the study villages in Thillai block calculated the interest incomes generated on their group loans and distributed the money equally among members at periodic

> intervals. In a few SHGs, the women used the money to make a purchase that embodied a spirit of collectivity and group identity (such as saris or household utensils) rather than distribute it as cash. The BDO and promoter NGOs strongly disapproved of the distribution of interest incomes and of the women's privileging of a social end (using interest income to strengthen member loyalty and group cohesion) rather than a financial end (uninterrupted rotation of the money in order to expand loanable funds). When an official of the BDO asked the women whose permission they had sought prior to distributing the interest income, the women defended their action and informed the official that they had the right to do so, just as 'shoe companies in the region provided bonus to their employees'.

In addition to the periodic distribution of interest incomes, the SHGs in the fieldwork villages in Thillai often distributed the accumulated savings amount (and the group corpus in its entirety) to all members at the end of a certain period and restarted group operations afresh. Drawing on their study of sample SHGs in Koppal taluk (Karnataka), Premchander *et al.* (2009) observe that the promoter NGO judged the distribution of the SHGs' financial corpus as detrimental to the women as it would lower the groups' creditworthiness from the financing banks' point of view. It was feared that the groups and the promoter NGO would earn a 'bad reputation' with the bank which would decide to finance other groups instead (Premchander *et al.* 2009).[10] The APMAS (2007) study report on 240 SHGs in eight districts of Andhra Pradesh also found that close to half (47%) of the groups had distributed their savings among members periodically. In one of the districts (Vizianagaram), in 70% of the sample SHGs, the savings had been distributed to the members several times. Interestingly, the report describes the return of savings to SHG members as 'disconcerting' even as it notes that this might be a 'sensible way out' for groups that find it hard to maintain accounts and supervise a large number of small transactions (APMAS 2007).

In Thillai block, the INGO explicitly forbid the SHGs it promoted to dissolve their capital, threatened to disown the groups that did so and warned the SHGs to eschew any practice that might diminish their group financial resources.[11] The INGO, which provided milch cattle and other forms of financial and material assistance to poorer SHG members, ordered the groups to return all financial assistance in case they chose to distribute the group corpus among members. While one SHG in Karisal village gave up the idea of distributing the corpus, two others decided to do so in secrecy and without informing the INGO. Having looked forward to the distribution of the corpus in order to finance a large-sized household or personal expenditure, the INGO's unrelenting stance greatly disappointed the women in the groups associated with it. The women, however, had greater success in resisting the INGO's directive that the groups raise annual interest rates (on internal loans) to 24% from the 12% rates it had recommended when the groups were formed. The INGO's rationale was that the capital accumulation capacities of the SHGs and their skills in financial intermediation had grown over time, making a progressive increase in interest rates both desirable and necessary. However, the women in Karisal refused outright to raise their interest rates, fearing difficulty in loan repayment. In the context of a livelihood crisis, the acceleration of the pace of capital generation was unthinkable for the women.

Conclusion

NABARD has expressed pride in the capacity for self-governance and the autonomous decision-making that the SHG model of microfinance is vested with, in contrast to alternative models that empower lending agencies (such as the MFIs) vis-à-vis the peer groups at the grassroots. In this chapter, I explore how SHGs fashion themselves as micro-banks and strive to autonomise and responsibilise their rural women members towards certain desired ends. Promoter agencies and financing banks that 'conduct the conduct' of the SHG collectives exhorted the groups to function as disciplined, credit-worthy entities and select financial practices based on a cost–benefit calculus. The case studies that I discuss in this chapter (drawing on both my fieldwork in Tamil Nadu and secondary literature from other states) suggest that SHGs self-assessed and collectively evaluated their capacity to save and to generate capital, taking cognisance of livelihood conditions in the village economy and the terms of lending that prevailed in the informal sector.

However, women made autonomous choices regarding the terms of their financial transactions, keeping in mind that the decisions could also affect their chances of securing bank loans. As the EDA and APMAS (2006) study of SHGs in four states finds, group-level 'adjustments' to the repayment schedules of internal loans as well as decisions to raise the savings amount could be taken in view of the groups' plans to apply for external (bank) loans. Likewise, the field staff of promoter agencies could influence the repayment cultures of SHGs, in particular their willingness to tolerate delayed repayment. It appears, therefore, that the decisional autonomy that SHGs enjoyed with respect to the generation and rotation of their micro-capital was never absolute but governed by the promoters' directives and stipulations, the groups' imperative to secure bank linkages and (as my field study from Tamil Nadu shows) the SHGs' own evolving mandate as a lender to generate an adequate loanable corpus and ensure its efficient and quick rotation/turnover, making thereby for a regulated autonomy (Rose 1999).

In Thillai block, the women members of those SHGs that attempted a quick turnover of their capital strove to 'capitalise the self' by restraining their bodily hungers and wants and incessantly working on their capital generation and repayment capacities. All the SHGs were urged and incited (by promoters) to increase the interest rates over time (if lower than 24%), to charge penal interest rates (if loan repayment was delayed) and to accumulate capital without interruption by eschewing practices such as the distribution of interest incomes or the periodic dissolution of the groups' corpus. The last, in particular, appears to have been insisted upon by promoter and financing agencies from other parts of the country as well, as the literature testifies. Promoter agencies have also strongly disapproved of balloon repayment practices that some SHGs adopted and of the women's ensuing unwillingness to even discuss loan repayment at group meetings or pressure each other to complete repayment, as the Premchander *et al.* (2009) study from Karnataka has shown.

As the discussions in this chapter indicate, promoter and financing agencies oftentimes envisioned disciplined financial intermediation in ways that did not resonate with the women's views on the matter. The SHGs' decisions, calculations and actions were motivated by diverse concerns that were not confined to maximising productivity, eliminating waste or conforming to a financial rationality in all contexts. These concerns included protecting women from repayment-related stress (by prioritising transactional practices that protected individual borrowers), strengthening social ties and solidarity within the groups (by using group revenues to make a uniform gift for all members), permitting women to quit their SHGs and start afresh only if they chose to (by dissolving the groups' corpus once every five years or so) and retaining group savings for emergency expenses and purposes, without making intra-group loans to members. As the bearers of a regulated freedom (Rose 1999), the SHGs sought to defend and expand the opportunities for autonomous action vis-à-vis promoters, even as individual members sought greater autonomy with regard to their transactional practices vis-à-vis the collective.

Notes

1 A very similar concept definition is found in Harper (2002b: vii–viii).
2 In order to facilitate quick identification of an SHG, I provide the name of the promoter agency and the caste composition of the group (SC or OBC) after the name of the SHG.
3 The Tamil Nadu Women's Development Corporation's Mahalir Thittam scheme likewise emphasises that all decisions regarding loans including interest payment and the mode of repayment be taken by each SHG keeping in mind the availability of funds, its stage of development and its circumstances (Mahalir Thittam n.d.).
4 The *taluk* or *tehsil* is the administrative sub-unit lower than that of district in many parts of India.
5 Sixteen of the 19 SHGs promoted by Mahalir Thittam, the BDO and the bank had 24% annual rates of interest. Of the remaining three, one SHG (bank-promoted) had 36% rates and two SHGs (Mahalir Thittam) had 12% annual rates.
6 Informal loans in the study villages in Thillai block were mainly of two types. (a) Finance *vatti* (translated as interest) loans were repaid fully in equal daily instalments, no matter the loan amount, over a strict period of 100 days, with the interest being deducted when the loan was given. A loan of Rs 1,000 was repaid daily (as Rs 10) over 100 days, with the interest (of Rs 110) deducted at the outset. Sometimes repayment was weekly, rather than daily. These loans were difficult to obtain, and prospective borrowers had to make repeat visits to the creditor's house and plead their case persuasively in order to secure the loan. Reputation was very important in securing these loans. (b) The *maasa vatti* (monthly interest) loans were those wherein interest ranged upwards from annual 36% to 120% rates. The interest was repaid each month, with no option provided to repay the loan principal in a staggered fashion (lump sum repayment alone was accepted). Usually the interest repaid was far greater than the loan borrowed, and the lender was not interested in loan principal recovery.
7 During my field study, the women of *Nelmani* SHG (Bank-BC) were repaying a monthly amount of Rs 895 per member, which included the payment on two bank-sourced loans and the monthly savings of Rs 40. In addition, eight women in the group who had received a third bank loan were repaying Rs 1,195 per member each month.

8 APMAS is a technical resource organisation that aims to promote a sustainable self-help movement in India by fostering self-reliant people's institutions such as SHGs and SHG federations and enabling them to realise their full potential to engage in microfinance and sustainable livelihoods (www.apmas.org).

9 The calculation of interest rates on a diminishing balance basis assumes that interest diminishes *only* if the loan principal is paid every month.

10 Not all promoters shared this view. The NGO PRADAN assisted the tribal SHGs it promoted in Jharkhand to calculate their income, distribute the corpus annually to members and dissolve the group with zero cash balance in the bank (Premchander *et al.* 2009).

11 The INGO was more authoritarian in its dealings with the SHGs vis-a-vis other promoter agencies due to its role as a purveyor of donor-funded largesse in the study region.

Chapter 3[1]

Evaluating the self

Distributing resources, containing risks

> I don't ask for loans as I have no family support. Anyway, the group doesn't give me a large amount even if I ask. For women without income like me, there is hesitation before loans are sanctioned.
>
> Chitra, an older single woman and member of Annai Janaki SHG (MaThi-SC)

NABARD (2006) anticipates that the experience of SHG participation will teach women to appreciate that resources are limited in relation to demand and that they bear a cost. As rational economic actors urged to ensure both the rapid growth of the group's capital and its safe distribution among members, the women had to make decisions on how best to apportion scarce resources prudently and in a risk-averse fashion. This chapter, thematically linked to the previous one, takes forward the discussion of how rural women constitute their SHGs as 'micro-banks' by exploring the group-level practices and dynamics that govern (a) the *distribution* of the groups' corpus through internal loans to women members and (b) the *preservation* of capital by expelling particular members whose fiscal indiscipline is perceived as a threat to the financial viability of the SHGs. I show that, to the SHG women, ascertaining the creditworthiness of loan seekers was central to the identification, assessment and the management of risk (of non-repayment endangering the group's capital) in SHG operations. In this instance, the SHGs constituted themselves as 'calculable spaces' (Rose 1999: 152) by provoking each member to self-evaluate the risk she was likely to pose the collective, even as the group incessantly and collectively assessed and deliberated upon the creditworthiness of its members.

In the study villages in Thillai block, only 2 (of the 27) SHGs rotated equal-sized loans to all members on the basis of a cycle of rotation (Rs 500 loans during the first cycle, Rs 1,000 during the second cycle etc.). All other SHGs sanctioned loans in response to borrowers' specific requests that were made during the group meetings, prior to cash withdrawal from the bank by SHG leaders. The only formal preconditions for loan sanction to a prospective borrower were her regular weekly (or monthly) savings payment to the group corpus and her full repayment of any previous loan borrowed from the SHG. However, the intra-group discussions that preceded loan sanction, either implicitly or otherwise, invoked the perceived repayment capacities of differently placed SHG member households. I found that SHGs subjected individual members' repayment ability/skill (*kattum thiramai*) to critical scrutiny prior to loan sanction, with borrowers often self-assessing the legitimacy of their claims upon group capital, prior to advancing them. I make specific mention of the terminology since *kattum thiramai*, in the manner in which it was used by the women, alluded to household incomes and the social class–derived status of the households that the women belonged to. In order to understand the distribution of loans within the SHGs and the possible ways in which socio-economic disparities among their members might have influenced this, I turn to data on the credit histories of the women from the (18) SHGs in Karisal and Prakasam villages and the livelihood and employment status of their households.

Household economic status and loan access: exploring the links

In Thillai block, the SHG women commonly described the severity of household poverty in terms of the ownership or absence of productive assets (mainly agricultural land holdings) and the instability and precarious nature of livelihoods. Consequently, the household information I sought included the economic activities and income source/(s) of all earning household members, headship of household (whether female-headed), land owned (if any) and enterprise/business activity (if any) managed by the household. In order to provide some data-backed context to my discussion of loan-related negotiations within the SHGs, I categorised the households to which the women members (of the 18 SHGs) belonged as those of *higher economic status* (*HES*) or *low economic status* (*LES*). Landless households wherein daily wage labour (in the farm or the non-farm sector) was the principal source of income were categorised as LES households. The classification of households as HES depended on whether they fulfilled at least one of the following three criteria:

1 Employment in government service of a household member (usually the husband of the SHG member), since public sector employment entailed a regular and secure monthly wage.
2 Management of 'own-account' enterprise (in service, trade or manufacture) that was regarded as a commercial success in the context of the village economy. In the three villages, these were home-based enterprises such as small grocery stores, home-based hotels, a soda-manufacturing factory, retail trade in ready-made garments. If the households eked out a livelihood through subsistence-level, self-employment activities in the lower end of the unorganised sector, they were placed in the same category as wage labour–dependent households. In doing this, I took my cue from the women who described sizeable enterprise activities as *thozil* (trade), whereas self-employment in the lower rungs of the informal sector was described as *coolie velai* (coolie work) on par with other forms of daily wage labour.
3 Ownership of agricultural land, of any size or irrigation status. As this study explores intra-group differences within each SHG of 16–20 members, the ownership of land per se (rather than the size of holding) was regarded as an important asset that could set apart land-owning SHG member households from those of the landless.[2]

The loan ledgers of the SHGs contained member-specific data on all the loans that had been borrowed, the monthly loan principal and interest amount repaid. I obtained data on the quantum of each loan borrowed by an SHG member since joining the SHG, including old loans that were fully repaid and the current loan being repaid at the time of my fieldwork. The data on the cumulative amount of all (internal) loans[3] borrowed by an SHG member enabled me to arrive at the cumulative total of all loans for the SHG as a whole. The cumulative loan amount of an SHG divided by the total number of members in the SHG yielded the average per member loan amount. Each member of an SHG was ranked as *high (loan) access* or *low (loan) access* depending on whether her cumulative loan amount was higher or lower than the average per member loan of her SHG. All members who had dropped out and those who had joined the SHGs in the place of the former were excluded when recording data on loan access. In the manner described here, information on loan access was collected for the 327 members in 18 SHGs in Karisal and Prakasam villages.

Table 3.1 provides a comparative picture of the percentage of SHG women from HES households, who have high loan access vis-à-vis their counterparts from LES households. This is shown for all SHG members, SHG members belonging to the scheduled castes and those belonging to the OBC-only SHGs. While all SHGs (barring two) are caste-homogenous groups, it is possible that the distribution of loan access among the household economic status categories may differ between the SC-only SHGs and the OBC-only SHGs. Hence, Table 3.1 shows this distribution by caste. The table shows that 64% of all SHG women from HES households have high loan access as against no more than 38% of women from LES households. Table 3.1 also shows that the percentage of SHG members with high loan access does not vary significantly between the caste groups. Table 3.2 further underscores the relative advantage of women from HES households with regard to loan access by showing the higher quantum of loan per member availed by an HES household member as compared to an LES household member.[4]

Table 3.1 Loan access by household economic status and caste: Karisal and Prakasam

Caste	*Higher economic status*			*Low economic status*		
	All members	*High-access members*	*Percent high access to total*	*All members*	*High-access members*	*Percent high access to total*
SC members	24	16	*67*	203	77	*38*
OBC members	31	19	*61*	69	25	*36*
All members	55	35	*64*	272	102	*38*

Note: The figures in italics are percentages.

Source: Fieldwork data.

Table 3.2 Loan size by household economic status: Karisal and Prakasam

Household economic status	*Cumulative loan (Rs)*	*Number of members*	*Average loan per member (Rs)*
Higher economic status	671,000	55	12,200
Low economic status	1,938,675	272	7,127
Total	2,609,675	327	7,981

Source: Fieldwork data.

The prevalence of disparities and inequities within SHGs with respect to access to group resources has been relatively under-examined in the literature. Two notable exceptions are Pattenden's (2010) ethnographic study of SHGs in two villages in Dharwad district (Karnataka) and the EDA and APMAS (2006) macro-scale study of 214 SHGs drawn from four states. Pattenden (2010) differentiates between SHG member households on the basis of whether they belong to the labouring class (all those who are net sellers of labour power) or the dominant classes (net-buyers of labour power who have an investable surplus and earn consistent agricultural profits). The former class is further differentiated as the labouring class poor and the labouring class vulnerable non-poor. While the dominant classes used 75% of the total amount lent from group savings in their SHGs, the labouring class vulnerable non-poor used the bulk of the remaining amount. The labouring class poor used no more than 10% of the total amount lent (Pattenden 2010).

Given the large data set it deals with, the EDA and APMAS (2006) study has approached this issue differently. It has aggregated the number of loans borrowed by all SHG members and the total amount of loans borrowed and found low standard deviation around the mean for both the indices, suggesting that the extent of inequality in access was fairly low.[5] The percentage of those who had never borrowed from their SHGs was found to be quite small, with non-borrowers constituting only 9% of the total sample of SHG members. The study reported that group members 'generally accepted' that poorer women borrow less and the non-poor borrow more, since they were better able to absorb large-sized loans and repay them. For those who did not accept the situation, the alternative was to drop out. Around 6% or more of those who left the groups had done so because they did not get a loan (EDA and APMAS 2006). My field study in Thillai block allowed me to closely examine how a similar consensus regarding differing claims to SHGs' resources had come into being and how it was sustained. First-hand examination of the dynamics that informed group transactions provided valuable glimpses of a set of practices by which unequal access to loans was made possible and normalised as I discuss in the following section.

Knowing one's place in the SHG

> As a widow raising two children single-handedly, I can only take small loan amounts unlike those who have husbands who earn or own milch cows and bullock carts.
>
> Member Vanitha of Annai Parasakthi SHG (MaThi-SC)

> My largest single loan from the group is no more than Rs.1000. This is because my daily wage earner husband is the sole breadwinner and my children are in school. In other families, the woman herself may work, older children may earn or husbands may have a business.
>
> Member Ruku of Annai Parasakthi SHG (MaThi-SC)

As these testimonies suggest, each woman assessed the validity of her loan-related claims upon her SHG using an amalgam of factors that included the number of income earners and the household's dependency ratio, the ownership of productive assets and the availability or reliability of male income support. The group's collective assessment of an individual member's *kattum thiramai* or repayment ability shaped her self-assessment and her sense of the appropriate claims that she could make upon the group's corpus. The case of Chitra of Annai Janaki SHG (MaThi-SC), an older woman who lived alone and sustained herself through daily wage work, hints at the complex ways in which women self-censored their loan-related demands, even as they anticipated that the collective would not accommodate higher-order claims, should they advance them (refer to quote at the beginning of this chapter). A study of 69 SHGs in Chitradurga district (Karnataka) and Kancheepuram (Tamil Nadu) makes a similar observation. It notes that women rarely ask for loans larger than the group is willing to give them since 'the women are aware of their repaying capacity and only apply for sums which others find reasonable' (Gadenne and Vasudevan 2007).

In the SHGs in Thillai, it was seen that the *size* of loans served to differentiate those perceived (by the collective) as credit-worthy from non-credit-worthy others. When the latter pressed their claim to loans on the grounds of dire or desperate household circumstances (*kudumba kashtam* or household distress), the SHGs sought to resolve the issue by sanctioning a 'smaller loan amount to poorer women based on their need ("*Kashtam*") and Rs.5000 to others based on their capacity *("thiramai")*' as a member of *Vennila* SHG (INGO-OBC) put it. A member of *Ganga* SHG (MaThi-OBC) who sought a loan of Rs 5,000 for her daughter's wedding was saddened when she received no more than Rs 1,000 since 'the group leaders looked at my livelihood (flower-vending) and decided that I cannot repay more'. The group leaders of Annai Janaki and Annai Parasakthi SHGs (MaThi-SC) that enforced short repayment duration of five months (hence larger-sized monthly repayment) minced no words when stating their SHGs' position on the sanction of loans of Rs 5,000 or more. Eligible candidates were 'the salaried' and 'owners of household assets' in Annai Janaki SHG and 'women with husbands or sons who earn' in Annai Parasakthi SHG.

Strategies of loan delay and denial

> When a prospective borrower's self-censorship (of her loan demands) was found inadequate, the group's leaders attempted to dissuade her from staking claim to credit on par with her better-off co-members. In one instance, the INGO stipulated a ceiling of Rs 3,000 on the size of internal loans that could be sanctioned by the SHGs it promoted. Although the SHGs continued to disburse large-sized loans, entirely disregarding the promoter agency's stipulation, the INGO's disapproval of large-sized loans was well known and selectively invoked by group leaders in specific cases. In the words of a member of Tamarai SHG (INGO-OBC), a widow and construction worker, 'Whenever I ask for a loan, the SHG president says she will have to ask the "manager" of the NGO and let me know if she can help me.' A few women expressed their bitterness at the propensity of some SHG leaders to readily resort to the excuse of 'no money in the SHG's bank account' when the former sought loans that the latter attempted to stall. The secretary of Annai Janaki SHG (MaThi-SC) admitted (to me) that she had lied to specific SHG members that the bank manager was not available during her visit to the bank.

The SHG leaders were seen to deploy what the literature on credit markets describes as 'credit-rationing' strategies to squeeze 'non-preferred' borrowers out of the credit market. According to the theorists of rural finance and credit markets, commercial banks use credit-rationing strategies (such as the processing of complicated application forms, untimely loan disbursement, making borrowers wait in long queues) to dissuade non-preferred borrowers (such as low-income cultivators) from seeking bank credit (Adams and Vogel 1986: 482). In this interpretive framework, credit rationing is presented as a rational response by banks that seek to minimise the risks of lending to low-income borrowers when governments impose restrictions on interest rates, precluding thereby the option of charging higher interest to those perceived as high-risk borrowers.

In the case of the SHGs, we may regard these strategies as attempts by the collective (enforced by group leaders) as *rational economic actors in the making* to preserve group capital against the perceived risks (of loan default) likely to be posed by equal claims upon the groups' loanable corpus by all members. Nevertheless, they were successfully enforced insofar as they reflected the societal power relations between women, with older women and/or poorer women without male income support facing the brunt of their co-members' suspicions regarding their repayment intent or capacities. Being called upon to exercise judgement in determining 'credit-worthy' others and to function as risk-averse investors of precious and limited capital resources, the women routinely invoked and inscribed social class, male-kin and household-mediated identities (of 'woman of no means', 'widow', 'mother of earning adult sons', 'woman without a man', 'wife of a habitual drunk, vagabond') in the assessment and evaluation processes that preceded the sanction of loans to co-members.

Competing discourses: 'capacity' versus 'power'

In Thillai block, the SHGs' positioning of (some) members in ways that constrained their access to group capital did not go unchallenged. If the group leaders invoked income and male kin-related identities to circumscribe the credit entitlements of specific SHG members, the latter positioned themselves as victims of discrimination, identified the delimitation of their credit entitlements as an act of power (*adhigaaram*) and/or underscored the desperate nature of their 'family's need' (*kudumba kashtam*) and by implication, their oppressed class status, to contest and resist the capacity discourse (*thiramai*) that was wielded against them. Member Kumari of *Pavalam* SHG (INGO-SC), an older woman and widow who lived on income from beedi-rolling, was furious at the rejection of her loan demand of Rs 2,000 by the group's leaders. Repudiating the group's assessment of her perceived lack of creditworthiness, she declared at a group meeting: 'The owners of money in the group are those who withdraw money from the bank.'

Assessing creditworthiness: difference or sameness?

> The request of Chitra of Annai Janaki SHG (MaThi-SC) for a loan (of Rs 3,000) to repair the roof of her thatched hut was met with scepticism from her co-members since she had delayed repayment of a previous loan of Rs 500. The SHG's president said to Chitra, 'How can you ask for Rs.3000? Do you have sons to help you repay? Take Rs. 500 or Rs.1000 instead.' Chitra fought back by asking why the group had accepted her membership if it would not meet her credit needs and whether her regular savings record did not entitle her to a loan. 'Am I not a woman like you all?', she retorted, strategically invoking *sameness* (both of female identity on which SHG membership was based and of her contribution to the monthly savings, uniform for all members) to counter the disparities of household incomes, (gendered) social status and perceived repayment capacities that were used to deny her loan. Chitra's loan was eventually sanctioned after her brother offered to sign a document to the effect that he would guarantee her loan repayment.

Chitra admitted (to me) that the group did possibly run a risk (of delayed or irregular repayment, but not default as she clarified) when sanctioning a large-sized loan to her given the fragility of her livelihood. The responsibilising of the women that the SHGs fostered was reflected in the emergent consensus that irregular repayment would disrupt the logic of efficient capital rotation and that the stakes were high, involving as they did women's own capital. All women, albeit to varying degrees, acted as prudent appraisers of their co-members' creditworthiness and vigilant monitors of loan repayment. Consequently, Chitra's struggle to secure a loan of an adequate amount and at the required time (as of other women from LES households) may be perceived as an implicit plea to the collective to be more willing to bear a shared risk, should the occasion warrant it.

Knowing when to self-exclude

The termination of SHG membership following poor financial performance either through an act of personal 'choice' (dropout) by an individual member or by the group's decree (push-out)[6] provides yet another entry point to explore the processes of self-making and the disciplinary techniques that co-constitute women's subjectivities. In two of the three fieldwork villages in Thillai block (Karisal and Prakasam), 17% of women had dropped out of 18 SHGs since their formation. The EDA and APMAS (2006) study of 214 SHGs in four states reports a dropout rate of less than 10% of group membership and observes that almost 50% of the SHGs had no dropouts. A study conducted by CGAP (2007) involving 150 SHGs in four states (Andhra Pradesh, Rajasthan, Jharkhand, Karnataka and Uttar Pradesh) found that 15% of members had dropped out over an average of five years before the study. Apart from reasons such as death, migration in search of work, fights with group members, family pressures to withdraw from membership, constraints of time and disappointment at not receiving expected benefits or loans, all studies report that women's inability to contribute to group financial transactions prompted them to leave their SHGs.

The EDA and APMAS (2006) study reports that about 27% of the total women who had dropped out from the SHGs left due to financial difficulties. This was the second most significant reason explaining dropout, the first being migration out of the village (accounting for 30% of all dropouts). Out of 68 women who dropped out of 18 SHGs in 2 of the 3 villages I studied in Thillai block, 41% quit due to financial stress (the most significant factor), followed by 22% who left for reasons of migration in search of work. The women generally used their accumulated savings to cancel out any (unpaid) overdues on SHG loans – a last resort option that enabled them to exit the group in a dignified manner. The liquidation of savings effectively terminated the claims that a woman could make upon the social and financial resources of her SHG and severed her ties with the group. Drawing on 29 dropout-related interviews in their northern sample (Odisha and Rajasthan), the EDA and APMAS (2006) study finds that in the majority of cases, the decision to quit the group was taken by the member herself (or by her husband). This does not appear to be an unusual finding, judging from my fieldwork in Thillai block. My interviews with women who had quit their SHGs revealed that the woman in financial distress was confronted with the question of what a 'responsibilised' individual should do if unable to fulfil commitments to self and to others.

I found also that self-knowledge was seen as a necessary part of accountability to one's co-members in situations of loan repayment–induced crisis. In this case, it entailed *knowing when to quit the SHG* so as 'to not stretch the SHG's tolerance' and 'even if no one speaks hurtful words', as two women put it. The women's self-evaluation also included assessing their prospects of (ever) rejoining SHGs and subjecting themselves again to the disciplinary pressures of peer group membership. The women who had dropped out of SHGs on account of temporary setbacks such as a sudden dip in household incomes following a collapse of livelihoods or other unanticipated stress-inducing events (requiring large expenses) actively sought to rejoin new SHGs, once they had weathered the crisis. For instance, Lalitha dropped out of *Ganga* SHG (MaThi-BC) owing to the dual burden of payment of monthly savings to the group and the school fees of her son. Once her son started to work in a shoe company, she joined a newly formed SHG in the village. Lalitha's decision to seek SHG membership was motivated both by her enhanced capacity to save following her son's employment and by her need for group loans and financial assistance, given the impending marriage of her daughter.

The EDA and APMAS (2006) study reports a case similar to the one described earlier from a village in Andhra Pradesh. A widow and SHG member, who was the principal earner of her family that included her daughter and son-in-law, quit the group and withdrew her savings after an illness. Two years later, an improvement in her health and her son-in-law's regular employment enabled her to start an SHG herself, motivated by a government fieldworker. In other cases, women estimated that SHG participation would forever remain beyond their capacities on account of the near-unbearable strain it imposed on their households. Two women, who had quit *Vanavil* SHG (BDO-SC) in Karisal village (Thillai block) due to the chronic illness of their spouses, declared that re-entry (to the same group or a new one) would never be an option for them. As one of them testified, feeding and educating four schoolgoing children with a diabetic husband on earnings from beedi-rolling was hard enough without having to meet SHG repayment deadlines as well. Some women decided to quit SHGs even in the absence of specific stress events or household emergencies. A 55-year-old agricultural labourer quit Vanavil SHG (BDO-SC) when she pledged jewellery to repay her first (and only) SHG loan of Rs 500. She decided to not seek SHG membership again. The discipline of regular repayment had been too stressful on her and her elderly husband who fended for themselves without support from their adult children.

Women, who were unable to reconcile the demands of SHG membership with the conflicts generated by violent and excessively oppressive marital relationships, avowed that they would never rejoin SHGs. A member of Tamarai SHG (INGO-OBC) described the hardship of supporting a family through her uncertain livelihood of coconut leaf thatching, with a husband whose relentless alcohol abuse had debilitated his health and the financial well-being of his household. After quitting Tamarai SHG, she made a feeble attempt to join a newly formed SHG in Karisal village, but withdrew the initiative soon after, fearing that her husband would again refuse to support her monthly savings and loan repayment. As these cases suggest, women from the poorest households and those vulnerable to male alcoholism-fuelled violence and/or neglect found themselves unable to endure the self-disciplining and the subjection to group discipline that the SHGs demanded.

The EDA and APMAS (2006) study of 214 SHGs in four states shows that women used similar criteria to assess if they would be able (or not) to join SHGs, even if they had never participated in SHGs before. Interviews with 100 non-members randomly selected in the villages studied found that all of them were aware of the existence of SHGs in their village. In particular, women non-agricultural casual workers, who travelled outside the village for daily work, could not see themselves as members on account of their irregular income and low ability to save, their 'lack of acumen for enterprise' and the limited time available given their employment outside the village. As with the case of access to internal loans in Thillai block discussed earlier, the perceptions of the non-members regarding their unsuitability for group membership were reflected and reinforced by those who were SHG members. For instance, in Chikiti block of Ganjam district (Orissa), SHG members excluded a woman who collected fuel wood to support her poor family. Poor and married to a man who was an alcoholic and did no work, she was judged uncreditworthy by the SHG members. In a village in Andhra Pradesh, SHG members expressed their sympathy for one of the poorest women in the village, an SC landless labourer with five children, by paying for a surgery she underwent. They were not willing, however, to have her join the group. The fieldworkers of the promoter agencies appear to have echoed, and not challenged, these concerns. In some cases (as in Orissa), NGO staff pursued a policy of systematically excluding the poorest when forming SHGs (EDA and APMAS 2006).

Resisting expulsion

While women usually recalled a 'voluntary' exit from the SHG with a lingering sense of regret, those who had experienced an expulsion or a 'push-out' expressed bitterness and a sense of betrayal. In the SHGs in Thillai block, the most fraught discussions regarding one's honour (*maanam*) and righteous anger or pride (*rosham*) took place around the issue of the expulsion of women from SHGs. A member of Annai Parasakthi SHG (MaThi-SC) quit the group due to the altercation that followed when she was unable to pay a month's instalment on a loan. Following her exit from the SHG, she overheard the women of the group discuss the crisis precipitated by the SHG's president, who had not repaid her loan for seven months. Unable to restrain herself, she shouted, 'You shamed me and made me leave the group when I did not repay. How hurt I felt! Let the president pay up her dues and leave with honour just as I did.' She later explained (to me) that her expulsion by the SHG had rankled long after her exit and had caused her outburst at the meeting, although she had forfeited her right to interfere in the affairs of the SHG upon quitting it, as her former co-members reminded her.

The women were fully aware that the relinquishment of SHG membership entailed the loss of opportunities that were not confined to financial exclusion. Besides subsidy-bearing bank loans explicitly targeted at SHGs, the functionaries of the BDO used SHG-centred social networks and contacts within rural communities in Tamil Nadu to make available state government–sponsored welfare programmes and schemes to targeted households and individuals. The Mahalir Thittam partner NGO, which was often required to identify targeted beneficiaries for schemes such as educational scholarships for the socially oppressed poor or financial assistance for physically disabled individuals, disseminated vital information about these schemes and sought the assistance of SHGs to identify eligible beneficiaries. Apart from the informal mechanisms of beneficiary selection, certain state government–promoted welfare schemes required SHG membership as a precondition for rural poor households to access them. For instance, the state government of Tamil Nadu offered a 'housing for the rural poor' scheme that provided subsidised bank credit to finance the upgrading of *kutcha* houses (thatched roofs and mud walls) to *pucca* or tiled roof houses. The eligibility criteria for the scheme included (among other criteria) SHG membership and a resolution signed by all SHG members endorsing loan sanction to selected beneficiaries in their groups.[7]

For these reasons, women struggled to retain membership, despite the high costs of doing so in contexts of household poverty and other forms of gendered vulnerability. Member Manjula of Vanavil SHG (BDO-SC) in Karisal village (Thillai block) suffered post-natal depression involving frequent bouts of 'extreme anger and confusion' following the birth of her child. Her family, which survived on income from beedi-rolling, struggled to meet the costs of Manjula's medical expenses. Describing her situation, Manjula said:

> Last week, my husband gave me Rs. 200 – 100 for my medicine and 100 to repay the SHG loan. I keep falling ill. The group leaders keep asking me to repay my loans on time. Unable to take it any more, I decided to leave the *Sangam* (SHG) twice. But my husband wants me to continue. Our names have gone right up to the government, haven't they? So we should stay.

An 'unreasonable' demand

> While several women quit their SHGs without a fight, despite the keen sense of loss they experienced, member Amulu of *Mullai* SHG (BDO-SC) was fighting what appeared to be a losing battle to retain membership, during the period of my fieldwork. Amulu supported her household of three schoolgoing sons through the daily collection and sales of firewood. Amulu's membership in Mullai SHG was a matter of dispute since she had not paid her monthly savings for a year to the SHG, nor had she repaid her (only) internal loan of Rs 200. The crisis had occurred when Amulu shifted residence to her natal village for a

> year after a fight with her alcoholic husband. When she returned to Karisal village, she requested the SHG for a loan (ranging between Rs 500 and Rs 1,000) in order to pay the year's savings amount that she owed the group. In her words, 'I don't want to leave the group. I have neither wealth nor relatives to turn to. My husband is useless. The only support I have is my Sangam.' The SHG's leaders regarded her plea as unreasonable and asked her to pay up the savings and repay the unpaid loan before making any further loan demand of the SHG.

The cases of Amulu and Manjula (and the cases cited by the EDA and APMAS [2006] cited earlier) suggest that both the costs of sustaining SHG membership and the need for the social and financial support it offered were higher for poorer women, in particular those whose marital relationships afforded little material security, and who were perceived therefore as lacking capacity. The plea, explicit or otherwise, that Amulu, Manjula or even Chitra (case described in previous section) made to the collective was to be more willing to show empathy, to set aside concerns of capacity, accommodating instead those of need, and to recognise that the special and different circumstances of their households merited a more compassionate response. Interestingly, as I show later (Chapter 5), (some) SHGs resorted to the same argument (of different and special circumstances) in the course of negotiating with bankers to secure bank loans.

Conclusion

In this chapter, I showed how the SHGs constituted themselves as calculable spaces (Rose 1999: 152) by provoking each member to constantly self-evaluate the risk (of non-repayment) she posed the collective, even as the group collectively deliberated upon how best to apportion scarce resources (as intra-group loans) in a risk-free fashion. Peer and self-assessments of a loan seeker's perceived repayment capacities shaped and reinforced each other, often provoking the woman in question to self-censor her loan-related claims, prior to advancing them. My fieldwork in Tamil Nadu and the literature on SHGs from other parts of the India suggest that the household economic status of the women and their embedding within household and kin-based social relationships (as widows living alone or women married to men judged as poor providers) mediated women's loan access within the SHGs.

While all women (in the study villages in Thillai block) self-evaluated the legitimacy of their claims upon the groups' financial resources, those who suffered dire economic stress and were consequently unable to make savings payments or repay loans on time asked themselves if their continuing membership would unduly strain the groups' resources, if their poor fiscal performance did not warrant a dignified exit instead and if their straitened financial circumstances would ever permit their re-absorption into SHGs. The constant self-evaluation and assessment that SHG membership fostered, therefore, included knowing when to self-exclude. As scholars of neo-liberal governmentalities remind us, technologies of the self require primarily that the self itself be isolated and made an object of knowledge and that intense self-scrutiny, self-dissatisfaction and self-evaluation accompany and facilitate the continuous project of self-improvement that an autonomous individual is expected to undertake (Rose 1999: 93). In constantly assessing the validity of their individual claims upon the collective resources and their membership worthiness, the women members of SHGs sought and found knowledgeable techniques to understand and practice upon their selves (Rose 1999: 93), in the process governing themselves and each other in ways that might contribute to the financial health and viability of their 'micro-banks'.

By and large, the women's consent to this project does not imply, as Cruikshank (1999) reminds us, the absence of power. Rather, by isolating and constructing a self to act upon, the women availed themselves of a terrain of action, exercising power over themselves. However, as I have also shown, the 'consensus' regarding what constituted prudent and risk-averse practices of resource distribution within SHGs was precarious and contested. The unequal distribution of group resources cannot be seen as an automatic or taken-for-granted outcome of socio-economic disparities among SHG members. It was produced through a set of practices that the group leaders often initiated and rationalised as necessary from the point of view of safeguarding the groups' financial resources. The leaders resorted to credit-rationing strategies of loan delay or outright denial that included lying about the status of the groups' funds in order to discourage particular non-preferred borrowers whose self-curtailment (of their loan-related claims) was found inadequate. Positioning themselves as the victims of discrimination and 'power play' within the SHGs, some of the women denied loans by their peer group members contested the capacity discourse that was deployed against them. A similar battle was waged by the women who struggled to retain group membership in the face of the collective scepticism regarding their abilities to 'capitalise the self' in required ways. Mindful of the potential risks (of delayed repayment) that the collective might incur on their behalf, they asked that their co-members be more willing to bear a shared risk, to empathise with their plight and stretch themselves to accommodate the special circumstances and needs of their impoverished households.

Notes

1 A part of the material in Chapters 3 and 4 of the book, drawing on the author's fieldwork in Tamil Nadu, have been discussed in a paper published by the author titled 'How Pro-Poor Is User-Owned Microfinance? Class, Gender and Group Dynamics in Self Help Groups, South India', *Indian Journal of Human Development* (*IJHD*) in 2011, 5 (2): 495–514.

2 The terms 'HES' and 'LES' denote the relational nature of the two economic status categories and highlight differences within the lower end of the income spectrum in rural society. The purpose of this classificatory tool is to understand how access to some form of regular employment or income-earning opportunity for a few households in a context in which the majority are unable to avail of it might serve as the basis for difference within SHGs.

3 Only loans that were borrowed from the SHGs' funds were included when calculating the total loans borrowed by SHG members. External or bank-sourced loans were distributed equally among SHG members and therefore excluded from consideration since the basis of their distribution was at complete variance with that of internal loans.

4 I add the caveat that the cumulative loan is also a function of the age of the groups, with older SHGs having a larger cumulative loan amount and vice versa. In case the distribution of women from HES or LES households is concentrated among the younger or the older groups, it could impact the reading of the table. Hence, a rank correlation was done between the age of SHGs and the percentage of women from HES households in each group. The coefficient was found to be less than 0.2, suggesting that the two household economic status groups are fairly evenly distributed among the SHGs of different age groups.

5 It calculated an aggregated standard deviation and average loan statewise for 60 SHGs in Andhra Pradesh, 51 in Karnataka, 50 in Orissa and 53 in Rajasthan.

6 The women clearly expressed the difference between a member who had left an SHG and another who was made to leave the SHG by using the active and passive versions of the same verb.

7 This was not unique to Tamil Nadu. Tankha (2012) notes that state governments in many states had several schemes designed for the welfare of the poor that were delivered through the SHGs and their federations.

Chapter 4

Managing micro-banks

How much autonomy? Whose responsibility?

In this chapter, I discuss the routine practices that underpin the management and governance of SHGs in order to explore further the 'financial rationality' that informs their calculations and actions when they distribute the costs, efforts and labour involved in managing the quotidian affairs of their 'micro-banks'. In Chapters 2 and 3, I showed how the SHGs constituted themselves as lender-collectives whose imperatives and mandates (of the rapid generation and quick turnover of capital or its risk-free distribution) could diverge from the needs and interests of particular members/borrowers. This is seen, for instance, in the case of poorer women whose financial claims upon the group were regarded as incommensurate with their income-earning and loan repayment capacities. In this chapter, I explore yet another instance of a constant undercurrent of unresolved tension within SHGs between collective and individual interests, albeit of a different kind. The endeavours of the group as a collective to manage its capital resources judiciously, prudently and in a waste-free fashion conflicted, as I show, with the needs of a few individuals (the group leaders in this instance), whose decisions and judgements were not exclusively guided by the impulse of preserving or growing the groups' capital.

In this chapter, I discuss the motivations and ambitions of group leaders who are autonomised and responsibilised to a greater extent than group members and the consequences that flow from the uneven sharing of the privileges and burdens of SHG management. I discuss this in the light of both the group leaders' access to the groups' capital (as borrowers themselves) and their role in managing the groups' finances, liaising with banks and keeping the books of accounts. I discuss whether other forms of privilege (such as relative social and economic status) sustained the autonomous decisions and actions of group leaders and how, and through what precise mechanisms and group routines, the discretionary power of group leaders played out within the SHGs. By mapping the tensions and conflicts that accompany the self-governance of SHGs as micro-banks and the women's self-fashioning as rational economic actors, I show how women's gendered subjectivities, never pre-given or determined prior to their entry into the world of social relations (Mohanty 1991), are produced by developmentalist projects in ways that are both conflicting and inequality-producing (Sharma 2010).

The dual privilege of group leaders

As the discussions and case studies in Chapter 3 suggest, the group leaders took upon themselves the responsibility of governing the conduct of group members and steering group functioning in desired directions by minimising perceived risks to their groups' financial resources, withholding credit from those deemed credit-unworthy and 'weeding out' certain members. This raises the question of whether the exercise of power by group leaders was fuelled by other forms of hierarchy (such as that of economic class), besides the decisional authority conferred by the formal position of leadership. Quite evidently, group leadership required a degree of literacy skills as well as some leisure time in order to make weekly visits to banks and attend meetings organised by the promoter agencies. The question, therefore, of which social classes of women are more easily able to secure leadership opportunities within SHGs has been discussed in the literature.

The EDA and APMAS study (2006) in four states (Rajasthan, Odisha, Andhra Pradesh and Karnataka) finds that 16% of total members in the 214 sample SHGs operating in nine districts were in positions of group leadership and drawn from all wealth ranks, caste groups and occupations. While the leaders' caste usually reflected the caste composition of the SHG itself, the leaders were more likely to be non-poor and have some schooling, when compared to group members. However, like group members, the majority of group leaders (60% compared to 74% overall) had no schooling and was unable to read or write (EDA and APMAS 2006). A study conducted by the NGO Nirantar on 2,750 SHGs in 16 states found little difference between the economic backgrounds of the group members and that of leaders; 49% of group members and 46% of leaders belonged to landless families. The chief source of family income for nearly 77% of the group leaders was wage labour and marginal farming. The principal difference between the two groups was the significantly higher literacy status of leaders. While 61% of all women joining the SHGs were non-literate, 69% of group leaders were literate; 54% of the group leaders who could read and write had studied at least up to the sixth standard. The literacy rate of group leaders from all caste groups was higher than that of group members and much higher than the national literacy rate of the women from their community (Dwivedi 2007).

Besides economic class and literacy status, proximity to local sources of political power could also set leaders apart from members. Pattenden's (2010) micro-study of SHGs in Dharwad district (Karnataka) found that of 12 groups in a village, 6 had officeholders (or group leaders) who had been gram panchayat members at the time of group formation, or who were immediate relatives of someone who was. One was the daughter of the District Council (*Zilla Parishad*) vice-president. A further two groups had officeholders who were immediate relatives of the president of the taluk panchayat. Of more than 30 officeholders whose socio-economic status was established, less than 20% were from labouring class poor households. Initial economic conditions, Pattenden (2010) observes, were reflected in the distribution of power within SHGs.

In Thillai block, 44 of the 327 members in 18 SHGs in 2 villages (Karisal and Prakasam) were the leaders of their respective groups.[1] As Table 4.1 shows, a higher percentage of SHG leaders belonged to higher economic status (HES) households (34%) as compared to all SHG members (17%).

Table 4.1 Household economic status of all SHG members and SHG leaders: Karisal and Prakasam

Household economic status	*All SHG members (including leaders)*		*SHG leaders*	
	Number	*Percentage*	*Number*	*Percentage*
Higher economic Status	55	*17*	15	*34*
Low economic status	272	*83*	29	*66*
Total	327	*100*	44	*100*

Note: The figures in italics are percentages.

Source: Fieldwork data.

The norms and criteria that underlay the selection of group leaders drew upon the existing forms and sources of gendered authority and power in Tamil rural society. The president was usually an older woman 'who commanded respect', 'whose words were heeded by all' and who was either married or an older widow whose household included adult earning children. The promoter organisations urged the SHGs to select a president whose personal attributes or the social standing of her household (implicitly understood as determined by the ownership of some land or a small business) would enable her to sustain 'consensual' decision-making given that 'matters of cash are prone to cause conflict', as a field staff of the INGO put it. Take the case of President Soosanna of Roja SHG (MaThi-SC), whose husband, having retired as a headmaster in a government school, managed a store that did good business in Prakasam village. Co-managing the store with her husband, the authority that Soosanna wielded in her SHG was bolstered, both by the relative economic prosperity of her household and by her reputation as a 'generous-spirited' woman who helped people in (financial) need, possessing, as she did, the wherewithal to dispense charitable assistance when called upon to do so. The secretary of an SHG was usually a younger woman with middle-level or higher-level schooling, who was expected to manage account-keeping and book-writing responsibilities and hold her own with bank personnel, government officials and NGO staff.

In her seminal critique of Western feminist discourses on Third-World women, Mohanty (1991) problematises the discursive representations of women as a coherent group or category prior to their entry into the process of development and their a priori constitution as subjects outside social relations. She asks that we demonstrate instead how women are produced as socio-economic political groups in particular local contexts through the complex interactions between multiple social relations and institutions. Drawing on Mohanty, Sharma (2010) argues further that 'women as material beings do not simply exist, but are made and re-made', their subjectivities the effects of multiple intersections in specific contexts, and that developmentalist projects constitute women's gendered subjectivities in conflicting and inequality-producing ways. In the discussions thus far (in Chapter 3 and above), I have suggested that the social relations of class, literacy status and aspects of (gendered) life cycle and household organisational dynamics have both shaped and intersected with group routines, practices and transactional activities. In doing so, they have influenced outcomes such as women's differing access to group loans as well as to leadership positions, constituting women as 'high (loan) access' and 'low access' and as 'leaders' and 'members'. In the next section, I show how these identifications, in turn, became the locus of conflicts and tensions within the groups, with high loan access women or 'those who take more' challenging and attempting to reverse the practice of the equal distribution of interest incomes in their respective SHGs. Subsequently, I turn to the question of how the identification of 'leader' versus 'member' also engendered new interests, needs, rivalries and alliances that the women sought to defend or to counter.

Contested practices of revenue sharing

My fieldwork in Thillai block suggested that high (loan) access and its converse were not merely the incidental outcomes of loan-disbursal practices within the SHGs. The women were able to accurately identify themselves and each other as being those who take more or 'those who take less' in terms of their cumulative loans relative to that of co-members in their respective SHGs. These were identifications that engendered struggles over access to another critical material resource that the SHGs made available to women, namely the interest incomes that were distributed equally among SHG members, as discussed in Chapter 2. The sharing of interest incomes in SHGs was often marked by the eruption of conflict between women differently placed in the 'loan access' hierarchy of the group. The women who initiated the disputes were those with high loan access (and usually from HES households), who had contributed in greater measure to the interest income of the group. Acting on the perception that the women with lower levels of cumulative loans stood to gain when interest incomes were equally distributed, the 'high-access' women in a few groups challenged the practice of equal distribution of interest incomes. They demanded instead a higher share for themselves, in proportion to the loans they had borrowed.

When the high-access members of Roja SHG (MaThi-SC) brought up this issue at a group meeting, a low-access member Sarada retorted, 'It's our money you have taken as loans. Without our savings, could you have done it? If we had not reduced our loans, could you have taken so many?' Contending that women with lower cumulative loans had done those with higher loans a favour by making available a sizeable volume of SHG funds, Sarada sought to make common cause with the other low-access borrowers like her in the group. The formation of these informal alliances and solidarities helped poorer women mobilise as low-access borrowers in order to defend (and secure) the equal distribution of interest incomes. In this case, Sarada positioned herself and others like her, not as women who had (in some cases at least) been judged and declared credit-unworthy, but as *diligent savers* who had surrendered their rightful claim to the low-priced credit that the SHGs offered. In doing so, the low-access women further undermined the privileging of the 'capacity' discourse and its unequalising implications. The unequivocal support expressed by the promoter NGO and the BDO for the principle of equal sharing of interest income (conveyed during training workshops and monthly meetings with SHG leaders) enabled low-access borrowers to ensure the equal distribution of interest incomes in their SHGs.

If women's self-identification as those who take more and those who take less crystallised through the periodic distribution of interest incomes, the identities of 'leader' and 'member' were often produced in sharply polarised ways through routine group transactional activities such as the approval and disbursal of internal loans, as I discuss here.

Group leadership and loan access

The question of whether positions of leadership within SHGs translate into pecuniary gain for the leaders is often at the centre of discussions about the democratic functioning (or otherwise) of SHGs and the extent to which SHG-based microfinance is embedded within local forms of power and politics. Pattenden's (2010) study of SHGs in Dharwad (Karnataka) finds that a disproportionate number of internal loans went to the group leaders' caste and kin fellows and political party allies. In a group presided over by a woman of the Maratha caste and a Bharatiya Janata Party (BJP) supporter, 89% of loans were made to BJP supporters in the year of the *grama* (village) panchayat elections, even though they constituted only one-third of the group's members. In another group, 46% of loans over a three-year period had been allocated to the group leaders themselves (ibid.). Analysing its large-scale data set generated from SHGs in four states, the EDA and APMAS (2006) study finds average data on the number of loans and the amount borrowed indicating a degree of bias in favour of group leaders (by a factor of 25%–30%) in all states, when compared to group members. In the sample drawn from the northern states (Odisha and Rajasthan), leaders had borrowed significantly more than other members, more than twice the number of loans in 8% of SHGs and more than twice the amount in 18% of SHGs.

My field study in Thillai block also points to the higher loan access of group leaders vis-à-vis members. Table 4.2 shows that a significantly higher percentage of SHG leaders of both household economic status categories (77%) enjoyed high loan access, as compared to all SHG members (42%). The EDA and APMAS (2006) study reports that even when the higher loan access of group leaders was widely known, this was not necessarily perceived as exploitative, judging from the discussions that the research team conducted with group members. The study observes that since leaders are more aware, have more education and are better off economically and socially, they are in a position to utilise loans better and hence take larger loans from the group. Nevertheless, it notes a few instances of 'questionable practices' involving the disbursal of the largest loans issued by the sample SHGs (amounting to Rs 80,000 and Rs 60,000) to group leaders. In contrast, I would argue that the higher loan

Table 4.2. Loan access of all SHG members and SHG leaders: Karisal and Prakasam

Household economic status	*All SHG members (including leaders)*			*SHG leaders*		
	Total number	*High-access number*	*Percent high-access to total*	*Total number*	*High-access number*	*Percent high-access to total*
Higher economic status	55	35	*64*	15	14	*93*
Low economic status	272	102	*38*	29	20	*69*
Total	327	137	*42*	44	34	*77*

Note: The figures in italics are percentages.

Source: Fieldwork data.

access of leaders cannot be rationalised as the automatic outcome of their socio-economic status or their presumed ability to utilise loans better. As with the unequal distribution of group loans to members (discussed in Chapter 3), this too was produced through a distinct set of practices that paved the way for discretionary actions and judgements on the part of group leaders, producing outcomes that were unintended by the policy advocates of SHG-banking, as I discuss here.

The power to sign and sanction loans

My fieldwork in Thillai block indicates that the impulse of capital preservation was not the sole guide of the actions of group leaders, especially on matters relating to their own loan requirements or those of their close kin. The formal rules of the SHG did not deter SHG leaders from obtaining the loans that they required. The case of Tamarai SHG (INGO-OBC) presented here provides an insight into the dynamics at play.

A matter of trust

> In Tamarai SHG (INGO-OBC), the secretary had not repaid a single instalment on a loan of Rs 5,000 when she sought and obtained the SHG president's sanction for a new loan (of Rs 5,000) to defray expenses relating to a household medical emergency. Commenting on this, the president offered the following explanation (to me): 'It is a matter of trust. If those who are trust-worthy ask, I will give it.' Nine months later, the secretary had an unpaid balance of Rs 3,000 on each loan of Rs 5,000. Planning to repay the balance on both loans shortly with the 'bonus' payment that her daughter was expecting from the shoe company where she worked, the secretary was confident that she would immediately secure a third SHG loan (also of Rs 5,000).

In the case described here, the secretary's multiple access to the group-generated corpus despite her delayed repayment contrasts, in stark ways, with the unsuccessful loan applicants belonging to poorer households whose probable repayment delinquency on a loan *they had not even received* deterred their SHGs from approving it in the first place.[2] The case of Tamarai SHG was not unusual.

In the INGO-promoted groups in Karisal village, poorly attended meetings that were held infrequently had created a situation in which the group leaders effectively monopolised the right to judge who posed a threat to group resources and who did not. Infrequent meetings and a waning of interest in group transactional activities had led to a situation that all promoter agencies had warned against, namely, the stagnation of idle cash deposits in the SHGs' bank account. Aware that bank interest rates on their deposit were significantly lower than those charged by the SHGs on internal loans, the group leaders made loans to each other and to a select few members, rationalising their actions as serving the financial interests of the collective (by ensuring the circulation of group capital) and being in conformity with promoter instructions.

The Mahalir Thittam, BDO and bank-promoted groups in Prakasam and Nalloor villages fared better in the matter of regular group meetings that were fairly well attended. And yet, regular transactional activities were not sufficient protection against what a member of Roja SHG (MaThi-SC) graphically described as the leaders' 'power to sign and sanction loans'. The president of Roja SHG reportedly withdrew a sum of Rs 8,000 (when the group-sanctioned loan amount was Rs 3,000) in order to secure a loan of Rs 5,000 for herself. Since her existing loan disqualified her from seeking the SHG's formal sanction, she attempted to record the loan in the secretary's name in the loan ledger. In this case, the secretary's unwillingness to accommodate the SHG president's unapproved loan marked a departure from the majority of cases in which the leaders usually assisted each other in similar situations. Occasionally, the SHG leaders openly staked their claim to a large-sized loan on the basis of their (time and labour) contribution to managing the groups' affairs. Upset that Roja SHG had approved only half of a loan (of Rs 10,000) that she had sought for her son's wedding, President Soosana asked the group, 'Am I like the others? What is the use of being president? I run around on group work.' Tired of being harangued and badgered by her, the SHG sanctioned an additional Rs 2,000 that she repaid in a month's time.

Holding leaders to account

The attempts of group leaders to secure loans for themselves without the approval of group members did not pass without challenge in the SHGs in Thillai block. This was seen, for instance, in the case of the women's resistance to Mahalir Thittam's instruction that concessional (or annual 12%) interest rates should be charged for particular borrowing purposes such as medical emergencies, child birth and the death of a family member. The majority of the groups firmly refused to observe purpose-differentiated interest rates. Besides the practical difficulties this practice would entail, the women feared that it would enhance the scope of their leaders' discretionary decisions and actions. The case of Annai Janaki SHG (MaThi-SC) bears this out. Member Sundari of the SHG was resentful that her request for a loan at 12% interest rates for house-building was turned down by the SHG's president, who allowed her own daughter-in-law (also an SHG member) the concessional interest rate for the latter's childbirth-related expenses. In Sundari's perception, her requirement of low-priced credit to build her house was no less important to her household than another's need for a medical expense. The hierarchy of needs implicit in purpose-differentiated interest rates made them a minefield of conflict, besides paving the way for potential abuses of power by group leaders.[3]

Responding to the perception that group leaders did not always seek the collective's approval for their own loans or inform co-members about the repayment status of their loans, (a few) members positioned themselves in ways that allowed them to hold their leaders to account. In Roja SHG, three group members took to regularly 'flipping the pages' of the account books at group meetings to signal that they had taken it upon themselves to keep watch over the leaders. In this case, the women in question were formally literate, making this an effective intervention. The group leaders of Ganga SHG (MaThi-OBC) had stopped sharing information relating to group accounts with their co-members who were formally non-literate. The self-positioning of two outspoken members as 'the ones who ask questions' enabled them to seek information regarding their group's financial status. In the words of one of them:

> We pester the leaders with questions at weekly meetings. We demand to know how much they deposit in the bank, how much they give as loans and to whom. The NGO tells us to not be mute spectators at group meetings. The NGO tells us to ask questions.

Matters came to a head in Ganga SHG when the bank permitted the group to circulate Rs 20,000 (part of a subsidy amount on a bank loan) as intra-group loans among all members, but this amount was withdrawn by the leaders without informing the members. The cash withdrawal was discovered more than a month later when the two proactive members, accompanied by the college graduate son of one of them, visited the bank to enquire about the subsidy funds. Furious that the group leaders had concealed the withdrawal of the cash, the group decided that the college graduate son would, henceforth, play a more active role in monitoring the SHG's accounts in return for a small fee. As the cases of Roja and Ganga SHGs suggest, the perceived privileges associated with the autonomising of group leaders had provoked the self-positioning of some members as the alert and watchful monitors of group accounting practices. During the period of my visits to Prakasam village, the women frequently discussed a news-worthy development in a neighbouring village. The president and secretary of an SHG, who had refused to permit the account books to be audited by anyone, had been shamed when group members marched into their homes and seized the books, on the advice of officials of the BDO. This development had caused some fear among the SHG leaders in Prakasam village.

Managing micro-banks: privilege or burden?

> Do you pay my wife a salary that you ask her so many questions about the group's expenses and accounts? If you continue to do this, I'll make her step down as your secretary.
>
> The husband of the secretary of *Kaveri* SHG (MaThi-OBC)

Besides the sanction and disbursal of loans, another dimension of group functioning that constituted the women as members and leaders with distinct and conflicting interests was the management of micro-banks, and the risks, costs and burdens they entailed for both parties, albeit in different ways. For group members, the issue was one of containing the risks of either deliberate pilfering by their leaders or the imprudent, wasteful management of their finances.[4] From the point of view of the leaders, the risks of being the custodians of group funds were high in an environment of alert watchfulness and amplified, in some cases, by their own low levels of formal literacy. Ensuring the repayment of multiple loans to the bank and the SHG and keeping accurate accounts could be daunting for the leaders.

The president of *Annai Indira* SHG (Bank-SC), who began to oversee the maintenance of group accounts after the SHG's secretary was incapacitated by her husband's illness, was terrified of handling money. She admitted to me that her 'timid' nature, her household's poverty (making it impossible for her to replace any money she might lose) and the extent of her responsibility filled her with constant dread and great anxiety. She was required to safely reach a total loan principal of Rs 12,000 (on two simultaneous loans) to the bank *each month*. The secretary of Bharathi SHG (Bank-SC), also the only group member who had class 10 level schooling, was often unavailable for SHG-related work. The SHG's president relied on her schoolgoing children to write out cheques and make entries in the SHG's resolution book before school time, causing tension in her household and earning her husband's rebuke. The costs of group leadership also included the sense of being constantly watched and the possible sullying of one's reputation through village gossip, should money be lost inadvertently.

The perils of being watched

> The group leaders, who managed small businesses, faced their co-members' constant suspicion that they might divert the SHGs' corpus in order to meet their own working capital requirements. Then-Koodu SHG (Bank-OBC) permitted its leaders to retain some cash for sudden expenses since quick withdrawal from the bank was not easy. The members of the SHG made frequent demands on the secretary (the owner-manager of a mosaic stone-manufacturing unit) for small amounts of 'change' (loose cash for petty expenses) to check if she kept the cash with her at all times. The president of Bharathi SHG (Bank-SC) postponed a visit to the bank to deposit the monthly loan principal amount, claiming that the delayed payment of her husband's salary had made it difficult for her to add her share to the corpus. The delay coincided with a period that her children, pursuing a diploma education elsewhere, visited the village. The women of her SHG reportedly gossiped among themselves that their president had probably sent the money back with her children as part of their fee payment. The SHG president said to me, 'Their words hurt me. Even the bank manager is more understanding than these women.'

The leaders lamented that none of the costs and the risks they bore were regarded as worthy of remuneration either by group members or by promoter organisations. The monthly meetings held by the Mahalir Thittam partner NGO at the block headquarters and the weekly deposit of cash in the banks warranted frequent travel outside the village on SHG-related work. Lunch was not provided at the NGO-organised meetings, and the time involved in making visits to the bank was unpredictable. In the Mahalir Thittam SHGs, all women paid a monthly amount of Rs 5 per member (and thus a total Rs 100) by way of a 'Group Maintenance Fund' in order to meet the SHG-related expenses. While SHG members expected that the leaders would use the fund for unavoidable expenses and add the remaining amount to the group corpus, the leaders regarded it as payment for their services and lost their temper when the women insisted that they provide a detailed account of group expenses.[5] The SHG leaders described the frustrations involved in being accountable to multiple actors – the NGOs, the bank, the BDO, group members and even their spouses. The husband of the secretary of Ganga SHG (MaThi-OBC) reportedly beat her severely when she returned from a three-day SHG-related event as she had not sought his permission before leaving the village. In this context, the leaders resented the public reiteration by the Mahalir Thittam partner NGO and the BDO that their services were voluntary and the invisibilising, thereby, of the time, efforts and skills they expended in SHG management.

In its handbook on how to form SHGs, NABARD (n.d. 2) instructs all group members to share the work of managing SHGs by 'rotation' of the responsibility and tasks of leadership, such as bookkeeping and organising meetings. In Thillai block, the SHG promoters issued a general instruction to SHGs (when the groups were formed) to periodically rotate the position of leadership, both to distribute work responsibilities and to preempt the formation of vested interests. However, none of the 27 SHGs had rotated leadership positions. The lack of formal literacy skills among members, the complications of bank-related paperwork involved in the formal change of leadership and the absence of initiative on the part of the existing leaders to discuss the possibility of change in leadership were cited (usually in combination) as the reasons that leadership changes had not been attempted. Similar issues were reported by Smriti Rao's (2008) study of SHGs in two villages of Mahabubnagar district (Andhra Pradesh). The bulk of the work of group management had fallen upon leaders, and the posts of leadership had not been rotated for years. The leaders described their responsibilities as burdensome and complained of the time and energies required to even make women turn up for meetings and to make their payments on time. When members failed to make monthly payments, group leaders dipped into their own funds to make up the difference, seeking reimbursement later (Rao 2008).

The political economy of promotional assistance

The absence of institutionalised arrangements for the routine auditing and financial oversight of SHGs' account books accentuated the general climate of suspicion within SHGs. Despite the presence of multiple actors (state and non-state) that competed with each other to enter the arena of SHG promotion in Thillai block (discussed in Chapter 1), the women reported dissatisfaction with the quality of the 'nurturing' they received from the promoter organisations; the latter were judged unaccountable to the women and unavailable when they required external intervention. The SHGs often found themselves subject to neglect and indifference even when they vigorously sought the motivational presence of sympathetic outsiders during periods of stress, whether related to failing livelihoods and irregular group transactions or intra-group conflicts between members and leaders.

No nurturing when needed

> The BDO in Tamil Nadu lacked the administrative wherewithal and financial resources required to provide support services to the SHGs that it had formed. The two BDO-promoted groups in Karisal village reported virtual abandonment by the rural welfare officer (RWO) who had formed the groups, contributing, in part, to the low morale of the women and irregular group meetings. Both the SHGs comprised women from landless households whose male kin were formerly bonded labourers in the beedi industry. During the period of my study, over half the women in both the groups were unable to repay a bank-sourced loan (amounting to Rs 1,250 per member) owing to the uncertain and meagre incomes they earned from beedi work. When the RWO was requested by the group leaders to meet the women and intercede, the official advised the leaders to manage their SHGs with the ten women 'who had the capacity to repay well' and expel the others. When I made contact with the groups for the first time, I faced a rather extraordinary request – to pose as a functionary of the BDO who had been deputed to monitor SHGs. The SHG leaders, who made this request, hoped to use my visits to create a semblance of external support in order to enthuse and motivate their co-members and counter the acute demoralisation of the groups.

The commitment of the Mahalir Thittam partner NGO to the SHGs it had formed in Thillai block suffered from the conflict-ridden relationship between the partner NGO and the TNCDW. The partner NGO was constantly anxious about the perceived impermanence of its role in Mahalir Thittam and the state's power to terminate the relationship at will. During my fieldwork, the head of the partner NGO in Thillai block affirmed that the absence of alternative funding sources had forced his (and other partner) organisation/s to endure the relationship with an 'overbearing' state partner. The partner NGOs identified three principal areas of discord in Mahalir Thittam, namely (a) the state's propensity to take all credit for work executed by the NGO, (b) the mounting work-related expectations and (c) the dwindling financial compensation. The tasks associated with SHG promotion included the burden of collecting and providing information (to the TNCDW) about group transactions at frequent intervals (nearly 15 times a year, as estimated by one of the NGO heads).

To add to the woes of partner NGOs, the 'NGO support cost' component of Mahalir Thittam was considerably scaled down after a change of state government during the first five years of the project.[6] While the partner NGOs were expected to regularly audit the SHGs' account books, constraints of personnel and funding had limited the frequency of audits. They were usually undertaken only before the 'grading' of SHGs by banks to assess whether the groups were fit to receive particular loans. When fights broke out in the groups due to suspected pilfering by the leaders, the women had to make multiple trips to the NGO's office, pleading that NGO staff visit the village to mediate and resolve the conflict.

In Thillai block, unlike the BDO and the Mahalir Thittam partner NGO, the INGO enjoyed consistent financial support from its headquarters office in Chennai. And yet, its communication with the SHGs it had formed in Karisal village, the periodic training of SHG leaders and visits by INGO field staff had greatly reduced, provoking allegations of abandonment by the women. In particular, the INGO's indifference galled the women since it coincided with a period of economic distress – an outcome of the near-drought conditions that prevailed during four successive years (2002–5) in Tamil Nadu. The absence of external institutional support from the promoter INGO during a period of livelihoods crisis was perceived (by the women) as no less than an act of 'betrayal' on the part of the promoter. Somewhat surprisingly perhaps,[7] the nationalised bank branch that doubled up as promoter agency of the groups in

Nalloor village had painstakingly cultivated the most valued relationships with the SHGs it promoted. The SHG leaders in Nalloor recounted with pride the (former) bank manager's concern for the SHGs' financial health, his regular monthly appearance at village-level SHG meetings and, in particular, the patience with which he had trained SHG leaders to take charge of accounts maintenance. The women regretted that the current bank manager did not display the diligence or interest in the promotion of SHGs that his predecessor had shown, pointing to the individual-dependent quality of SHG promotion when performed by commercial banks.

The issues regarding promotional support that I found in my fieldwork resonate elsewhere and appear to be a common concern in the literature. A study conducted by the NGO Nirantar on 2,750 SHGs in 16 states points to the overall inadequacy in meeting the basic training requirements of SHGs. Nearly 56% of the groups had not been given training of any kind, not even on themes such as group formation or functioning. Of the government-promoted groups, 70% had not received any kind of training, including group building or management skills (Dwivedi 2007). The poor performance of government actors as promoter agencies is frequently commented upon in the literature. The EDA and APMAS study (2006) of 214 SHGs in four states found that while 37% of sample SHGs in all the four states had received low inputs of any kind (whether related to microfinance or other development inputs), government-promoted groups accounted for the highest proportion of SHGs (77%) with low inputs of any kind. The report observes that this reflects the target-driven approach of government programmes that add SHG promotion to the existing tasks of field staff, without providing additional resource or infrastructural support (ibid.).

A study of 109 sample SHGs drawn from nine blocks in four districts of Assam likewise found that the district rural development administration fared poorly as promoter agency on account of numerous vacancies in its field posts, woefully inadequate travel allowances provided to fieldworkers of the BDO and the quick formation of SHGs so that they might qualify for the SGSY loans. The DRDA/BDO structure was reported to have frequently 'lured away' SHGs promoted by NGOs and MFIs on the promise of disbursing subsidies, grants and bank loans (APMAS 2009a). Drawing on her study of SHGs in two villages of Mahabubnagar district (Andhra Pradesh), Rao (2008) reported that the government staff member ('sevika'), who had signed up women to form new SHGs, subsequently left it entirely to local NGOs and the male kin of the SHG members to provide assistance in securing bank loans or other services the groups might require.

Pattenden (2010) found that the anganwadi worker (attached to the Integrated Child Development Services centre) in one of his study villages in Dharwad district (Karnataka) could not name the village's SHGs that she was ostensibly responsible for, although she had been in her post for six months. During the period of his fieldwork, many anganwadi workers were refusing to supervise SHGs because they were offered no more than Rs 25 per group on a monthly basis. If government fieldworkers suffered from the tendency of government programmes to overload them with additional work responsibilities and little or no monetary compensation, the reliance of NGO promoters on donor funding or, alternatively, support from NABARD was equally problem-ridden. The study of 109 SHGs in Assam found that almost all the 34 NGO promoters in the sample reported insufficient funds for promotion and capacity-building inputs either from NABARD or from other apex NGOs (APMAS 2009a).

Conclusion

The secondary literature on SHGs and my fieldwork in Tamil Nadu suggest that group leaders were autonomised and responsibilised to a greater extent than members and that the intersection of broader societal power hierarchies with routine group functions and transactions underpinned the discretionary powers of leaders. Economic class, literacy skills and, in some cases, proximity to local sources of political power were found to bolster the authority of group leaders within their SHGs. In this chapter, I detailed the processes by which group leadership translates to higher loan access within SHGs and showed that this did not go unchallenged by group members who sought to hold their leaders to account, with respect to both the leaders' own credit access and loan repayment and their management of group accounts. While NABARD (2006) expects that SHG participation will teach women to handle large sums of cash and manage accounts, this particular pedagogic function of SHGs constituted *group leaders* as the autonomised managers of micro-banks and *group members* as the alert and watchful monitors of group accounts, with some performing the role more proactively than others.

Although vested with ensuring the waste-free, leakage-free rotation of group finances, the group leaders did not adhere to an exclusive financial rationality aimed at maximising productivity. Instead, their calculations, judgements and priorities were influenced by their acute sense of the 'unfair' expectation (of their co-members and of promoter agencies) that they toil without reward. Aggrieved at the taken-for-granted manner in which a considerable degree of volunteerism was expected from them, the leaders siphoned off small (and sometimes larger) amounts of petty cash from their SHGs and lost their temper when group members demanded transparency or full disclosure of group finances. Even as the SHG leaders resisted the efforts of members to contain the scope of their autonomous decision-making, they drew attention to the skills required and their greater responsibilisation vis-à-vis the others. Handling large sums of cash required skills and imposed risks and costs that were borne disproportionately by group leaders and could not be easily transferred to others or shared equally within the groups. The low prevalence of formal literacy skills among SHG women, the demands of daily wage work and the near-absence of the periodic auditing of SHGs' financial transactions by promoter agencies shaped the social and institutional context in which the management of micro-banks took place.

In this chapter and Chapter 3, I have shown that the weekly SHG meetings were sites of contestation wherein women positioned themselves and each other in multiple ways, and strove to refute a positioning that did not serve their interests and to fashion instead a counter-positioning of the self that expanded their spaces of manoeuvre. I show therefore how women do not come into development programmes as pre-constituted subjects (Mohanty 1991; Sharma 2010), but are produced as 'the women who take more' whose views on the distribution of interest incomes conflict with 'the women who take less'; as group leaders who bring to bear a 'collective' judgement upon all and invoke a capacity discourse to evaluate the creditworthiness of prospective borrowers; as the 'women who live alone' and 'women of no means' from poorer households who draw attention to the webs of 'power' that pervade SHG operations and limit their credit entitlements; as 'push-out' women who decry the absence of empathy and compassion on the part of the collective; as the women who 'ask questions' about money so as to not be 'mute' spectators at weekly meetings; as 'thrifty savers' who demand a constant flow of information about the decisions made on their behalf; and as 'overworked', 'under-appreciated' managers of micro-banks and 'uncompensated', 'risk-bearing' leaders who withhold information and refuse accountability-related demands.

The outcomes of the numerous micro-struggles engendered by the autonomising and the responsibilising of the SHGs were never known in advance. The overall loan access of women belonging to poorer households was lower vis-à-vis their co-members from economically better-off households (Chapter 3). However, low-access borrowers (also usually poorer members) did win the right to the equal distribution of interest incomes. The SHG leaders, who were generally regarded as unaccountable with respect to the management of group finances, were (on occasion) successfully tamed by group members who sought the support of bank managers, the BDO, their male kin and promoter NGOs to be able to do so.

Notes

1 In Karisal and Prakasam villages, the ten groups promoted by Mahalir Thittam and the BDO had two group leaders each (president and secretary), while the eight INGO-promoted groups had three leaders each (president, secretary and treasurer). Thus, there were 44 leaders in the 18 SHGs.

2 Tamarai SHG, like the other groups in Thillai block, used the evaluative criteria of *kattum thiramai* (repayment skill/capacity) to judge if particular loan seekers were eligible for the group loans they sought. This was discussed at length in Chapter 3.

3 The occurrence of life cycle events that required lump sums of expenditure elicited other forms of solidarity from the SHGs. The SHGs usually raised a special collection to make a gift (cash or kind) during occasions such as the birth of a child, a puberty function and a wedding in the family. In case of death in a woman's family, several SHGs sanctioned fresh loans for funeral expenses even if a current loan was not fully repaid and had a large-sized balance. *Pushpam* SHG (INGO-mixed caste) provided ten kilograms of rice and a sari to any member who lost her husband. These actions always followed collective decisions taken at group meetings and approved by all members.

4 The secretary of Vaigai SHG (MaThi-SC) allegedly used up Rs 15,000 of the group's corpus, citing expenses relating to weekly visits to the bank. The secretary's husband routinely handled the tasks of accounts maintenance and liaison with the bank. The money used up by the secretary was never returned to the group.

5 I heard stories of SHG leaders who used the money to buy 'cool drinks' and 'snacks' when they visited the bank on SHG work. In one case, a group leader was accused by members of using the money to feast on 'chicken biriyani' whenever she travelled out of the village on SHG work!

6 The statewide expansion phase of Mahalir Thittam was launched in 1997–98 during the DMK regime. The SHG women members received a daily allowance of Rs 45 for attendance at training sessions, while the NGO received a daily allowance of Rs 30 for each woman who attended the training. After the state assembly elections of 2001 (in which the AIADMK was voted to power), payment to SHG leaders, SHG members and the NGO per training day were reduced to Rs 20, Rs 7.50 and Rs 15, respectively. Shortly, after being voted to power in April 2006, the DMK state government restored the training allowance paid to SHG women and partner NGOs to pre-2001 levels.

7 Banks have generally been reluctant to undertake SHG promotion on account of the costs, efforts and labour involved as well as the perception of bankers that NGOs were better suited for 'social intermediation' (Harper 2002b; Satish 2001).

Chapter 5[1]

The 'imperfect translation' of SHG-banking

Autonomised bankers, 'vulnerable' women

In Chapter 1, I argued that the policy documents (of Reserve Bank of India [RBI] and National Bank for Agriculture and Rural Development [NABARD]) have constituted women of poor households as the ideal responsibilised subjects of peer group–based lending projects in ways that resonate with the commercial interests of the banking sector in the post-reforms era. The central idea that informed SHG-banking (via the direct linkage scheme) was that rural women organised into grassroots collectives who save and rotate micro-capital, 'imbibe' the skills of 'financial intermediation' and demonstrate responsible financial behaviour may seek and obtain bank loans. Through unceasing activity, the SHGs were expected to manifest an active citizenship and work on themselves ('capitalise the self'), fashion themselves as prudent savers and disciplined borrowers and demonstrate (to banks) that they are fiscally responsible agents who 'handle large sums of money well', thus working their way to bank credit. The underlying idea of the SGSY scheme was that, in addition to all of the aforementioned points, the women members of SHGs would show willingness and capacity to initiate and manage an income-generation enterprise in order to secure the 'anti-poverty' assistance available through the SGSY scheme.

However, rural women's access to bank loans did not depend' only on their disciplined financial behaviour or the smooth functioning and successful management of their 'micro-banks' as I show in this chapter. I show how the 'imperfect translation' (Mosse 2004) of the 'policy idea' of SHG-banking into the intentions and ambitions of the collaborating agencies, their institutional interests and organisational cultures produced multiple unintended consequences, with autonomised bank officials steering women's decisions and actions in ways that were not anticipated by policy mandates. I complicate the discursive construction of gendered citizenship (of women as the desired and sought-after clientele of group-based lending) by the 'centres of calculation' (the RBI and the NABARD) by showing how *branch-level* bank personnel address and position SHG women or the 'denizens' of political society (Chatterjee 2004) who seek to 'leverage' the banking sector. I show how the women, in turn, counter-position themselves as certain kinds of development actors, even as they appeal to and position (particular) bank officials in ways that bolster their claims to state developmental resources.

The distribution of bank loans in the study villages

In this chapter, I draw on literature assessing the SHG-bank linkage in the states of Rajasthan and Andhra Pradesh through large-scale data gathering and analysis, besides my own fieldwork in Tamil Nadu. The first study on the linkage programme in Andhra Pradesh, conducted by APMAS in 2003–4, included 400 SHGs in eight districts[2] (Reddy 2005). Some of these districts, along with others, were part of a recurrent study conducted in Andhra Pradesh in 2006–7 that covered 240 SHGs from 96 villages in eight districts[3] (APMAS 2007). Whereas 54% of the SHGs covered in the 2003 study were on their first bank linkage, only 25% of the SHGs in the recurrent study were on their first linkage; 34% of SHGs in the recurrent study had obtained three or more linkage loans from the financing banks and over one-tenth of the SHGs were experiencing their fourth or fifth credit linkage with the banks during the period of the study. The district-wise linkage figures showed that the average first linkage loan was smallest in East Godavari district at Rs 14,700. However, by their fifth linkage, the SHGs in the districts were drawing an average loan of Rs 112,500. The average loan sizes were found to have increased with every linkage.

In Rajasthan, the study included 202 SHGs in 89 villages from five districts.[4] A total of 151 of the 202 sample groups had received bank loans. Of 151 groups, 141 SHGs had received the linkage loans and 10 SHGs the SGSY loans. SGSY loan amounts were substantially higher than the linkage loans. The average loan size of SGSY groups in the sample was over Rs 300,000. The average loan size for all 151 groups receiving bank loans was found to be Rs 45,000. For the 141 groups that had received the linkage loans, the average loan was Rs 27,000 (APMAS and CMF 2006). In the three villages of my fieldwork in Thillai block, 25 of 27 SHGs had received the Revolving Fund (of Rs 25,000) component of the SGSY scheme[5] and 13 had received the SGSY loan-cum-subsidy. A total of nine SHGs had received the direct linkage loan. Table 5.1 shows the village-wise distribution of the SHGs that received these loans.[6]

The total financial assistance ranged from Rs 50,000 to Rs 200,000 per SHG for the 15 groups that received or were sanctioned the SGSY loan. The quantum of the linkage loan received by the nine SHGs ranged from Rs 40,000 to Rs 200,000 per SHG. The sanction of the direct linkage loan was relatively smooth for the banks and the SHGs since it required neither proof of enterprise activity (being untied with regard to borrowing purpose) nor the conduct of the 'grading' exercises that involved the DRDA and BDO (as there was no subsidy component). And yet, as Table 5.1 shows, of 27 SHGs in the three villages, only 9 SHGs (all in Nalloor village) received the linkage loan, suggesting that bankers may not have been inclined to finance SHGs, without a targeted scheme that mandated such linkages.

The promoter NGOs in Thillai block affirmed that banks were generally reluctant to make large-sized loans to SHGs that were four times the groups' own savings as permitted under the bank linkage scheme. They opined that the linkage scheme was 'pointless' if the loan sanctioned was considerably less than the 1:4 ratio permitted by the norms of the scheme. From the point of view of the women as well, the attraction of the subsidy-bearing SGSY

Table 5.1 Number of SHGs receiving bank loans by village: Karisal, Prakasam and Nalloor

	Karisal	*Prakasam*	*Nalloor*	*Total*
Total SHGs studied	10	8	9	27
Of total, SHGs that received Revolving Fund	8	8	9	25
Of total, SHGs that received SGSY assistance	5	6	2	13
Of total, SHGs sanctioned (not yet disbursed) SGSY assistance	–	–	2	2
Of total, SHGs that received direct linkage loans	–	–	9	9

Source: Fieldwork data.

financial assistance outstripped that of the non-subsidy loans. The women reconciled themselves to the linkage loan if the SGSY assistance was not available. In the following sections of this chapter, I discuss the negotiations that ensued between the SHGs and bank personnel, when the women staked their claim to the direct linkage and the SGSY loan schemes.

A Hobson's choice

NABARD's operational guidelines on SHG-banking encouraged branch-level officials to make autonomous decisions with regard to determining the terms on which they would finance SHGs (NABARD 1992, 1996). The autonomising of branch-level personnel took place in an environment that valued loan recovery, repayment performance and portfolio quality, a fallout of the banking sector reforms.[7] In Thillai block, when sanctioning bank loans (whether through the direct linkage or the SGSY scheme), the bank officials made the disbursal of these loans contingent upon SHG members' repayment of the unpaid overdue on older *individual-targeted* bank loans, made through (long-defunct) schemes such as the Integrated Rural Development Programme (IRDP). These loans were borrowed directly by particular SHG members or, as was more commonly the case, by their male relatives (husband, son and even in-laws). The propensity of bank managers to hold SHGs accountable for poor repayment on older loan schemes has been reported in other parts of India as well. A study of SHGs sponsored by the NGO *Grama Vikas* in 20 villages of Kolar district (Karnataka) reports that banks did not provide loans to SHGs if anyone from the household of a group member was an IRDP defaulter. The groups had to choose between making the households repay the bank or forego the linkage loan. While the SHGs chose to convince members to repay these loans, this was a difficult task for group members and leaders alike. The women concerned had to talk to their spouses who were convinced that the loans had been waived under a previous political regime at the centre (Rajasekhar 2004).

In the villages surrounding Thillai town, an SHG that applied for a loan from its financing bank was required to produce 'no-objection' certificates from all (five) banks in Thillai town to the effect that no group member or her relative/(s) had an unpaid loan from any of the banks.[8] The banks threatened to stall loans to the SHGs unless they *expelled* members who were unable to repay an unpaid balance on individual-targeted loans, although these pressures were not sanctioned by the official norms of the SHG-targeted loan schemes. The guidelines of the direct linkage scheme clarify that defaults by a few members of SHGs and their family members to the bank should not matter so long as the SHG is not in default to it (NABARD 1996).[9] The resurrection of long overdue loans created the phenomenon of bank-induced 'push-outs' from the SHGs. In 27 SHGs in the three villages, eight women dropped out of membership following the banks' pressures to repay individual-targeted loans. Of the eight, no more than three were direct borrowers of bank loans. An elderly widow quit her SHG when urged (by the bank manager) to repay her deceased husband's loan to the bank.

Sometimes SHG members became the targets of bank pressures even if they (or their spouses) were not direct borrowers of bank loans and had merely co-guaranteed a loan (as *jameen* signatory) made to a friend or relative. In some cases, exclusionary pressures from the banks preceded credit linkage and were exerted even during group formation. When SHGs sought to open savings bank accounts as part of group formation, the bank managers stipulated that the groups deny membership to women with defaulter male relatives. Some women consequently tended to self-exclude from SHG membership, anticipating that they would face bank-induced pressures to repay the loans borrowed by male relatives.

The spectre of old loans

> The husband of member Swarnamma of Kaveri SHG (MaThi-OBC) had borrowed a sum of Rs 2500, 16 years ago from the cooperative society to buy goats. This had grown to Rs 10,650 over the years, when Kaveri SHG was sanctioned a bank loan. Swarnamma claimed that her husband had ceased repayment of his loan when he learnt that the (then) state government had waived the loan. All the women members of Kaveri SHG accompanied Swarnamma to the bank to persuade the manager to not make the sanction and disbursal of the loan they sought contingent on the repayment of her husband's old loan, but to no avail. The Mahalir Thittam partner NGO endorsed the bank manager's position and counselled Swarnamma to repay the loan. Using a lump sum of money that her daughter-in-law had received from the shoe company she worked in, Swarnamma repaid Rs 6,500 and informed the manager that she could pay no more.

When faced with bankers' intransigence on the repayment of individual-targeted loans, several SHGs mobilised their financial resources to provide emergency loans to particular group members to enable the repayment. Then-koodu SHG (Bank-OBC) paid Rs 45,000 to the bank to complete repayment of individual-targeted loans borrowed by (the male kin of) eight group members. At least one-half of this amount was financed by the SHG's loans to the individual members in question. Opinions were divided regarding the perceived fairness of the bankers' loan recovery prerogatives. The president of Roja SHG (MaThi-SC) was zealous in her efforts to ensure that women fully repaid the money owed by their male kin to the bank. 'Making the women repay the bank is our achievement,' she said. Some SHGs resorted to subterfuge mechanisms and sought to deceive the bank by providing a formal letter declaring that the women in question had quit the group, even when they continued to remain members. The strategy of deception, which carried the risk of discovery by the bank, demanded a high degree of group solidarity and willingness on the part of the collective, to bear the risk of protecting a few members. In one instance, an SHG president, when asked by the bank manager to provide the names of fathers-in-law of her co-members, provided false names foreseeing correctly that the enquiries pertained to unpaid bank loans!

The banks also enlisted SHGs in the task of enforcing community-wide financial discipline by inciting the women to function as 'debt collectors' and undertake house-to-house campaigns for full loan recovery in their village or panchayat on behalf of the banks. For example, an SHG 'earned' a bank loan by persuading five families of village co-residents *who were not related to SHG members* to repay a sum of Rs 25,000. The leaders of the SHG subsequently challenged the bank manager saying, 'We have kept our promise to recover your money. You keep yours and give us our loan.' Even as the women struggled to fulfil loan repayment targets that were (informally) set by the bank, they recognised that bank managers were manipulating SHGs' community-level social networks and their goodwill to complete a task that could not have taken place otherwise. The president of Then-Koodu SHG (Bank-OBC), who ensured the full repayment of all individual-targeted bank loans by her group members, said to the manager: 'You are earning the salary. Will you pay me for this work?' Though her response was made in jest, the issue that she raised was entirely serious and reflected her cognisance of the bankers' mobilisation of SHGs' (and particularly SHG leaders') unremunerated labour to settle their outstanding debt.[10]

In several instances, the women vigorously countered the bankers' deployment of their gendered household and kin-mediated identities (as wives, daughters and mothers of defaulter males) and positioned themselves instead as 'savers' and 'borrowers' whose credit histories and disciplined rotation of their capital testified to their creditworthiness. For the most part, the bankers overrode SHGs' protests as they were able to draw upon a widely shared understanding of the embedded nature of women's familial identities – an understanding that cut across institutions including government bureaucracies, NGOs and the households of SHG members. Eventually, when all other strategies failed, the SHGs succumbed to bank pressures and expelled particular members.

Poverty, social context and financial intermediation

The 'paradox' of SHG-banking outlined in the Introduction of this book involves women from formerly unbanked households seeking and securing bank credit in the era of financial liberalisation and banking sector reforms that had effectively terminated the social and developmental banking era. The literature on the banking sector in the post-reforms era suggests that the institutional cultures of nationalised commercial banks were significantly impacted by the reforms. For instance, a study of 60 bank branches (48 commercial and 12 regional rural banks [RRBs]) in three districts of Madhya Pradesh included interviews with both branch managers and senior officials to ascertain their views on rural banking (Jones *et al.* 2003). While this study was not specific to banking with SHGs, some of its observations are telling nevertheless. Over half the managers viewed lending to the poor as 'high risk', and nearly all managers associated the poor with high diversion of loans. The large majority felt that poorer borrowers thought that it was the branch manager's responsibility to ensure the repayment of their loans. Branch managers perceived an acute conflict between the mandate of rural development and the business objectives of banking. The conflict had demotivated them, besides producing high levels of stress. Both branch managers and the senior staff emphasised that performance appraisal systems within the banking sector focused on deposit mobilisation and recovery performance, with little recognition of development-related lending. Given the post-reform emphasis on profitability, many branch managers feared that their own worries about risk and repayment were likely to negatively impact their lending to the rural poor (ibid.).

In Thillai block, the financing banks were fully aware that SHG-banking linked them to women from households and communities that had been the targets of social banking–type schemes associated with poor credit discipline in the past.[11] Consequently, the banks were sceptical of the women's abilities and/or willingness to honour repayment-related deadlines and commitments. While the SHGs demanded that their credit history be the sole criterion for loan sanction (in the face of bank pressures to retrieve loans made to male kin), they found that the banks' minute inspection of the repayment record of their internal loans could also have deleterious consequences. The SHGs' books of accounts contained details about the weekly savings made by each member and all loans made by the SHG to individual borrowers, the amount of monthly repayments and the interest paid. The women were expected to write down details of their financial practices and generate knowledge about the savings and repayment performance of individual borrowers, to keep track of inflow and outflow and to use the knowledge thus generated to preserve and accumulate their micro-capital in prudent and responsible ways.

The information in SHGs' savings and loan ledgers was crucial insofar as it informed the bank officials to judge regarding the creditworthiness of the group as a collective as well as of individual members. We might see SHG accounting books as a calculative technology (Rose and Miller 1992) installed by government in the heart of the private sphere (an enterprise, school or even family) that embeds new methods of calculation linking 'private decisions' and 'public objectives'. Rose and Miller (1992) observe that making people write things down and count them or inscription can itself be a form of action at a distance, even as power flows to the centre or agent who determines the inscriptions and contemplates, compares and evaluates them in their aggregated form. In this case, power flowed to the banks that made decisions about allocating resources on the basis of the information aggregated.

Problems arose when banks refused loans to a group if a few of its members had delayed repayment on an internal loan or had not made an interest payment that was due. The NGOs that engaged in SHG promotion in other parts of Tamil Nadu also testified that some bank officials displayed zero tolerance for any form of delayed repayment of internal loans. This stringent scrutiny disadvantaged groups drawn from economically and socially marginalised communities that were more likely to show poor financial performance on their internal loans and savings. It was generally felt that this was more evident with respect to the direct linkage loan that did not mandate loan disbursal to socially marginalised sub-groups of the population, unlike the SGSY scheme. The Dalit woman head of an NGO promoting SHGs that I interviewed (as part of the first phase of my field research) reported that the bank manager frequently criticised her publicly in his office saying, 'Your people are always like this. They do not repay on time.' She said to me, 'I find this humiliating as I know he is referring to my caste.'

Ethnographies of SHG-banking, to the extent that these are available, have not adequately explored the processes by which caste mediates women's access to bank resources or shapes 'inclusive banking' schemes in particular ways at the grassroots. However, Rao's (2008) study of SHGs in two villages of Mahabubnagar (Andhra Pradesh) does make some important observations in this respect. The study found that the male kin of SHG members played an important role in mediating between the women and state institutions and that men from the higher castes used their knowledge of official procedure to facilitate interactions with bank and other officials. These networks enabled them to secure bank loans for the SHGs that their female kin were part of. Since Dalit and tribal men did not have the education or the confidence to deal with state structures and could not perform this mediating role, the quality and consistency of support from NGOs and their staff was critical for the functioning and bank linkage of SHGs consisting of scheduled caste (SC) and scheduled tribe (ST) women. Where such support was uncertain or withdrawn after a period of time, those SHGs that were dependent on this support suffered (Rao 2008).

While Rao's (2008) study is micro-scale, two large-scale quantitative studies conducted by APMAS on the SHG-bank linkage scheme in Andhra Pradesh have examined the question of whether the quantum of bank loans received by groups varies markedly in keeping with the social composition of the groups. The 2003–4 study of the SHG-bank linkage scheme covering 400 SHGs in eight districts of Andhra Pradesh reported poorer linkage of SC and ST groups in comparison to open category (OC) SHGs (Reddy 2005). The study found that only 5% of SC SHGs received cumulative loans beyond Rs 105,000 and no ST SHGs had received such loans. In contrast, 22% of OC groups had received loans beyond Rs 105,000. The average current loan size was highest among OC SHGs at Rs 44,585, and lowest among STs at Rs 27,059 (ibid.).

The recurrent study (2006–7) involving 240 SHGs in eight districts of Andhra Pradesh found that the SHGs comprising SC and ST members did receive loans regularly from banks but that their loan size did not grow at the rate of other (more advantaged) groups. The largest loan size in the fifth linkage was accessed by SHGs that had a majority of members from the backward classes, while the second-largest loan sizes went to SHGs with members wholly from socially advantaged castes. In contrast, no SHG with members drawn from the SCs in the sample had received a fifth linkage loan (APMAS 2007). A comparison with the older study (2003–4) indicated that the difference between the size of the loan accessed by SHGs with SC and ST members and that accessed by more advantaged groups had, in fact, widened over the years. The report concludes the discussion by calling for more analysis to understand if overt discrimination on the part of bankers or a 'low resource base' (referring perhaps to the accumulated savings) of the SC SHGs had contributed to the observed disparities.

Contesting the 'evaluative' power of bankers: deception and defiance

In the three villages of Thillai block, the SHG women who faced the bank managers' close scrutiny of their financial accounts when applying for bank loans attempted to make the officials see that irregular savings or delayed repayment (of internal loans) were, to an extent, inevitable due to poverty and uncertain livelihoods. More commonly, the women fudged SHG account books before bank supervision to create a semblance of timely repayment. Reports from other parts of the country suggest that this practice may have been more widespread. For instance, a study of 109 sample SHGs in nine districts of Assam found that the books of accounts in some groups did not tally with the oral information given by the group members. While the members of one group said that they were saving at the rate of Rs 20 per member each month, the amount was recorded as Rs 50 per month in the books. In the same group, the numbers of internal loans and repayment figures were far higher in the books than what was reported by the members. The study observes that the records were being maintained 'attractively' so that the groups might obtain bank loans (the SGSY loans in this case) (APMAS 2009a).

In the study villages of Thillai block, the promoter NGO played the critical role of 'setting right' the account books by camouflaging repayment irregularities, prior to bank evaluation of the SHGs' loan ledgers. Being directly promoted by the financing bank, the SHGs in Nalloor village (unlike the groups in Prakasam and Karisal) were deprived of this dimension of promotional support.

Keeping the peace: a practical improvisation

> When the five OBC-only SHGs in Nalloor received a loan of Rs 200,000 per group through the linkage scheme, the women in the SC-only SHGs also sought the linkage loan. Arguing that the 'irregular' repayment of their internal loans demonstrated diminished capacity to repay bank loans, the bank manager firmly turned the women away. One of the more tenacious of the SHGs was sanctioned a (smaller) sum of Rs 150,000 when the women wore down the manager through their repeated visits and requests. Eventually, some women in the other SC-only SHGs also secured the linkage loan owing to a serendipitous development. The bank was required to disburse loans under the state government–sponsored *kutcha* house upgradation scheme, which was targeted to (only) those SHG members whose families lived in thatched huts in order to finance the construction of tiled roofing. Fearing that the disbursal of the house loans to a select few would cause heartburn and resentment, the bank manager devised a strategy of keeping the peace. This involved the simultaneous disbursal of the kutcha house loans to eligible members in the SC-only SHGs and of the linkage loan to those (in the same groups) ineligible for the house upgradation scheme. The manager publicly announced that the kutcha house loan was for those who lived in thatched huts and the linkage loan for those who lived in tiled houses!

The disbursal of the linkage loan was clearly not anchored to any policy-derived understanding of the scheme and yet served as a 'practical improvisation' (Mosse 2004) intended to maintain institutional and political relationships between the bank and the SHGs, besides enabling the bank to implement two divergent schemes targeted at the same population group. The women members of the SC-only SHGs in Nalloor were aware that the compensatory impulse that underlay the sanction of the linkage loan demarcated their entitlement to the loan from their OBC counterparts.[12] Moreover, the linkage loan was sanctioned after a change of guard at the bank and under the aegis of a new manager. The president of Ilam Pirai SHG (Bank-SC) commented, 'The former manager was too strict in judging our repayment record. But the new man has a conscience. He is more humane. He understands our poverty.'

Interestingly, the women did not always concede the bank's right to govern their financial decision-making through its evaluation of their savings and loan histories and its attempted regulation of their responses to livelihood and other crises. The president of an SC-only SHG in Nalloor challenged the manager (who had denied their linkage loan) saying, 'We have no employment now and have not repaid our loans. But it is *our* savings money that we haven't repaid. And that is not your business. You have a right to question us if we don't repay *your* loans.' By denouncing the bank's authority to 'contemplate' and 'evaluate' their credit histories, the women contested the power that the bankers exercised over them and their attempts to link private decisions to public objectives (Rose and Miller 1992). The women asserted instead their right to autonomous decisions vis-à-vis the rotation and the repayment of their group-generated corpus.

Other studies suggest that bank officials, grading SHGs to ascertain their suitability for bank loans, have had to accommodate (internal) loan repayment practices that the SHGs observed. The recurrent study of 240 SHGs in eight districts of Andhra Pradesh found that only in 38% of the groups visited were passbooks updated and in no more than 22.5% were loan ledgers up to date (APMAS 2007). Besides the non-maintenance of books and records, several SHGs did not repay internal loans until they required the next one and did not therefore monitor internal loan repayment either. Notwithstanding this, many of these groups had received 'A' grade (the highest grade) from the financing banks and had drawn several bank loans in succession (ibid.). While this study does not provide a 'thick description' of the negotiations and interactions between bank personnel and the SHGs so that we might understand better the processes at play, this finding does suggest that bank assessment and evaluation practices have had to take into account and adapt themselves to some of the 'private' decisions that the women have taken, in keeping with their priorities and preferences.

In sum, the dynamic of SHG-banking constituted women in various ways. Positioned as the female kin of defaulter males, the women vigorously repudiated their 'embedding' in kin and social relationships, positioning themselves as disciplined savers and borrowers whose creditworthiness merited evaluation on independent grounds. When the bankers brought to bear an intense scrutiny of their internal loan repayment, the women from the poorest SHGs drew attention to the economic oppression of their households and communities. They framed their entitlement to the linkage loan, not in terms of their efficient performance in this case, but of the dire and pressing nature of their need for development resources from the state. They reminded the bank officials that household poverty and the vagaries of livelihoods inevitably mediated the forms of financial intermediation their SHGs displayed. They appealed to the bank managers to show compassion and be mindful of their poverty, regardless of whether the credit assessment the bankers undertook was part of an anti-poverty scheme or not.

Valued clientele or potential defaulters?

The bank officials' anxieties regarding loan repayment and the strategies they fashioned to allay their anxieties constituted women as potential defaulters and portfolio risks, not the valued customers that RBI and NABARD policy documents envisaged. In Nalloor village, the manager's anxieties continued even after the linkage loans were disbursed and were reflected in specific measures to ensure foolproof repayment. He strictly instructed the women to *not* sanction internal loans out of the group-generated funds, until the linkage loans were fully repaid. The bank's efforts to prevent SHGs from rotating their own funds contravened the intended aim of the linkage scheme, which was to supplement the groups' own funds and increase the total loanable resources at the groups' disposal at any point of time. The bank's move to monopolise women's repayment capabilities towards servicing bank loans angered the women who were deprived of their internal loans even during an emergency requirement. The bank had stalled internal loaning selectively in the case of the SC-only SHGs in Nalloor village, reflecting again the bankers' assessment of the relative market and credit worthiness of women from the poorest communities.

Similar practices have been reported by a study of the bank linkage programme involving 202 SHGs in five districts of Rajasthan

(APMAS and CMF 2006). The study found that the financing banks had impounded the savings money of the SHGs in their bank accounts as collateral for bank loans in blatant violation of the formal rules of the linkage scheme. In four out of five sample districts, the banks insisted that the SHGs regularly deposit their savings amount (without withdrawal for intra-group lending) as precondition for sanction of bank loans. The amount of loan sanctioned was dependent on the deposited amount at the time of sanction and not on aggregate group savings, as required by the norms of the linkage scheme. Moreover, it was unclear if the financing banks were paying interest on the amount deposited in the saving account of the SHGs and other deposits, adding to the effective cost of bank loans for SHGs. The Rajasthan study found that, in some cases, a part of the bank loan sanctioned to the SHGs was impounded as well, with no interest being paid on the impounded loan amount either (ibid.). Banerjee and Sen's (2003) study of the SGSY scheme in three districts of West Bengal (Haora, Hoogly and Paschim Medinipur) reported that the banks interpreted the back-ended subsidy[13] of the scheme in ways that protected their own capital investment. Rather than release the full financial assistance, the banks in West Bengal withheld the subsidy component as collateral, therefore making available only about 50% of the total finance to the groups.

Banking with the denizens of political society

Besides anxieties regarding (bank) loan repayment by SHGs, the message that the SHGs were not valued bank customers appears to have been conveyed in other ways as well. An early NABARD-sponsored evaluation of the SHG-bank linkage programme in the three states of Uttar Pradesh, Odisha and Karnataka drew attention to the propensity of bankers to be patronising and disrespectful to SHG customers. Harper (2002b) cautions that bankers' attitudes to SHGs could threaten the social empowerment dimensions of SHG programmes. The SHGs in the study villages in Thillai block resented the prolonged period of frequent bank visits they were required to make when applying for bank loans. In their experience, the routine visit to the bank to deposit and withdraw cash could be trying enough, owing to the bankers' impatience with the women's low literacy skills and unfamiliarity with bank procedure. When the secretary of *Alamelu* SHG (INGO-SC) asked why she was required to sign her name thrice on the withdrawal cheque, the manager barked at her: 'Bring the joint signatory with you or else just shut up and sign. You speak too much.' On a second occasion, she was instructed by the bank manager to return with a fresh cheque since the one she brought had an ink stain (accidentally tipped by her young child). She came away in distress unable to inform him that the entire cheque book was drenched in ink!

The leaders of Pushpam SHG (INGO-SC) had refused to accept a sum of Rs 2,500 as one rupee denomination coins fearing that the women would not be able to keep track of small change or even store it safely. The manager was enraged and informed the women, 'If you ever make a mistake in bank procedure in future, see how I treat you.' The women were also greatly frustrated by the bankers' assumption that their time and energies carried zero opportunity costs. The secretary of Alamelu SHG (SC) was sent back home on three different occasions with the money she carried to the bank when the staff had declared themselves too busy to accept her deposit. The bank's stipulation that all group members (and not leaders alone) in Nalloor village take turns to make the weekly cash deposit was resisted most vigorously by the SC-only SHGs owing to the daily wage labour of Dalit women in shoe companies. When the women informed him that the companies penalised workers who missed one day of work by suspending them for four successive days, the bank manager sarcastically suggested that the only 'solution' possible was the expulsion of all daily wage earners from SHG membership.

From the point of view of the women, the contempt with which they were treated was most evident in bank personnel's unwillingness to explain the terms of credit contracts. Most SHGs remained uncertain about the actual rate of interest payable on the SGSY loans. The banks did not state up front what the rate of interest was, nor did they provide women loan documents clarifying the terms of repayment.[11] Not infrequently, bank propensity to withhold information about interest calculation was perceived by the women as harassment and extortion.

Reviving a corpse?

> The three-year official duration of an SGSY loan (of Rs 100,000) borrowed by *Jeyam* SHG (INGO-SC) had ended in December 2003. In March 2004, the bank demanded a lump sum interest payment of Rs 3,600 and in August 2004, the women

> were asked to make insurance payment as well. Since the women had paid interest on a monthly basis while repaying the loan, the bank's demand that they make additional interest payment, after completion of repayment, aroused their suspicion. The SHG's secretary asked the bank manager: 'Can you feed oil tomorrow to a child that died today, and make it come alive?' Referring to a practice in rural Tamil Nadu of placing a few drops of (cooking) oil in the mouth of a dead person in the belief that it would preserve the corpse longer, the SHG's secretary attempted to inform the manager that the life of the loan, having lapsed, could not be revived by feeding it interest after completion of repayment. Her poser to the manager reflected her attempt to initiate a dialogue regarding bank procedure with reference to the conceptual universe familiar to her. The manager exploded with anger at her question saying: 'Village women understand nothing. If you don't shut up, I will get even more abusive.'

In the absence of any initiative, on the part of the bank or the promoter NGO to demystify bank procedure, the women experienced an acute sense of vulnerability to individual bank officers' caprices. Complaining bitterly of the insensitivity that the banks displayed to their life circumstances and their livelihood-related imperatives, the group leaders, when applying for a bank loan, often declared (to me and to group members) that this was the last loan they would ever seek from the bank.

Servicing bank loans: bending over backwards

In Thillai block, the bankers' misgivings regarding the non-repayment of loans by the SHGs in the study villages were belied by the timely repayment of bank loans (both the linkage and SGSY loans) by *all* SHGs, resulting from the severe disciplinary pressures mounted by the group leaders and sustained by intra-group peer dynamics. In the face of bankers' scepticism regarding women's willingness or ability to repay bank loans, the women strove to demonstrate proof of disciplined repayment, even at considerable cost to themselves. The Mahalir Thittam promoted SHGs in Prakasam village aimed to finish repayment of the SGSY loan (of Rs 100,000 per SHG) in 18 months or less, although the permitted period was three years. Vaigai SHG (MaThi-SC) sought to fully repay the SGSY loan over ten months, goading and pushing the women to sustain a frenetic pace of repayment. The sooner-than-required repayment of bank loans was driven by (a) women's fear that the interest payment on bank loans – inflexible and outside of group control – might increase if the duration was extended, (b) their concern regarding the likely vulnerability of households over a long duration to life cycle crises and other events that debilitate loan repayment capacities and (c) the prospect of securing a higher-order loan from the bank which served as a powerful incentive to quicken the pace of repayment.

The SHG leaders strove to cultivate an atmosphere of fear and discipline that might aid the repayment of bank loans. In one instance, the group leaders lied to their co-members that the bank had taken the former's property documents (the house ownership papers), which would be forfeited, if the women failed to repay the SGSY loan. The leaders of two other SHGs in Karisal village insisted that each member sign a loan agreement form, with her husband and two other members co-signing it. Although the women were unhappy about the costs and the involvement of their husbands, the group leaders were firm. The SHG's president asked, 'What happens if a woman dies and her husband disowns responsibility for the loan? Who will answer the bank?' Punitive practices such as verbal abuse and the payment of fines for late repayment were deployed even by those SHGs that normally eschewed such measures in the case of internal loans. Bharathi SHG (Bank-SC) permitted each borrower to determine the repayment schedule on internal loans based on her convenience and ability. When Bharathi SHG received a direct linkage loan and the group decided that each woman should repay a monthly instalment of Rs 500, three group members protested. Although they claimed that their poverty made this a difficult proposition, their co-members overruled them.

Defaulting on a bank loan was inconceivable since the bank was a highly valued external contact that no SHG could afford to antagonise. In all the SHGs that received bank loans in the study villages in Thillai block, several women were repaying internal loans when bank loans were disbursed. In all the SHGs without exception, *the women prioritised the timely repayment of bank loans over group loans*. If group leaders found that some members delayed bank loan repayment despite the many pressures, they used the savings corpus of the collective to make good the deficit. Banks also directly transferred funds from the SHGs' savings bank account to the bank loan account, whenever an occasion to do so arose. In the eventuality of a delay in repayment by the SHGs, the bank appeared well placed to protect its investment, due to its dual position as banker and financier of SHGs. The APMAS (2007) study of 240 SHGs in eight districts of Andhra Pradesh also finds that the recovery rate of bank loans was highest among the different types of loans borrowed by SHG members. About 64% of the SHGs were found to have over 75% recovery rate on bank loans. The repayment of internal loans was much lower, with over 57% of SHGs having a recovery rate of less than 25% of loans that had become due.

The APMAS report observes that the SHGs appeared to have focused only on bank loans in terms of bookkeeping, monitoring and repayments, with the loan principal and interest collected and remitted directly into banks. The bankers interviewed reported that they had almost no problems with loan recovery from the SHGs. Group savings were commonly used to settle bank loans in the sample SHGs in districts such as Guntur, Vizianagaram, Adilabad and East Godavari. Around 10% of the sample SHGs in East Godavari, Kurnool and Nalgonda districts borrowed from other sources to repay bank loans. The bankers' strategies to recover loans from SHGs included directly transferring funds from the SHGs' savings accounts and relying on promoter agencies (especially government agencies) to pressure SHGs to repay loans (APMAS 2007). The APMAS and CMF (2006) study of 202 SHGs in five districts of Rajasthan collected data on SHG operations from 30 bank branches (14 commercial, 11 RRBs and 5 cooperative banks). The study found that non-performing assets and overdue loans were very few and limited to a few banks and branches. The branch managers interviewed affirmed that SHG lending was sound commercial operation from the point of view of repayment, besides other parameters.

It appears, as both my fieldwork in Tamil Nadu and the literature on SHGs from other parts of India testify, that the peer dynamics that underpin the rotation of bank and internal loans were qualitatively different, with the women attaching different and unequal meanings to bank loans and internal loans. By privileging the repayment of bank loans ('cold money') over their own capital ('warm money'), women inverted the anticipated relationship between cold money and warm money. In so doing, they signalled that banks were powerful institutional actors whose goodwill and patronage must be sought and secured by all the means at their disposal.

Good manager, bad manager

Many instances discussed thus far (such as the coercive repayment of individual-targeted loans, the impounding of savings or the casual disregard of the women's livelihood and other imperatives) suggest that asymmetrical relations of power and authority marked the terms of engagement between SHG women and the banks. However, the women were not merely acted upon by bankers but endeavoured in many ways to direct their discretionary actions towards the quick sanction of SHG-targeted loans. During the course of my field study in Thillai block, I heard several narratives of the 'good manager' and the 'bad manager' distinguished from each other on the basis of the civility and patience with which they treated women struggling to make sense of bank procedure. The secretary of Kaveri SHG (MaThi-OBC) explained that the manager who disbursed the Revolving Fund loan was 'rude and sharp-tongued', whereas his successor, who sanctioned the SGSY enterprise loan, was 'patient with women like us', attending to SHG women first at the bank. The transfer of a good manager was an occasion of great loss and marked a period of anxiety while SHGs awaited the new manager, an unknown entity.

Given the discretionary powers that bank managers enjoyed with respect to the sanction (or not) of bank loans to SHGs, the women in the fieldwork villages in Thillai block experienced bank linkages as patronage extended by a benevolent manager. Not infrequently, they expressed their profuse gratitude to good managers through strategic gift-giving intended to reward them. For instance, a bank employee who received effusive praise from the SHGs was the (former) manager of the bank that also doubled up as the promoter agency in Nalloor village. The SHGs collectively organised a lavish farewell party on the occasion of his transfer with gift-giving (including the gift of gold jewellery) and oratory celebrating his 'good deeds'. The women sometimes sought to cement social ties with bank officials by presenting gifts whenever a loan was disbursed. This practice prevailed even in the case of the direct linkage loan which was subject to a purely market logic on account of the absence of capital subsidies. Seven of the nine SHGs, which received the linkage loan in Nalloor village, invested in the purchase of gifts (of clothing) offered to all bank employees as a token of gratitude. While the bank personnel made a formal show of protest to the effect that it was neither proper nor necessary for the women to offer a gift, they did accept the gifts.

On the other hand, the women sought to punish bad managers and impose reputational costs on them by complaining about them constantly to other SHGs, to their colleagues (other bank managers) and, more occasionally, to higher-level government officials such as the lead district manager (of NABARD). Wherever possible, the SHGs abandoned bank branches that were unwilling to finance them and flocked in large numbers to branches that had acquired a reputation for the smooth sanction of SHG-targeted loans and for extending a warmer welcome to rural women customers. In Thillai block, the branch of a nationalised bank that was perceived as 'SHG-friendly' had attracted more than a hundred SHG account holders from the surrounding villages. By dedicating one day each week exclusively to servicing SHG customers, the bank signalled that it valued their transactions. The SHGs, in turn, demonstrated that they could be valuable allies of the banks (who served them well) during difficult circumstances. When the rural branch office of a nationalised bank, which served the villages adjacent to Prakasam, faced the threat of closure on the ground of declining users, the SHGs in the surrounding villages mounted a successful campaign to 'save the bank' by encouraging individuals and other SHGs to open accounts in the bank. The bank was particularly grateful for the lead role that the older and long-standing women's SHGs had played in spearheading the campaign.

Conclusion

As the discussions in this chapter suggest, SHG-banking has been shaped by the financing banks' institutional interests, organisational cultures and ambitions (Mosse 2004) produced, in turn, by the situated policy histories of social banking and the current context of banking sector reforms. SHG-banking autonomised branch-level officials in an environment that privileged portfolio quality and recovery performance. Branch-level officials were acutely conscious that SHG-banking required them to make loans to women of rural households and communities that had received credit-based anti-poverty assistance associated with poor repayment during the social banking era. This conjuncture paved the way for an array of discretionary actions by branch-level officials who mistrusted women's intent to repay bank loans and attempted to secure, by all means, the foolproof repayment of SHG-directed loans and even of long-overdue loans made to individuals (mostly men) in the pre-SHGs era. Branch-level bank officials, who sought to 'enterprise' themselves (Burchell 1996: 27) via SHG-banking by enhancing the efficacy of their loan recovery mechanisms, steered the conduct and actions of SHGs in ways that were not anticipated by policy mandates. The social policy and institutional contexts framing the bank–SHG relationship generated tensions and conflicts (overt or latent) between the two actors.

Despite the discursive constitution (by the RBI and the NABARD) of the direct linkage scheme in a manner that removed it from the 'stigma' of social banking,[15] bank personnel at branch levels did not treat the SHGs as bodies of citizens on par with the other 'civil society' clients of banks (Chatterjee 2004). The marginal social status of the denizens of political society that the SHGs represented and an institutional legacy of traditional 'poverty-lending'-type schemes associated with poor credit discipline in the past informed bank–SHG transactions, often leaving the women with an acute sense of being disempowered partners in an unequal transaction. The power of the cold money provider over women was manifested in the 'making up' (Rose 1999: 92) of women as the female kin of defaulter males, as potential defaulters and portfolio risks themselves and as customers of lower social worth on account of their class-, caste- and gender-based disenfranchisement.

In responding to the bankers' strategies, the women positioned themselves as the members of credit-worthy collectives who repudiated kin-based identities; as bankers' allies who took pride in enforcing financial discipline in their communities; as the needy poor who staked legitimate claims to bank resources, despite irregular repayment of internal loans; as autonomous entities whose group-level decisions regarding the repayment of internal loans must be respected by bankers; and as hyper-responsible borrowers who bent over backwards to repay bank loans ahead of schedules. When responding to the idiosyncrasies of the individuals who headed branch offices, the women identified and actively positioned branch managers as good managers and bad managers, attempting to reward the first through gift-giving and public acclaim and to censure the second.

If the women's self-representations alternated strategically between positioning themselves as disciplined financial actors and as needy beneficiaries staking a claim to rightful entitlements, what effect might this have on the RBI and NABARD's representations of the direct linkage and the SGSY schemes? I argued (in Chapter 1) that RBI and NABARD policy documents constituted the direct linkage scheme as antithetical to the 'distortions' and the 'stigma' of poverty-oriented lending and as enhancing, instead, the efficiency of rural credit markets. The constitutive principles of the linkage scheme were aligned with the 'new thinking' on rural finance that privileged non-directed lending, the absence of capital subsidies, the linkage between loan finance and group savings and the de-linking of banks from poverty-alleviation-oriented lending. Despite the constitutive differences between the linkage and the SGSY schemes, I have shown, in this chapter, that the boundaries between the market orientation of the former and the 'poverty' orientation of the latter were blurred in practice. Bank pressures to repay loans made to male kin were directed towards SHGs, whether they sought the SGSY or the linkage loan. The women members of SHGs were regarded as supplicants of state largesse and treated with contempt as operators of small-sized accounts, regardless of whether they sought the SGSY or the linkage loan. Equally important, the blurring of boundaries was effected by women's initiatives. In certain contexts, women pressed claims to the linkage loan, not on the grounds of their efficient or disciplined financial performance as required by policy, but the dire nature of their need for development resources from the state. In Chapter 6, I discuss at length how women further blurred these boundaries in the manner in which they negotiated the entrepreneurial impulse of the SGSY scheme.

Notes

1 A part of the material in Chapters 5 and 6 of this book, drawing on the author's fieldwork in Tamil Nadu, has been discussed in a paper published by the author titled 'Economic Entitlements via Entrepreneurial Conduct? Women and Financial Inclusion in Neo-liberal India', *Journal of World Systems Research* (*JWSR*) in 2015, 21 (1), Winter/Spring: 50–68.

2 Andhra Pradesh was bifurcated into the states of Andhra Pradesh and Telangana in June 2014. The eight districts included in the 2003–4 study were East Godavari, Vizianagaram, Prakasam, Chittoor and Kurnool (currently part of Andhra Pradesh) and Nizamabad, Mahabubnagar and Warangal (part of Telangana).

3 The eight districts included in this study (2006–7) were East Godavari, Vizianagaram, Guntur, Kurnool and Cuddapah (currently in Andhra Pradesh) and Mahabubnagar, Adilabad and Nalgonda (Telangana state).

4 The districts were Bharatpur, Bhilwara, Dungarpur, Jalor and Bikaner.

5 The SGSY financial assistance consisted of a Revolving Fund that was disbursed to the groups prior to the approval and disbursal of the enterprise loan or the loan-cum-subsidy. The purpose of the Revolving Fund was to augment the loanable resources of SHGs and develop their capacity to use externally sourced funds. The fund could be used for any borrowing purpose and rotated among members on the same principle as internal loans (GOI n.d. 2).

6 The annexure shows the amount of the SGSY financial assistance and the direct linkage loan received by each SHG in the three villages.

7 This was discussed in detail in Chapter 1 in the section titled 'Aligning "the fate" of SHGs and banks: constructing consonant interests'.

8 SHGs across Tamil Nadu have been pressured by their financing banks to furnish this documentary evidence. Bankers' pressures that SHG members settle overdues on individual-targeted loans made to male kin were widely reported and not unique to Thillai block (source: interviews with promoter NGOs).

9 On the issue of the SGSY loan sanction to the defaulters of bank loans in SHGs, the RBI guidelines make a distinction between 'wilful' and 'non-wilful' defaults. Wilful defaulters are not permitted benefits under the SGSY scheme until a loan overdue is cleared. However, they may be permitted to participate in the normal savings and credit activities of the SHG. Moreover, the group may be financed under the SGSY scheme, excluding wilful defaulters, while non-wilful defaulters are permitted to access the SGSY loan (*RBI* 2011a).

10 The injustice of these pressures is striking when we consider that the popularity of SHGs with commercial banks derives primarily from the substantial transfer of screening, loan recovery and other transaction costs from banks to the poor themselves.

11 Poor repayment of loans in schemes such as the IRDP is attributed to the weak institutional incentives for repayment, including the tendency of political leaders to announce loan write-offs during elections and inattention to repayment criteria and asset productivity when selecting enterprise activities (Kabeer and Murthy 1996).

12 Of 58 members in three SC only SHGs in Nalloor, 23 received the direct linkage loan and 35 the kutcha house loan. On the other hand, of 95 women in five OBC-only SHGs, all were sanctioned the linkage loan. In addition, the kutcha house loan was sanctioned to 30 women deemed eligible in these SHGs.

13 According to the scheme's norms, the loan and subsidy amount should be fully transferred by the banks to SHGs. The subsidy would be repaid by SHGs in entirety and subsequently returned by the bank to SHGs, making this a 'back-ended' subsidy.

14 As per RBI guidelines during the period of my fieldwork, interest rates on 'priority sector' lending (which includes loans to SHGs) must not exceed the prime lending rate (PLR) of the bank for loans up to Rs 200,000. The PLR varied annually between 10% and 12.5% for the period that bank loans were borrowed by these SHGs.

15 This was discussed in Chapter 1.

Chapter 6[1]

Female entrepreneurship and the SGSY

Subverting policy, surviving poverty

In 1997, a Microcredit Summit held in Washington, D.C., supported by the World Bank, private commercial banks and hundreds of leading non-governmental organisations (NGOs) across the globe, adopted a resolution to reach credit assistance to 100 million of the world's poorest families (especially the women of these families), by 2005, to finance income-generating enterprises (The Microcredit Summit 1997). This was an early and powerful expression of faith that microcredit programmes would provide market-oriented and private entrepreneurship-driven solutions to global poverty, a key tenet of neo-liberal policy prescriptions. Globally dominant microfinance imaginaries have foregrounded appealing images of the hardworking poor, and poor women in particular, carving a niche for themselves in the informal segments of market economies by initiating and sustaining micro-enterprises in harsh economic environs and striving for upward economic mobility. Such imaginaries are conceptually grounded in what David Hulme and Paul Mosley (1996) describe as a self-evident and unmediated relationship between credit access and entrepreneurial successes or, in other words, the expectation that the poor, using their micro-loans to finance micro-enterprises and small businesses, will bootstrap themselves out of poverty. They fail to take adequate cognisance of contextual variables such as the initial asset position of borrowers, their life circumstances and the role of the macro-economic and policy environment in mediating the commercial success of credit-financed micro-enterprises (ibid.).

In this chapter, I discuss how state policy seeks to steer the rural women members of SHGs towards managing self-employment-based income-generating enterprises and women's negotiations with the entrepreneurial impulse of these initiatives. I do this by mapping the women's responses to the SwarnJayanti Gram Swarozgar Yojana (SGSY), which used SHGs to extend subsidy-bearing bank loans to rural poor households in order to finance income-generating economic activities. The SGSY may be seen as part of governmental endeavours to increase the reliance of rural poor households on self-employment activities that are sufficiently capital-intensive and large-scale enough to enable them to cope with economic adversity without making additional demands of the state or private capital. As an emergent technology of neo-liberal governmentality (Rose 1999), the SHG phenomenon, through its intersection with the SGSY scheme, urges rural communities (their responsibilised women members, in particular) to willingly bear the risks of collectively managing enterprises, thereby generating local employment and absorbing surplus labour in the informal sector (Weber 2002). In this chapter, I show how the women's calculations, decisions and actions, which were hardly in consonance with the formal goals and objectives of the scheme, constituted the SGSY as 'policy (that) primarily functions to mobilise and maintain political support, that is to legitimise rather than to orientate practice' (Mosse 2004), making it necessary therefore, as Mosse argues, to ask how the 'authoritative interpretations' that underpin (SGSY) policy are socially produced and sustained by its 'interpretive communities'.

SGSY: overview from the states

The process of integrating women in state-sponsored economic development projects was under way for a period of about two decades when the SGSY was introduced in April 1999. The Integrated Rural Development Programme (IRDP) was withdrawn and its successor scheme, the SGSY, introduced after rural women had consistently delivered high rates of loan repayment through the SHG-bank linkage project initiated by NABARD in the early 1990s.[2] In the starting year of the scheme (1999–2000), 60% of the 292,426 SHGs formed through the SGSY scheme were women's groups. By end of March 2011, 69% of the total (4,019,641) SHGs formed were women's groups. By March 2011, the total credit and subsidy disbursed through the scheme amounted to Rs 380.95 billion, with SHGs receiving 64% of the total amount. However, of the total SHGs formed through the scheme up to March 2011, only 29% had taken up economic activities, after passing through two stages of grading, receiving and rotating the Revolving Fund and securing the loan-cum-subsidy assistance (Tankha 2012: 126, 128). As the data indicates, the SGSY appears to have had greater success in mainstreaming women within anti-poverty projects than in promoting entrepreneurial activities.

By way of addressing some of the shortcomings that had prevented the emergence of IRDP-financed entrepreneurship, the SGSY guidelines prescribed that resources be concentrated in a few selected economic activities (i.e. the choice of enterprises available to *Swarozgaris*) in a block – the 'cluster activity' approach. The rural development administration, commercial banks and the panchayat structure were required to collaboratively undertake comprehensive planning to ensure the viability of enterprise activities selected under the scheme. While the scheme permitted individual-owned enterprises, it prioritised group-managed enterprises, anticipating easier provision of market linkages and support services to group economic activity (GOI n.d. 2). However, field reports on the functioning of the SGSY from various parts of the country have pointed to critical lapses with regard to selecting enterprise activities in the light of available infrastructure, markets and beneficiaries' capacities as well as multiple shortcomings in the provision of economic assistance such as the absence of forward and backward linkages and the poor response from commercial banks to credit-financing the scheme (Dasgupta 2009; GOI 2009).

In Sabarkantha district (Gujarat), the issues reported were bankers' delays in disbursement (up to 90 days) after sanction of the loan, lack of any support from Panchayati Raj institutions and government departments in helping the beneficiaries use the funds for the prescribed purposes, the inadequate and delayed supply of inputs, the absence of marketing support and nil training assistance to participants to facilitate any transfer of technology. In Maharashtra, interviews with 400 Swarozgaris or beneficiaries across seven districts revealed that 47% had not started any income-generation activity with the loan funds, while 52% had received no training in enterprise development (Shylendra and Bhirdikar 2005). Drawing on their observation of the SGSY in three districts of West Bengal (Haora, Hoogli, Paschim Medinipur), Banerjee and Sen (2003) report that there were no provisions to check if the multiple agencies (line departments, panchayats, NGOs, banks) involved were available and willing to commit time and energies towards implementation of the scheme and no incentives offered to them to do so. Further, the design of the scheme tilted the axis of power against the beneficiaries who were unable to appeal against the performance of these agencies and forced to accept the decisions of the authorities 'watching over them'.

Studies from many parts of the country point to the poor and inconsistent quality of the economic activities financed by the SGSY. The West Bengal study reported that, of those groups (in Haora district) that had received financial assistance under the scheme, almost all the members were involved in small, home-based activities (such as mushroom cultivation, making puffed rice or lentil cakes, poultry, tailoring, knitting) that were a continuation of what they had been doing before joining the group. Though the additional finance had expanded the scale of activities to an extent, no new skills were introduced nor were old skills upgraded. It also appeared that the SGSY-financed activities had increased women's physical labour overall, rather than enhancing the remunerative potential of their economic activities (Banerjee and Sen 2003). An evaluation of the SGSY in 16 villages of Ramnagar block of Jaunpur district in Eastern Uttar Pradesh also found that the recipients were usually encouraged to start traditional individual-managed activities (such as purchase of a cow or buffalo) and that no infrastructural or any other form of support was offered to the groups to enable them to initiate micro-enterprises. About 74% of the loan recipients had received no training whatsoever, 8% had disposed of their assets at the time of the study and 25% had created no assets at all (Pathak and Pant 2008).

Besides highlighting the predominance of traditional activities (dairy activities, goat rearing and agriculture) financed, a study involving 6,904 SGSY loan recipients in North India (Bihar, Chhattisgarh, Odisha, Uttar Pradesh) and 1,738 in South India (Andhra Pradesh, Kerala, Tamil Nadu) raised serious questions about the sustainability of the activities (Chintala and Mani 2009). Only 31% of total sample units/activities financed were intact during the period of the study, with the percentage of intact units being even lower (at 17.7%) in the case of group (relative to individual) beneficiaries in the northern states studied. In more than 85% of the groups financed through the scheme, the loan finance was divided among group members who were pursuing their business independent of each other, rather than undertaking group activity. For the most part, the activities (such as paddy processing, *khali* leaf stitching, broom making, collection and sale of minor forest produce and *sawai* rope making) did not require capital investment.

Consequently, the loan recipients had used most of the bank loan to finance their other needs (ibid.).

Notwithstanding the many systemic shortcomings that marked the operation of the scheme on the ground, all the studies of the SGSY underscore the great temptation of a subsidy-bearing loan scheme from the point of view of the SHGs. Given a programme context in which women received little or no support to initiate and manage viable enterprise activities, but were required to show willingness to do so in order to access subsidy-bearing bank credit, it appears that some degree of manipulation and machinations on the part of the borrowers had enabled them to draw benefits from the scheme. A nationwide review of the SGSY undertaken by the National Network of Resource Organisations found that it was not uncommon for the beneficiaries to 'manipulate' the process of asset acquisition and use. In Andhra Pradesh, for instance, groups that claimed to have purchased cattle sent their own to their friends or relatives' homes a day before the transaction and acted as if they were purchasing the 'new' livestock before the officials on inspection. In other states, it was seen that the groups disposed of the capital or the livestock immediately in order to repay the bank loan and distributed the subsidy amount among group members (APMAS 2009b).

In the subsequent sections, I show the workings of the SGSY scheme in the three fieldwork villages of Thillai block, outlining how manipulation and subversion of the project goals motivated the women SHG members to participate in the SGSY, sustaining thereby the operation of the scheme at the grassroots. Before I proceed to the theme of the SGSY, I discuss the micro-enterprise/small business scenario that prevailed in these villages.

Class, caste, gender and micro-enterprises

In the three fieldwork villages in Thillai block (Tamil Nadu), the SHG women and their household members engaged in a range of petty market activities that included petty hawking, vegetable, fruit and flower vending and beedi-rolling, in order to supplement incomes earned from wage work in the farm and non-farm sectors. Requiring rudimentary skills and marked by low entry barriers, the bulk of these market-oriented activities were survival activities (Ghate, Ballon and Manalo 1996) that are usually overcrowded and clustered at the bottom of the informal sector. Where SHG women did own and manage small businesses or micro-enterprises, these were household-based activities in trade and services (such as home-based eateries and petty stores) that were jointly managed by household members (usually a husband–wife team) and were heavily reliant on the intensive use of family labour. Single women rarely managed commercially viable enterprises, and when they did so, they managed secondary businesses that supplemented the primary income sources earned by other family members. For instance, two elderly widows who lived with their adult sons in Karisal village engaged in moneylending at informal sector lending rates.

SHG participation per se did not induce the women or their family members to initiate enterprise activity. SHG member households, which did not own capital assets (that could attenuate the effects of a business downturn) nor had prior entrepreneurial experience, were unwilling to make investments in new business activity.[3] The case of Karpagam of Vennila SHG (INGO-OBC) illustrates the social and kin-based networks, supportive relationships and material resources that were required to help households sustain enterprises through periods of crises.

Business recovery and sustenance

> Karpagam and her husband Sundar managed the most popular hotel for breakfast and evening tea and snacks in Karisal village. Karpagam and Sundar started the hotel (more than a decade before the inception of SHGs in the village) in order to overcome the desperate financial straits brought on by the simultaneous collapse of their earlier business (a grocery store) and the wedding expenses of Sundar's sister. (Karpagam: 'Our debts were huge. Our creditors were ready to beat us up. People thought we would flee the village. We didn't have enough to eat sometimes.') Early support from a friend-cum-local patron (of their grocery store) boosted their confidence and encouraged them to recover from their business debacle and initiate a new venture. Cooking vessels were bought by a friend, a grinder by Karpagam's brother and a tiled roof (replacing the thatched roof over the front portion of the house which doubled up as hotel) was installed by a local patron. These loans were repaid gradually with income from the business. Eventually, the hotel did well, enabling Karpagam and her husband to pay off their debt and acquire household assets. Karpagam's SHG loans were used largely as working capital to buy provisions for the hotel

in addition to paying back informal loans. While Karpagam and Sundar continued to rely on informal loans, their business activity had given them the financial strength to do so on favourable terms. They dealt with just one lender who was 'like a family member' and even helped them with non-interest loans for sudden expenses.

In Thillai region, caste relations and ideologies were constitutive of local markets. Of the 327 women members of 18 SHGs in Karisal and Prakasam, 4% of the SC women's households relied on own-account enterprises as their principal livelihood as compared to 18% of their OBC counterparts.[4] Women from Dalit communities pointed out that non-Dalits were willing to buy milk from them, but not milk-based products such as buttermilk or curd, thereby circumscribing enterprise-related options and opportunities. Kala, a resident of the *Arunthathiyar*[5] habitation of Karisal village, used an SHG loan of Rs 3,000 to help her husband start a 'bunk'[6] store selling beedis, sweets and other eatables. Kala was forced to shut down the store when they continuously sustained losses. Sulochana of the same SHG used a loan of Rs 1,000 to start a vegetable vending business but gave it up soon after it ran up losses. Neither Kala nor Sulochana could hope to extend their market beyond the spatial confines of the small Arunthathiyar habitation comprising the poorest and most socially marginalised caste group in the village economy of Karisal.

In marked contrast to the small stores and home-based hotels located in the Dalit (Parayar and Arunthathiyar) habitation,[7] the businesses managed by OBC households were more likely to be located in the 'public' spaces of the village – close to the bus stop, the panchayat office – and drew customers of all communities. The case of Soosanna, a Dalit woman and the president of Roja SHG (MaThi-SC) of Prakasam village, was a notable exception. Soosanna and her husband owned and managed a successful grocery store located on the pathway leading from the main road to the village. Soosanna's husband had managed a private chit fund business and worked as the headmaster of a government school. Besides, the family owned four acres of wet (irrigated) land in the village. The store, which was started with a capital investment of Rs 100,000, was reportedly 'grabbed' by a family member during a difficult period when her husband sustained a heavy loss in his chit fund business. By selling their land and seeking voluntary retirement ahead of time, Soosanna's husband used the bulk-sum retirement money to pay off his debts. Subsequently, they set up a second store with a smaller capital investment that did good business, nonetheless, owing to its favourable location. Whereas the business recovery of Karpagam and Sundar (case discussed earlier) was made possible through financial support from kin and relatively affluent friends and neighbours in the OBC habitation of Karisal village, it is telling that Soosanna and her husband had not relied on similar sources of support.[8]

Since women's abilities to invest loans in enterprise activities were never autonomous of village livelihood conditions and constraints or their social positioning in terms of class, caste and gender-specific life cycle status, they vigorously sought autonomy with respect to the end-uses of the loans they borrowed vis-à-vis promoter and financing agencies. In particular, the women valued the ability to use SHG-sourced loans for income generation *only* when they judged the environment favourable and their household circumstances conducive to permit such use. During the period of my field study, it was widely believed that the use of SHG loans to initiate or finance new income-generation activities was non-viable. The failure of the monsoon for about four years concurrent and prior to the period of study (2001–5) had led to the scaling down of agriculture and of other activities such as brick kilns that depended on water. The ensuing situation of 'no rains, no work' attenuated effective purchasing power and threw a number of small (non-farm) businesses into crisis as well. Apart from the general scepticism regarding the prospects of initiating household-owned small-sized businesses, the women rejected in toto the entrepreneurship model advanced by the SGSY scheme for the reasons discussed in the following section.

'Policy that does not orientate practice'

SGSY policy linked the sanction of subsidy-bearing financial assistance (by banks and the BDO) to women's proven willingness and capacity to initiate economic activity, selecting from the list of enterprises pre-approved in each block. If we regard development projects as seeking to maintain themselves as coherent policy ideas by stabilising the interpretation of events (Mosse 2004), we see that SGSY policy does so by establishing causal links between (a) the provision of financial assistance to targeted groups of women beneficiaries and the emergence of female entrepreneurship and (b) the collective management of enterprises by rural women (organised into SHGs) and the generation of business incomes/revenue that enable rural poor households to cross the income-poverty line. In Thillai block, the women in the study villages dismissed as far-fetched and impractical the posited linear relationships – the underlying premises of the SGSY.

The decisions of 'calculative actors'

> The saturation of local village markets by existing small businesses, the evident disinterest of the rural development administration in assisting the women with market linkages and the perceived non-viability of *group*-managed business activity had strengthened women's resolve to not initiate enterprise activity as stipulated by the SGSY scheme. In the three villages, all the SHGs comprised women who undertook diverse self and wage-employment-based livelihood activities as well as others, who for reasons of household care work (in particular the care of young children) or personal ill health did not engage in wage work outside the household. In the face of the heterogeneity that marked the household and livelihood circumstances of the women, the collective ownership and management of a capital-intensive enterprise activity was inconceivable. If the proposed enterprise failed, the SHG could collapse since the financing bank (also the SHG's account holder) would seize the women's accumulated savings corpus, built at great cost over a period of time. Urged (by promoter agencies and financing banks) to be calculative actors when setting the terms and conditions that govern group financial transactions, the women estimated the risks of initiating group-managed enterprises, the uncertain gains they offered, and judged the costs of managing group-owned enterprises as being unacceptably high.

Nonetheless, the SGSY scheme was greatly sought after on account of the coveted subsidy component, inducing the women to invest considerable energy and resources in making the scheme work for them. Instead of investing the loan-cum-subsidy assistance in a group enterprise, 11 of the 13 SHGs that received the loan *equally distributed the cash among all the members* on the understanding that it would be used for a variety of household-related needs (as was the direct linkage loan) and repaid to the bank on a collective basis.[9] Even as women repudiated the official borrowing purpose of the SGSY loan package, they strove to sustain the myth of female entrepreneurship financed by the scheme. In doing so, they constituted the SGSY as policy that helps stabilise the interpretation of events, even as it may not, in actuality, generate events (Mosse 2004). In the face of this radical divergence between policy and practice, I show, in the following sections, how the 'practical interests' of the interpretive communities or supporting actors (Mosse 2004: 646), namely bankers, officials of the BDO, NGOs and women's SHGs, came to be tied up with the particular interpretations presupposed by SGSY policy, inducing them therefore to 'participate in the established order as if its representations were reality'.

The costs and risks of scheme subversion

The case of Pavalam SHG (INGO-SC), which proposed to manage a brick kiln business, illustrates the modus operandus, involving a three-way nexus between the SHG, the bank and a local business owner.

The back-door entry of business owners

> The SHG contacted a brick kiln owner in the neighbourhood and struck a deal with him. The owner provided documentary evidence to the bank stating that the SHG had acquired a brick kiln and leased it to him to manage. The documents declared that he had received a total amount of Rs 100,000 (the SGSY amount) for a truckload of coal and for procuring clay, mud and water. The SHG women paid the brick kiln owner Rs 4,000 for providing the document and extending his cooperation. The staff of the financing bank inspected the brick kiln thrice for purposes of verification and photo documentation. And yet, as the SHG's secretary said to me, 'Of course the bank knew that we were not managing the brick kiln!' The fiction of make believe enterprises owned and managed by the women was created and sustained by the SHGs with the collusion of promoter NGOs, financing banks and the officials of the BDO, all of whom were mandated by the SGSY guidelines to ensure that an annual 'quota' of loans allocated under the scheme was disbursed to women who were neither willing nor able to engage in loan-financed income generation.

The case of the brick kiln demonstrates how the back-door entry of locally based, small-scale business operators was crucial in sustaining SGSY policy on the field. Commenting on this development, the secretary of Thangam SHG (BDO-SC) remarked, 'These days, the owners of coconut groves, shoe companies, tailoring units and poultry farms have woken up to the possibility of doing deals with SHG women who run around and beg for their documents in order to get bank loans.'[10] Identifying willing enterprise owners could be difficult, especially if they feared seizure of their enterprise by the bank, in case of a loan default by the group. (The only collateral allowed by the SGSY scheme was the asset generated by the economic activity financed under the scheme). Some business owners feared that the SHG might claim ownership of their enterprise since it possessed the legal documents authenticating purchase of the business through the SGSY loan. While business operators remained the *de facto* owners, the *de jure* ownership of the business was vested with the SHGs.

To assuage their fears, the business owners demanded large-sized payment from the SHGs as compensation for the perceived risks they bore. A case in point was Vaigai SHG (MaThi-SC) that identified a small business owner willing to provide corroborative evidence for a tailoring unit after a laborious search of two months and payment of Rs 9,000. Another example is that of *Mangalam* SHG (Bank-OBC), which was sanctioned a loan of Rs 300,000 (not disbursed during the field study) for the stated purpose of cement stone manufacture. The owner of a cement stone making factory in the village demanded a payment of Rs 50,000 for providing the required fake documents. The raw materials supplier demanded a payment of Rs 15,000 to cover the sales tax, which he claimed that he would have to pay, given that the bills submitted to the bank would record a large transaction, even if he did not actually make a sale to the SHG.

In the case of the SHGs that successfully obtained the loan, the costs that the women incurred did not end with loan sanction and disbursal. The SHGs were required to participate in government-sponsored exhibitions that celebrated the emergence of women micro-entrepreneurs and SGSY-promoted livelihoods. Such exhibitions demanded that the fiction of managing enterprises be sustained over a longer period and at higher cost. Two groups, which claimed to manage shoe-making units in Prakasam village, bought footwear at a cost of Rs 2,000 per SHG from a wholesaler for the purpose of display at an exhibition organised at the BDO headquarters. Vaigai SHG (MaThi-SC), which was given a two-day notice to prepare itself for participation in the exhibition, was asked by the Mahalir Thittam partner NGO to buy clothes for Rs 2,000, since the management of a tailoring unit was the professed enterprise of the group. However, the women's 'quick thinking' saved them, and they rented the apparel from a garments retailer for an amount of Rs 750. Officials of the BDO directed the SHGs to participate in these exhibitions with sufficient evidence of enterprise activity and threatened to withhold the subsidy on the SGSY loan if the women were reluctant to do so.

The tensions between the SHG members and leaders were amplified during the period an SHG sought bank loans owing to the considerable time and work on the part of the leaders who made multiple visits to the financing bank, other banks in the vicinity (in order to secure 'no-objection' certificates declaring that no group member owed the bank any unpaid overdue),[11] the Block Development Office and the owners of businesses who provided ownership documents to SHGs. In the absence of the regular remuneration of group leaders, the SHGs in Nalloor village made a token payment (of Rs 50 per member) to their leaders to present them with a gift of *saris* when the bank loans were sanctioned, in appreciation of their services to the collective. In addition, the women of Annai Indira SHG (Bank-SC) paid Rs 240 each to meet all the expenses related to the simultaneous sanction of two bank loans. The women were enraged when they subsequently discovered that of the total sum (of Rs 4,800) collected from the SHG, the group leaders reportedly paid Rs 700 to the Block Office (as bribe) and retained the remaining amount. In a few SHGs, the women suspected that the leaders overstated the expenses they claimed to have incurred when dealing with banks, business owners and block-level bureaucracy. It appeared that the multiple negotiation processes that preceded the sanction of the SGSY loans further autonomised group leaders and reinforced their perceived non-accountability to the members.

Bank manager autonomy and the 'enterprise' mandate

Much of the criticism of the SGSY has been directed at commercial banks for failing to provide the credit required to finance commercially viable enterprise activities, whether individual or group-managed. Drawing from their study of the SGSY in three districts of West Bengal, Banerjee and Sen (2003) observe that the groups had to face the hostility and indifference of financing banks that were unwilling to release the funds even when the groups were ready. They point out that the banks had the power to obstruct the project at any stage, given that the SGSY guidelines mandate that they be involved in all stages of scheme implementation. No other agency appeared to have the authority to challenge or question the banks (ibid.). In Thillai block, the bank managers did not withhold cooperation in the project. In the three fieldwork villages, they responded to the organised presence of the SHGs and the women's sustained demand on the banks for the 'subsidy scheme'. Nonetheless, they exercised considerable autonomy in conforming to or disregarding the scheme's mandate that the loans be used exclusively for the purpose of financing enterprise activities with serious consequences for women's ability to secure the loan.

For instance, the manager's insistence that the SHGs manage enterprises could increase the costs of fabricating proof of enterprise activity and even exclude SHGs from accessing the subsidy-bearing loans. This was evident in the case of the SC-only SHGs in Nalloor village. The prevalence of sizeable enterprise activities in the OBC habitation of Nalloor enabled the SHGs therein to more easily secure loans by 'showing proof' of the enterprises that already existed, while the absence of comparative enterprise activity in the SC habitation of the village disadvantaged the women in the SC-only SHGs. The secretary of Annai Indira SHG (Bank-SC) remarked, 'When we suggested trade in readymade garments as a possible enterprise activity, the manager asked us to produce the retail store.' While coconut leaf thatching was a common income-generation activity in the SC habitation, the bank manager informed the women that it would not do as credible economic activity to warrant financial assistance through the SGSY scheme.

On the other hand, the bank manager's flexibility sometimes eased the labour involved in feigning productive use of the loans. Two SHGs in Prakasam village, which proposed 'coir rope-making' and 'coconut grove-leasing' as their business activities, were greatly relieved when an 'understanding' bank manager brushed aside their documents and laughingly remarked that he knew all about their enterprises. In this case, a 'good manager' understood women's reluctance to initiate enterprise activity and responded to their need, whereas a 'bad manager' insisted on implementing policy by demanding that the women actually initiate and manage enterprises. The latter was regarded as a great misfortune, as the case of two SHGs in the OBC habitation of Karisal village demonstrates.

The misfortune of a bad manager

Two SHGs in Karisal village that proposed to manage cement stone manufacturing units were flummoxed when the bank manager made the release of the subsidy component (of the SGSY loan) conditional on the women purchasing the cement and equipment and initiating production activity. The SHGs were in a quandary, as there was no cement stone manufacturer in the vicinity of their village, whose enterprise could be passed off as their own. While the SHGs had initially chosen 'brick kiln management' as their proposed enterprise activity, officials of the BDO had changed it to 'cement stone manufacture' as the groups had scored well in the grading exercise and 'deserved' a 'higher-order' enterprise. A new bank manager, who insisted on substantive proof of enterprise activity and was less flexible than his predecessor, compounded the problem. The leaders of the SHGs visited the bank, the BDO and the president of their village panchayat several times to resolve the crisis. When this failed to yield results, the president of one of the SHGs attempted to use her membership in the local branch of the AIADMK to exert political pressure on the bank manager. The women tried to take the matter to the district collector too but returned after spending a day at his office waiting for an audience with him. Eventually the women gave up when the manager upbraided them for repeatedly disturbing a 'government worker' and threatened to report them to the police if they continued to press him about the loan. The two SHGs had spent Rs 11,000 each on their multiple visits, bribes and other expenses for a loan that eventually did not materialise. The women were demoralised to the extent that routine group business such as weekly meetings was adversely affected. Eight other SHGs in the same village had successfully obtained the SGSY loan (with none of them managing a group business), shaming the two groups and making their failure appear stark and singular.

The many faces of rent seeking

The payment to business owners was not the only cost incurred by the SHGs seeking the SGSY loan. The BDO demanded and extracted payment for processing the subsidy component of the SGSY loan. In Thillai block, this was viewed as part of the customary bribe payment routinely extracted by block-level bureaucracy for any of the functions it performed. Payment to the BDO to process the SGSY loan was not unique to the three study villages but widely reported in Tamil Nadu as well as in other parts of the country. For instance, in Assam, a study of 109 SHGs in four districts observes that the disbursement of the Revolving Fund and the SGSY loan finance was marked by illegal cash transactions (APMAS 2009a). The officials took Rs 1,000 to form an SHG and register it at the Block Office. In some places, bank staff also charged Rs 1,000 to route the Revolving Fund through the bank. Factoring in other transaction expenses, an SHG might have to spend close to one-third to obtain a Revolving Fund loan of Rs 10,000. Likewise, a group might spend between one-third and one half of the subsidy amount to secure the SGSY loan. In 45 of 109 SHGs, the total value of groups' assets was found to be less than that of their liabilities, with a deficit of Rs 4,59,000. The research team speculates that this could be one estimate of bribes paid by the sample SHGs. While 21 of the 109 groups contacted in Assam admitted that they paid bribes close to Rs 90,000, the research team admits that the quantum of payment and its prevalence were probably far more than what they had uncovered (ibid.).

In Thillai block, I was informed that officials of the Block Office reportedly demand bribes on a 'percentage' basis from the SHGs. For instance, a payment of Rs 10,000 could be extracted for an SGSY loan of Rs 100,000 (hence 10%). In the three fieldwork villages, the amount each SHG paid ranged from Rs 200 to Rs 2,000, with the majority of the groups paying Rs 500 each. In a few cases, the officials of the BDO skilfully exploited the SHGs' imperative to manufacture evidence of enterprise ownership to create additional avenues for rent seeking. Where the SHGs were required (by the bank) to produce an invoice (referred to as 'quotation' in local parlance) detailing the cost of raw materials and other inputs for a proposed business activity, the officials of the BDO set themselves up as brokers who mediated between the women's groups and local business interests to secure the invoice required to authenticate project proposals.

In Karisal village, Jeyam SHG (INGO-SC), which was required to show proof of a wedding decoration rental business, paid Rs 7,000 to block officials, who claimed to have procured the necessary invoice at great cost from a store in the neighbouring township. In this case, the bank manager himself supplied an invoice worth Rs 50,000 for the purchase of chairs – a service that earned him a fee of Rs 3,000 from the SHG. The women of Jeyam SHG were rudely shocked when the manager turned up at the village for supervision a day after disbursing the loan. The branch manager's unexpected supervision visit conveyed the message (to all groups in Karisal village) that he expected the women to buy his compliance and willingness to overlook their fabrication of enterprise activity. The women's payment to bank officials depended on the branch manager in question, unlike payment to the BDO for sanction of the subsidy; the latter was regarded as a routine affair that had little to do with individual officials.

The process of preparing SHGs for the grading exercise, undertaken by banks and the BDO, involved much work for promoter NGOs. In contrast to the INGO which was recognised and valued by the women as a benevolent purveyor of largesse, the Mahalir Thittam partner NGO evaluated itself (and was judged by the women) in terms of its efficacy in securing bank loans for the groups it promoted. The Mahalir Thittam–promoted SHGs made a 'gift' to the NGO whenever a subsidy-bearing loan was disbursed, in contravention of the official norms of Mahalir Thittam, which explicitly forbid any payment to the partner NGO, by the SHGs. For instance, Annai Janaki and Annai Parasakthi SHGs (MaThi-SC) spent Rs 300 per member to buy furniture for the NGO's office when their SGSY loans were sanctioned. The expectation of a gift was institutionalised in the relationship between the partner NGO and the SHGs it promoted and constituted an important supplement to the dwindling financial support the NGO received through the Mahalir Thittam scheme.

Table 6.1 shows the costs incurred by the SHGs that sought the SGSY loan by way of payment to the different actors involved. The table provides data for a total of 14 SHGs that included the 13 that had received the SGSY loan and one of the two SHGs in Nalloor village that was sanctioned the loan but had not received it yet. The total expense is shown as a percentage of the subsidy component since these expenses were usually adjusted from the subsidy on the SGSY loan. The SHGs are organised in the descending order of total expense as percentage of subsidy. As the table shows, Mangalam SHG was likely to have spent close to 90% of its subsidy amount to make payments to the owner of the cement factory and supplier of raw materials (as discussed earlier). While Roja SHG (at second position from bottom) gained from the bank manager's flexibility and made no payment to business owners, Then-koodu

Table 6.1 SHG-wise expense incurred to access SGSY loan: Karisal, Prakasam and Nalloor

Serial number	*SHG name*	*Stated business activity*	*Subsidy amount**	*Payments and expenses*						*Expense as percentage of subsidy****
				Business owner	*BDO*	*Bank*	*NGO*	*Miscellaneous expense***	*Total expense*	
1	Mangalam	Cement stone manufacture	75,000	65,600	2,000	–	–	–	67,600	90
2	Vaigai	Tailoring	35,000	9,000	500	–	–	2,300	11,800	34
3	Ganga	Shoe-making	35,000	2,000	500	–	–	4,706	7,206	21
4	Kaveri	Shoe-making	35,000	2,000	500	–	–	4,706	7,206	21
5	Annai Parasakthi	Rope-making	35,000	–	500	–	5,700	485	6,685	19
6	Annai Janaki	Fertiliser manufacture	35,000	–	500	–	4,800	392	5,692	16
7	Tazampoo	Retail trade	16,000	–	600	–	–	2,000	2,600	16
8	Jeyam	Wedding decoration rental	100,000	10,000	0	2,000	–	–	12,000	12
9	Pavalam	Brick kiln	50,000	4,000	500	500	–	–	5,000	10
10	Pushpam	Milch cattle purchase	100,000	1,600	6,000	–	–	–	7,600	8
11a	Annai Meenakshi (loan 1)	Milch cattle purchase	25,000	400	1,500	–	–	–	1,900	8
11b	Annai Meenakshi (loan 2)	Coconut grove leasing	50,000	2,000	500	500	–	1,000	4,000	8
12	Alamelu	Coconut grove leasing	50,000	2,000	500	1,000	–	–	3,500	7
13	Roja	Coconut grove leasing	35,000	700	300	–	300	300	1,600	5
14	Then-Koodu	Retail trade	16,000	–	200	–	–	–	200	1

(All the figures in column titled 'Payments and expenses' are in rupees.)
* The total quantum of the loan is provided SHG-wise in the annexure.
** This includes primarily the costs of participation of the SHGs in the exhibitions that showcased SGSY-financed enterprises.
*** Percentage figures.
Source: Fieldwork data.

SHG (at the bottom) invested its loan in enterprise activity under great pressure from the bank manager and therefore did not transact with local businesses.

Appropriations and resistances

> If you want men to be present at public meetings, you need to provide *sappaadu* (lunch), *saarayam* (liquor) and *savaari* (transport). SHG women, on the other hand, organise their own transport, bring cooked meals and come free – all expenses are met by the SHG.
>
> Member of Thangam SHG (BDO-SC)

> We spent Rs 1000 from the group's money to buy handloom-woven saris to wear to a meeting that the chief minister attended. The BDO said we have to do this. We were told of the handloom crisis in the state – it seems that the (SHG) women are saving the handloom weavers in distress.
>
> The secretary of Roja SHG (MaThi-SC)

If the Ministry of Rural Development sought to instil entrepreneurial subjectivities via the enterprise-management clause of the SGSY scheme and the NABARD sought to foster disciplined financial intermediation via the women's management of their 'micro-banks', the 'conduct of conduct' of women SHG members assumed other forms at the level of the district and the block. The DRDA's central role in the implementation of the SGSY scheme made it possible for the BDO to mandate that the women members of the SHGs participate en masse at public events organised at the block and district headquarters and graced by prominent dignitaries. In Thillai block, the appropriation of women's time and energies did not go unopposed. A staff of the Mahalir Thittam partner NGO said to me:

> The women get angry with us when we 'invite' them repeatedly for these meetings. 'Do you think we have no work to do', they ask. We say to them, 'They (the BDO) are your officials and they want to see you. What can we do? We are the messengers.'

While the NGOs that partnered with the state were particularly susceptible to these pressures, the non-partner NGOs could not entirely resist them either for fear of antagonising the local administration.

The bank-promoted SHGs in Nalloor were not as frequently required (as the Mahalir Thittam groups) to attend public events outside their village. On one occasion, the officials of the BDO summarily informed them that two bus-loads of women from the village were required to participate at a meeting to be attended by the chief minister in the district headquarters. Since the meeting was scheduled during a period of exceptionally heavy rainfall in Tamil Nadu (end of 2005), the women refused outright and clarified that they would meet the chief minister or any other minister only if the concerned dignitary visited their village, given the inclement weather. The women in several SHGs described the pressure to attend these meetings, usually organised at short notice, as a significant cost associated with SHG participation.

The women's resentment was further fuelled by the efforts of the BDO to position them as enthusiastic actors in the management and execution of village-level governmental schemes. The expectation that the SHGs would manage government schemes at the grassroots is not limited to Thillai block or to Tamil Nadu. NABARD (2013) notes that a large number of government services across the country have been contracted to SHG members in preference to private contractors prompted by their 'devotion' and 'efficiency'. In the fieldwork villages in Thillai, the women vigorously repudiated their 'participation', which they denounced as thinly disguised efforts to commandeer their time and labour towards managing programmes, some of which were plagued by flawed implementation.

Who wants a sanitary complex?

> In several villages in Thillai block, the SHGs protested against the BDO's order that they assume responsibility for managing the panchayat-level women's sanitary complex, which provided for toilets and facilities for bathing and washing under one roof.[12] The SHGs were required to collect Rs 5 per household from the village community for regular maintenance of the complex – a job that was perceived as impossible since no one was willing to pay. The fact that the electric motor, pipe and tap of the complex in Prakasam village had been stolen and the 'finishing' poorly done compounded the women's anxieties of being saddled with an unworkable scheme. The women claimed that they might have actively monitored the construction of the complex, had they known that it would be their responsibility to maintain it. The president of Roja SHG (MaThi-SC) refused

to accept the keys of the complex (that the BDO attempted to hand over) and, by implication, the responsibility for its management. She alleged that pressures to maintain the complex had become a form of 'torture' of the SHGs by the block development administration.

Bank loans and internal loans: coping with poverty

Notwithstanding the considerable social and financial costs, the stress and the risks associated with the SGSY scheme, the women in the fieldwork villages in Thillai block greatly valued the subsidy-bearing, low-cost bank credit that was used to finance a diverse range of end-uses in keeping with the particular requirements of their households. As discussed earlier, the autonomy that the women valued above all was the right to make decisions regarding the use of the loans that they borrowed from their SHGs. Insofar as internal loans were concerned, the SHGs (as well as the promoter NGOs and financing banks) made no attempt to legitimate some loan uses above others, making it possible for their members to use the loans for a variety of consumption and household-survival-related purposes that included the payment of rent and electricity charges, and the purchase of clothing or even food when required. The women sought and used internal loans to defray emergency expenses such as the replacement of a thatched roof blown away by a heavy spell of rain or, more commonly, medical expenses. The financial resources of the SHGs were often drawn upon to assist the women and their household members cope with ill health in the face of the poor performance of public health institutions, both the designated primary health centres and the secondary-level, tertiary-care centres.

The women also used their loans to strengthen inter-household reciprocal ties of mutual assistance and solidarity by making gifts and extending non-interest-bearing loans to kith and kin during periods of need. The loans borrowed for the purpose of meeting kin-related obligations were often used to assist an SHG member's siblings or the siblings of her husband, in particular, her husband's sister. This reflects the social sanction in Tamil rural society for relying on one's brother for assistance during life cycle events and periods of crisis. Single women and those in conflictual spousal relationships prioritised the use of SHG-sourced loans to cement social ties with their natal kin. Vanitha of Alamelu SHG (INGO-SC), a single mother of two young children, used six loans totalling Rs 12,700 for the assorted marriage and childbirth-related expenses of her nieces and nephews, indicating the value she placed on the maintenance of reciprocal relations with her extended natal family. Member Kanti of Roja SHG (MaThi-SC), who lived alone with her young daughter after abandonment by her husband, regularly borrowed small-sized loans to send gifts and sweets to her sister's marital family during the *Pongal* and *Diwali* festivals. Since her sister had provided critical support to her by helping raise her daughter, it was of great importance to Kanti that the relationship be sustained after her sister's marriage.

The SGSY and the direct linkage loans, which were always equally distributed among group members, were sometimes the only opportunity for women from poorer households to borrow relatively large-sized loans of Rs 5,000 or Rs 10,000 (depending on the total loan amount). As discussed in Chapter 3, the informal norms that governed the sanction of internal, group-sourced loans restricted the size of loans borrowed by those generally perceived (by co-members) to be less credit-worthy. Yet another difference between the bank loans and the internal loans relates to borrower control over the timing of loan access. Bank loans were supply-driven since the SHGs exercised no control over bank and BDO-determined processes of loan sanction. Hence, when an SGSY loan was distributed within an SHG, not all the women had a pressing or immediate requirement for a loan at that point of time. Several women were consequently able to use their bank loans to fulfil the *long-term* needs of households (as distinct from immediate or emergent needs) such as the acquisition of assets, the purchase of jewellery in particular, the redemption of old debt and improvements to housing. One SHG member used her SGSY loan to plaster with cement a newly constructed brick-walled part of her house; another used the loan to replace the thatched roof that 'constantly dripped water' with cement roofing; a third invested her loan of Rs 5,000 in gold jewellery and a steel cupboard; a mother and daughter (members of the same SHG) pooled their loans of Rs 5,000 each to raise the compound wall of their house and build a toilet and bathroom; yet another mother and daughter used their loans of Rs 10,000 each (supplemented by an informal loan of Rs 15,000) to buy a plot of homestead land.

The internal loans borrowed for medical expenses were used for sudden, unanticipated medical emergencies, whereas the bank loans used to finance medical treatment enabled rural poor households to seek elective medical care for conditions deriving from chronic, long-term illnesses. A case in point was an SHG member who was gradually losing her mobility and used her SGSY loan to consult doctors at a private hospital in the district headquarters and the principal government hospital in Chennai. Another member of the same SHG used her SGSY loan (of Rs 5,000) to seek treatment for her daughter for delayed puberty. A third member used her SGSY loan to cover the doctor's fees for a hysterectomy surgery performed at the 'free' government hospital in order to secure treatment of better quality. The value that women attached to sustaining SGSY policy on the field (Mosse 2004) was reflected in their efforts to ensure disciplined, on-time loan repayment, enabling banks to reap the rewards of scheme subversion as well.[13]

Conclusion

In this chapter, I used the case of the SGSY to discuss how state policy seeks to steer the rural women members of SHGs towards setting up capital-intensive micro-enterprises and acquiring the entrepreneurial capacities necessary to profitably manage these as collective or group activities. Reports on the SGSY from several parts of the country testify to the many systemic flaws such as the meagre training, marketing or infrastructural support offered by government agencies, the absence of any value addition to the existing livelihood activities of the poor (where these loans were invested in income-generating activities) and the failure of the group approach in ensuring the profitability of the enterprises financed through the scheme. The literature also indicates that manipulation of income-generating assets ostensibly acquired through the scheme had enabled its beneficiaries to draw some benefits from participation in the scheme.

In the fieldwork villages of Thillai block, the social relations of caste, class and gender mediated women's ability and willingness to initiate and sustain household-based enterprise activities. As the case studies suggest, prior entrepreneurial experience, some degree of asset ownership (especially in the case of Dalits) and the presence of a supportive male household member who co-managed the enterprise appeared to be prerequisites. The women's general reluctance to initiate new enterprise activity in an overall climate of failing livelihoods and diminished purchasing power was compounded in the case of the SGSY. The women refused outright to manage collective enterprises in keeping with SGSY policy. The SHGs that applied for financial assistance through the SGSY scheme contacted locally based, small-scale business owners and acquired their ownership documents for a fee. The fiction of enterprise ownership and management was sustained by the SHGs with the full knowledge of the promoter NGOs, financing banks and the subsidy-sanctioning BDO. The collusion of the promoter and financing agencies was prompted by their mandate to distribute an annual quota of loans, allocated under the scheme, to women who were neither willing nor able to engage in loan-financed income generation. Besides the back-door entry of small business operators, I showed that cash payment by the SHGs to *all* the actors involved in the scheme (business owners, [some] bankers, officials of the BDO, NGOs, group leaders) was central to sustaining SGSY policy on the field.

The success of a policy idea in development can never be taken for granted, is never given a priori, but is constantly being produced by the unceasing business of 'translation' of a project's central concerns or policy goals into the practical interests of its supportive actors (Mosse 2004). Sustaining SGSY policy on the field required the translation of its policy goals into the practical interests of its interpretive communities, whether these corresponded to the organisations' public transcripts or hidden transcripts (Scott 1990). The SHG women in Thillai block instrumentally reshaped the SGSY package of financial assistance in ways that enabled them to shore up and diversify household assets that could be drawn upon in times of need. The women's participation in the scheme – albeit on their terms – enabled the BDO to fulfil its mandate of implementing anti-poverty schemes on the field (the 'public transcript'). The SHGs also presented the BDO with new opportunities and channels for rent seeking, accentuated, in some cases, by the women's imperative to manufacture proof of enterprise activity. The latter, in particular, may be described as a windfall opportunity for the BDO. Through control over the subsidy component of the SGSY scheme, the BDO acquired sufficient leverage to appropriate and direct women's collective energies, thereby using the SHGs to stage and demonstrate popular support for state developmental initiatives at the grassroots.

In the public transcript of the SGSY scheme, the SHGs are ideal organisational channels that enable commercial banks to deliver income-generating loans to rural poor households in a cost-effective manner. These loans also enabled the banks to fulfil their priority sector lending targets and were refinanced (by NABARD) at lower interest rates. The hidden transcript included the bank perception of SHGs as socially effective channels to retrieve long-overdue loans made to the male kin of SHG members and even to village co-residents not related to SHG members (discussed in Chapter 5). The Mahalir Thittam partner NGO in Thillai block sought to sustain institutional relationships with the SHGs it promoted by facilitating access to bank (in particular the SGSY) loans, besides expecting remuneration for this intermediary function. In each case, some part of the practical interests that spurred the bank, the BDO and the Mahalir Thittam partner NGO to participate in the SGSY scheme was in direct conflict with the SHGs' interests. As Mosse (2004) points out, common narratives of development or 'commanding interpretations' are supported for different reasons by different actors in development and can serve a diversity of interests that may contradict and even conflict with each other.

Notes

1 An older version of this chapter (focused on the Tamil Nadu case studies alone) has been published as 'Subverting Policy, Surviving Poverty: Women and the SGSY in Rural Tamil Nadu', *Economic and Political Weekly* (*EPW*) in 2011, 46 (43): 50–57.
2 The policy context in which the SGSY scheme originated is discussed in Chapter 1 in the section titled 'The SGSY: re-assertion of poverty lending?'.
3 That the poorest microfinance borrowers are unwilling and unable to use credit to initiate new enterprise activity is well recognised in the literature on microfinance (Hulme and Mosley 1996). Karim's (2011) study of microfinance in Bangladesh also points to how social class–related factors shape women's use of loans for micro-enterprises.
4 This was discussed in Chapter 1 in the section 'Institutional context: SHGs in the study villages and fieldwork methods'.
5 As mentioned in Chapter 1, the Arunthathiyars were a sub-group within the scheduled castes, who were traditionally placed lower than the Parayars (of northern Tamil Nadu) in the caste hierarchy of the region.
6 These were tiny shops that did not deal with groceries or rice that distinguished the bigger stores in the villages.
7 Guerin, Kumar and Agier (2013: 84) also point to the restricted markets for micro-businesses located in the Dalit colony of villages in Tamil Nadu.
8 Soosanna's husband's protected job as a schoolteacher and eventually headmaster had enabled the upward economic mobility of his family. When Dalits owned land, it was almost never inherited or ancestral

land and the acquisition had been made possible through a public sector job in the army or clerical positions in post offices, banks, government schools, etc.

9 Two bank-promoted SHGs in Nalloor invested the loan in business activity under great pressure from the bank manager to conform to the objective of the scheme. They chose retail trade (as opposed to any manufacturing activity) to minimise risks.

10 The full list of stated business activities is provided SHG-wise in Table 6.1. The SHGs chose their activities from the bank and BDO-approved list of enterprises for Thillai block.

11 This was discussed in Chapter 5 in the section titled 'A Hobson's Choice'.

12 The Integrated Sanitary Complex scheme was introduced in 2001–2. While water consumption charges were borne by the village panchayat, the daily maintenance of the complex was entrusted to women's SHGs (GOTN n.d.).

13 As discussed in Chapter 5, the women in the fieldwork villages in Thillai block demonstrated exemplary repayment on both the direct linkage and the SGSY loans. This was not however the case with other studies that point to poor repayment of subsidy-bearing loans by women's SHGs (APMAS 2009a, 2009b).

Chapter 7

Learning about the state

A pedagogic reversal

In this chapter, I build further on the arguments in Chapters 5 and 6 in order to flesh out better the ways in which the women members of SHGs experienced and perceived 'the state'. Drawing from scholarship on how the poor engage the *sarkar* (Chatterjee 2004; Corbridge 2007; Corbridge *et al.* 2005; Gupta 2006), I show that women's multiple and conflicting perceptions of the state and their variegated encounters with diverse state agents enabled them to fashion strategies of resistance, of subversion and of appeal and to work the dissonance among multiple state agents to their advantage. In particular, I draw upon Partha Chatterjee's account of the mobilisational strategies of 'political society' when it seeks access to state-mediated resources or public amenities/services to which it lacks legal entitlements. I do so in order to identify points of congruence between these and the modes of engagement that the SHGs displayed during their interfaces with diverse state personnel, actors and institutions.

Both the SHGs and the associations of political society that Chatterjee (2004) describes have emerged in response to the governmental functions of the state, albeit bearing marked differences. The self-organised forums of squatters and the urban poor, which spring from the violation of property law and civic regulation, defend their illegal occupation of public land or the tapping of electricity supply lines and demand that local state agents declare an exception (through the negotiation of rental settlements for water or electricity) in order to deliver essential public amenities and other state-mediated resources vital for the survival of the poor (Chatterjee 2004). The other important means by which the poor seek and claim state developmental resources, which I have described in this book, involve the participation of the 'denizens' of political society in civil society–type associational activities that involve the conduct of periodic group meetings, the maintenance of books of accounts and minutes books and the management of disciplined financial transactions in order that these denizens might produce themselves as fiscally responsible and efficient actors, who are judged credit-worthy and found deserving of financial inclusion.

In stark contrast to the quintessential forms of political society organisation and action that Chatterjee describes, the arrangement of SHG-banking is top-down and has state backing and endorsement, with state institutions (directly or via NGO intermediaries) engaged in the formation, financing and the provision of promotional support to SHGs. However, as I argue in this chapter, the women's endeavours to secure bank loans and their multiple negotiations towards this end point to the 'irreducibly political' (Chatterjee 2004) nature of the transactions they conduct with state actors. They also produce the effect of blurring the distinctions between political and civil society that Chatterjee appears to overemphasise (Corbridge 2007; Corbridge *et al.* 2005). In this chapter, I also offer some glimpses of other forms of citizenship claims (besides claims to economic entitlements) that SHGs have made possible for the women of rural poor households, addressing thereby the question that Corbridge *et al.* (2011) pose, namely what forms of politics and what forms of citizenship claims are open to different groups of the poor in post-reform India?

Encountering the state

Corbridge *et al.* (2005) argue that the proliferation of opportunities for 'sighting the state', which participatory development programmes open up, creates new spaces for 'state-poor' encounters and exchanges, through which the marginalised claim citizenship entitlements. They make the important observation that men and women experience the state differently and that opportunities for encountering the state tend to be mediated through the male head of household for poor women given the targeting of the household unit by welfare and developmental schemes aimed at the poor. In India, several studies observe that new physical and institutional spaces have opened up for rural women, post-SHGs, and that these amplified their opportunities for 'encountering the state'. Interviews with a sample of 83 SHGs, formed as part of the South Asia Poverty Alleviation Programme, in three districts of Andhra Pradesh (Kurnool,

Mahabubnagar, Ananthapur) found that a significantly higher proportion of members (66%), as compared to non-members, reported visiting new places in the five years prior to the study. These places included the mandal development office, the mandal revenue office, the panchayat office, the collector's office and the government block office (Murthy *et al.* 2005).

Micro-studies of NGO-promoted SHG programmes in Malappuram district of Kerala (Anand 2002), Nuapada district of Orissa (Rajagopalan 2005) and Latur and Osmanabad districts of Maharashtra (Parthasarathy 2005) have also commented on the striking ways in which women's mobility has increased since the advent of SHGs and the range of government departments and institutions that SHG members have interacted with. In Thillai block, the presence of multiple actors in SHG promotion and financing permitted the SHG women in Prakasam, Karisal and Nalloor to encounter an array of officials – rural welfare officers (RWOs), officials of the Block Development Office, bank managers and other bank staff and, more occasionally, Mahalir Thittam staff from the Project Implementation Unit office at the district level. My field study and the secondary literature on SHGs confirm that the SHG phenomenon has dramatically increased direct interfaces with the state for women whose sightings of the state may have formerly been 'at a distance, episodically, roughly and through intermediaries' (Corbridge *et al.* 2005: 150).

Experiencing the state at local levels, not as a coherent entity, but in a 'discrete' and 'fragmentary' manner (Gupta 2006: 220) through interaction with officers belonging to a range of diverse bureaucracies and departments, generates highly individualised perceptions (on the part of the poor) of particular government officers and 'discontinuous' or 'fractured' views on the responsiveness and empathy of the latter (Corbridge *et al.* 2005: 119). In Chapters 5 and 6, I discussed the women's narratives about 'good' and 'bad' managers distinguished from each other on the basis of the civility and respect with which they treated SHG women and their willingness (or not) to collude with women's subversion of the SGSY scheme. The disparate, discontinuous and fragmentary sightings of the state by SHG women shaped the way they constructed the state and served an important purpose. It enabled the women to see state institutions as constituted by different fractions, which the women could appeal to as allies or rally against as adversaries and to thereby act in strategic ways, as I discuss in the following section.

Spaces of manoeuvre

The women frequently appealed to one actor to mitigate the perceived excesses of the other. In Thillai block, certain RWOs had gained notoriety for their ruthless extraction of bribes by making late evening/night visits to the homes of the SHG leaders and promising quick sanction of subsidy (on the SGSY loan) if the women immediately paid the concerned official. Under pressure from the women, the Mahalir Thittam partner NGO raised the issue several times with the block development officer and even with the district collector, although to no avail. While the women generally perceived the BDO as a corrupt agency primarily interested in securing bribes, they saw that it could be an important ally when required to manage difficult bankers. Following the sudden visit of the bank manager to inspect the wedding decoration rental business ostensibly managed by Jeyam SHG in Karisal village (discussed in Chapter 6), the women appealed to the BDO to intervene. Officials of the BDO, in turn, played their part in convincing the manager to go easy on enterprise inspection.

The SHGs also attempted to use their relationships with some (not all) bank managers to reduce the payments they made to the BDO. The secretary of an SHG in *Velpatti* village[1] (also in Thillai block) had successfully minimised the bribe her group paid the BDO, when their subsidy-bearing loan was sanctioned. In this case, the manager of the bank that financed the SHGs encouraged the group leaders to report (to him) demands for payment from the BDO. The bank manager repeatedly reminded the women that neither the bank nor BDO officials could treat themselves to 'a cup of tea' using women's savings money. In two other instances, the SHGs in Prakasam village reported demands for bribes that appeared unreasonable (for instance, having to pay a new BDO functionary when his predecessor was transferred) to the bank manager, who was known to take an interventionist stance. The BDO was wary of the disapproval by conscientious bank managers of the payment that the women made. This was reflected in the BDO's standard instructions to the SHGs to not expect a receipt for the payment they made, to never record details of the payment in the Resolution Book of the SHG and to not report it to the bank manager!

In addition to providing some protection to the SHGs from the rent-seeking proclivities of the Block Development Office in Thillai, the presence of multiple institutional actors made possible other forms of autonomous action on the part of SHGs. In case of perceived victimisation by a promoter NGO, the SHGs did 'vote with their feet' by dispensing with the existing relationship and seeking a new one as did the nine groups in Nalloor village.[2] A few SHGs in Prakasam continued to remain formally associated with the Mahalir Thittam partner NGO even as they chose to signal a growing distance by avoiding NGO-sponsored meetings; instead, they prioritised relationships with bankers. As an NGO staff explained, the NGO–SHG relationship was strong for the first six to eight months of the SHG's life, that is until the sanction of the Revolving Fund, and weakened once the SHG established an independent relationship with the financing bank.

The literature on SHGs has frequently alluded to the 'capture' and 'hijack' of NGO-promoted SHGs by the rural development administration and other state agencies, charged with the responsibility of SHG promotion (Harper 2002a; Sinha 2000). However, a few studies have observed that the movement of SHGs from one promoter to another could also be an act of conscious choice on the part of the women. For instance, a study of 109 sample SHGs in four districts of Assam found that the promoter agencies had limited their supervisory functions and that this had happened by default, not design. Almost all the groups had moved away from their original promoters to the DRDA in order to obtain the Revolving Fund and subsidy-bearing loans (APMAS 2009a). It appears then that women's decisions with regard to sustaining a relationship with a promoter agency were informed by their assessment of the relative costs and benefits of the relationship in question, as well as the choices available. Where the costs outweighed benefits or where a particular relationship had outlived its usefulness, the women manoeuvred strategies of disengagement. In Thillai block, the women's actions and decisions as 'rational economic' actors in this instance provoked the anger and displeasure of promoter NGOs who lamented the 'fickleness' and 'ingratitude' of the women, their 'opportunistic' readiness to 'embrace' whichever agency sanctioned Form 3 (the subsidy approval form of the SGSY loan) and their propensity to 'forget' the NGO once they had secured a bank loan.

Learning about the state

In Thillai block, the women members of SHGs experienced the state through their direct interaction with banks and the BDO or second-hand, in the case of the group members who did not routinely travel outside the village on SHG-related work, through the exchange of news and stories at the weekly group meetings. Narrativised as specific incidents that highlighted the characteristics of good and bad managers, 'more' and 'less' corrupt BDO officials, these stories were bandied about not only at the village-level meetings of the SHGs but also at public events and spaces where the women routinely gathered. These included the monthly training workshop organised by the Mahalir Thittam partner NGO, public meetings organised at the Block Development Office, the waiting rooms of banks, when women from different villages waited for their turn at the counter, or even bus stops. The women would recognise each other through the account books they carried and strike up a conversation asking, 'Which group are you? From which village?'

By sharing stories about the contradictions, the inconsistencies, the divergent personalities and styles of functioning of different officials, women constructed the state in public culture (Gupta 2006) in ways that disseminated valued information such as which particular official might be approached for loan schemes, who should be guarded against, who was a bribe-seeker and who was not, who needed to be managed tactfully or who was a lost cause. They represented the state to each other in ways that allowed them to negotiate more effectively within a universe of shifting alliances, by seeking contingent partnerships with an organisation or individual (such as a sympathetic bank manager), denouncing and condemning another, deserting a third and cultivating temporary allies in order to move a specific loan.

If NABARD and the RBI envisioned SHG-banking as a pedagogic exercise that teaches women of rural poor households the skills of optimising valuable resources (micro-capital, both group and bank-sourced) in contexts of scarcity, the most important dimension of SHG-banking as a pedagogic exercise, from the point of view of the women, was the opportunity it gave them to *learn about the state*. That women valued this opportunity was evident from the many group discussions in the fieldwork villages in Thillai on more evenly distributing the responsibilities of SHG management and especially the tasks that required visits to the bank or the BDO. The group leaders, who sought to motivate group members to accompany them on visits outside the village, constantly underscored the value of 'seeing' the state from intimate vantage points and of understanding its internal dynamics. The leaders also desired that their co-members experience first-hand the toll it took on them to continuously sustain points of contact with the state.

Besides understanding the inner workings of state bureaucracies in order to more effectively pressure specific state actors for financial resources, the literature suggests that women also valued other learning opportunities that proximity to the state entailed. Drawing on a study of SHGs in Latur and Osmanabad districts of Maharashtra, Parthasarathy (2005) emphasises that women valued access to information on a range of issues, including government development schemes, Panchayati Raj procedure and the workings of the Public Distribution System (PDS) or the ration shops that supplied food and commodities essential for household survival. Information and discussions on the operation of the PDS enabled the women to monitor availability, quantity and quality of the stocks and provisions, confront shop owners on a number of occasions, take up the issue at the *taluk* level and lobby the administration. The women were able to use the information collated and place it before the head of the *Zilla Parishad* (the district council or panchayat) at an open forum meeting conducted by the district administration. By doing so, they gained entry as special invitees to the ration committees where they could report errant functionaries. Parthasarathy (2005) observes that women used these learning opportunities to set themselves up as community-level watchdogs monitoring schemes that were vital to the well-being of economically vulnerable communities, such as programmes of poverty alleviation, food security, health and education.[3]

Seeing the state from intimate vantage points also rendered visible the state's desperate quest for legitimacy via association with a popular 'pro-poor', 'pro-women' rural development initiative. In Thillai block, the SHG women understood that multiple state actors (the BDO, the Mahalir Thittam partner NGO and other departments of the state government) often undercut each other and competitively sought to promote women's SHGs.[4] Through the experience of coerced participation in the BDO-sponsored exhibitions celebrating women micro-entrepreneurs, the women, who were required to fabricate evidence of fake enterprises for these exhibitions (discussed in Chapter 6), came to see that their collusive presence was indispensable for sustaining the official narratives of poverty alleviation and demonstrating the visible successes of state-mediated female entrepreneurialism.

Interlocking political practices

Chatterjee (2004) points to how groups in political society make a large array of connections outside the group – with other groups in similar situations, with more privileged and influential groups and with government functionaries, political parties and leaders in order to win and sustain their claims to state resources. In the case of the SHGs, their mobilisational potential had rendered them obvious targets for the cultivation of some of these linkages. Several studies have pointed to the emergence of SHGs as potential 'vote banks' and the political pressures that they were consequently subjected to. The EDA and APMAS (2006) study of 214 SHGs in four states finds that in the southern states (Andhra Pradesh and Karnataka, in particular) local supporters of political parties closely interacted with the SHGs that had emerged as a 'rallying point' for all political parties. Besides transporting SHG members in large numbers to political meetings, parties distributed money to the SHGs, which, in turn, demanded funds and benefits. In Rajasthan as well, political parties had begun to pay attention to the SHGs given the impending state assembly elections during the period of the study. In one of the study villages, local politicians had promised the women a community hall in return for their votes during the election (EDA and APMAS 2006).

In his study of SHGs in two villages in Dharwad district (Karnataka), Pattenden (2010) observes that almost all the SHG members had been summoned to attend political rallies and that resources were routinely channelled to SHGs in exchange for votes or support. The political ties of the SHGs' leaders could also determine which groups accessed the SGSY financial assistance. The president of an SHG in one of the study villages that had received the loan was the wife of a grama panchayat member. The president of the taluk panchayat had actively supported the SHG's application for the SGSY loan in the expectation that the women would canvass for him during elections (Pattenden 2010). A perusal of the literature suggests that even if these alliances and ties to outside groups and actors were not chosen or sought after by their women members, they had begun to use them to extract some benefits for themselves and their groups.

It appears then that while SHG-banking coopted rural women of landless and land-poor households, the members of political society within civil society–type associational activities, it simultaneously required that they hone the skills of negotiation and cultivate tactical friendships and alliances with highly placed individuals and agencies in order to 'pick their way through an uncertain political terrain' (Chatterjee 2004). My discussion (in the first section of this chapter) on how the SHGs in Thillai block proactively identified empathetic allies and crafted strategies of manoeuvre and manipulation in order to press their claim to bank loans also bears this out. The negotiations that the women members of SHGs relentlessly conducted with a range of state (and non-state) actors in order to secure their credit-related entitlements mimic in some respects the strategies of political society when it seeks resources that are *not* endorsed by the state or legally guaranteed. Not unlike the urban squatter groups that encroach on land illegally and yet negotiate rental settlements with governmental agencies for water, electricity and other amenities (Chatterjee 2004), the SHG women in the fieldwork villages in Thillai block were able to successfully secure the SGSY loan finance, despite the manifest illegality they displayed with regard to the formal intent and purpose of the scheme.

The SHG women's claims to the SGSY and the direct linkage schemes may be regarded as 'irreducibly political' as they were fought and won (or lost) through 'contingent', 'contextually dependent' negotiations waged on a *political* terrain informed by the calculations of political/electoral expediency in a representative democracy and the obligation of governmental bodies to make some provision for the poor (Chatterjee 2004). Calculations of political and electoral dividend were particularly pronounced in the case of the SGSY scheme. In Tamil Nadu, the implementation of the SGSY acquired explicitly political overtones in the weeks and months that preceded a state assembly or Parliament election. A quicker-than-usual sanction and disbursal of the Revolving Fund and the SGSY loan finance commonly took place, with the ruling party (at the state level) taking credit for the dispensing of the funds to SHGs. For instance, in the run-up to the 2006 state assembly elections, the rural development administration in Thillai block put out the message that the quick response to new and pending applications (from SHGs) for the SGSY loan finance was a 'gift' from the (then) ruling dispensation (the AIADMK).[5]

However, the political negotiations that I describe also complicate Chatterjee's dichotomised representations of civil and political society that some scholars (Corbridge 2007; Corbridge *et al.* 2005; Sundar and Sundar 2012) have critiqued in other contexts.

Critiquing the 'oil' and 'water' nature of the distinctions that Chatterjee makes between civil and political society, Corbridge *et al.* (2005: 214) suggest that they be perceived instead as a 'set of interlocking political practices that are arranged along a continuum'. This is exemplified by the field-level operation of the SGSY. Despite the illegality of women's actions with respect to feigning enterprise management, the SGSY did not involve the open declaration of an exception (Chatterjee 2004) and required instead a considerable investment of resources to sustain the façade of collective enterprise management by the women. For their part, bankers, BDO functionaries and the NGOs recognised that their collusion in the flouting of the scheme's formal objective was a necessary precondition for its implementation and the distribution of resources to a target population group. The multiple collusive alliances that sustained SGSY policy on the field suggest that 'routinised legal practises and associations, and contingent political negotiations (may) segue into each other' (Sundar and Sundar 2012: 286), rather than standing distinctly apart from one another. To define civil society solely in terms of adherence to law (as Chatterjee does) is to miss the contested nature of law itself and how the state violates its own laws all the times (Sundar and Sundar 2012). It might be added that it is to also miss how state agents have to violate, subvert and overlook laws to deliver services when policy mandates diverge significantly from target beneficiaries' life circumstances and in contexts where 'policy does not orientate practise' (Mosse 2004).

Democratising political society

The state-women encounters that I have described in this book were, more often than not, fraught and contested. And yet, the women valued the opportunities to cultivate links to state actors for reasons that extended well beyond access to microfinance or anti-poverty schemes. As I argue in this section, the SHGs not only encouraged women to stake legitimate claim to development resources but also permitted other 'sightings of the state' (Corbridge *et al.* 2005) that the women effectively mobilised to pursue ends that were unrelated to credit disbursal. For instance, the SHGs in Tamil Nadu functioned as a legitimate organisational means that represented women at village- and block-level public forums. On the orders of the state government, the SHGs were routinely invited to participate in all public events relating to local governance such as village-level panchayat meetings. The extent of SHG involvement in village-level developmental issues was sometimes (but not always) reflected in fairly dynamic interfaces between the SHGs and village-level panchayat structures.

Resolving jurisdictional issues

> The SHGs of Velpatti village (in Thillai block) drew up petitions listing the names of the elderly poor excluded from old-age pensions, of households without ration cards, of women who had been denied the widow's pension and demanded the immediate measurement of land in order to allot house sites to the homeless scheduled caste poor. The SHGs insisted that the meticulously prepared petitions be made part of panchayat agenda for discussion on the day of the *grama sabha* (the village assembly).[6] Close to 100 SHG women attended the grama sabha by way of pressuring the panchayat to take their petitions seriously. The traditional village headman of Velpatti village, already angry at the SHGs' increasing role in mediating local disputes, was incensed at the seriousness with which the women (Dalit women's SHGs in particular) engaged the grama sabha and hurled caste-specific abuse at them, besides challenging their right to participate in panchayat meetings. The SHGs reported this to the district collector (the head of the rural development administration), who ordered the BDO and the district superintendent of police to intervene. Police officers as well as officials of the BDO warned the headman to cease interfering in the SHG's affairs and rebuked him for 'overstepping' the limits of his 'jurisdiction'.

The case of the SHGs in Velpatti village suggests that the women used the official support for SHGs both to navigate local vested interests and power structures and to gain access to other state institutions, in particular the police. It was uniformly reported that police stations were more willing to register cases of sexual harassment, marital violence and dowry-related abuse, when these were referred by the SHGs. Some women had even used the threat of complaining to the police through the SHG ('file a complaint using the SHG letterhead') against abusive husbands or sons-in-law. A member of Ganga SHG (MaThi-OBC), whose daughter was harassed by a village co-resident, warned him that she would file a case through the SHG. She explained that this was the most effective threat she could have made since no one would fear her husband – a man of advanced age and poor health. A member of Roja SHG (MaThi-SC) asserted that even the police feared and respected SHGs and that this fear was echoed in the rhetoric her husband used when abusing her (As she put it: '"What can you do? Can you send me to jail through your *Sangam*?", he says. I know he speaks out of fear.') The men, in turn, complained about a 'nexus' between women's SHGs and all-women police stations.[7] A few men even complained (to me) about perceived SHG propensity to 'harass' and 'shame' husbands and in-laws by reporting against them to the police, at their 'whims and fancies' and for 'small offences'.

The EDA and APMAS (2006) study on 214 SHGs in four states (Rajasthan, Odisha, Karnataka, Andhra Pradesh) discusses 20 instances of collection action undertaken by the SHG women. The issues involved were confronting husbands during bouts of drunken violence, bigamous marriages, the remarriage of a separated woman, dealing with a dowry death, preventing child marriage and protection of a woman from sexual harassment (by a father-in-law). In Rajasthan, the SHG members defied the *jati* (caste) panchayat (comprising elder males in the village from the Gujjar caste) in supporting a woman's decision to walk out of her marriage after her husband took a second wife. They assisted her in filing for a legal divorce and persuaded her to marry again within a year, despite the public humiliation heaped on her by the jati panchayat. In a village in East Godavari district (Andhra Pradesh), the SHG persuaded the committee of elders to revoke their permission to a man to divorce his wife (an SHG member), arguing that the woman must also be permitted to remarry if the decision on the divorce was to stay. In all the cases discussed, the SHG members had acted as a group, going together to the police station or a man's house or initiating a legal case. The actions were initiated in villages wherein the promoter agency (government or NGO) had proactively supported such action, with field staff providing strategic guidance and helping interact with the police. These actions were also more likely to be seen in villages that had a clustering of SHGs, enabling the women to come together in larger collectives (EDA and APMAS 2006).

Several studies note that one of the more common forms of action that the SHG women undertook related to male alcoholism, with the women, once organised, refusing to overlook or tolerate it (Dwivedi 2007; EDA and APMAS 2006; Murthy *et al.* 2005;

Sanyal 2009). Drawing from her interviews with women from 59 SHGs in two districts of West Bengal, Sanyal (2009) observes that a key community-wide intervention of the 'normative'[8] kind initiated by women included anti-liquor action. In two villages, the SHGs' action on liquor involved haranguing the police for their inaction with respect to liquor sales in the village, seizing liquor barrels and setting them on fire and patrolling the streets at night with bamboo batons to keep village outsiders from patronising the village liquor trade, thereby shutting down the liquor business in their villages (ibid.). My fieldwork in Tamil Nadu also uncovered instances of collective action, initiated and led by the SHGs, on this issue.

The SHG members of Prakasam led a procession to the homes of the families who sold illicit alcohol and extracted letters from the sellers that they would stop sales once they exhausted the existing stock. The sympathetic station inspector of the local police station invited the women to alert him to the presence of any of his subordinates who came to collect a bribe from the sellers (even giving the women his mobile phone number and asking them to call him any time) and promised immediate suspension of the police personnel involved. The women's partnership with the station inspector on the issue of illicit alcohol sales and consumption sharpened their criticism of the double speak of the state. Discussing this issue with me, the women ruefully pointed to the contradiction between state rhetoric declaring support for women's public action in defence of their interests and the direct retail vending of alcohol through a public sector undertaking – the Tamil Nadu State Marketing Corporation Limited (TASMAC). A woman said to me, 'Will the police stand by watching if we attack a TASMAC shop or agitate for it to be closed?'.

All forms of interaction between state institutions and the SHGs were not exclusively synergistic, with the women effectively harnessing the powers of benign or neutral officials in their favour. Sometimes, women's organised collective action brought them into direct conflict with state functionaries, especially when the women challenged the entitlements of economically powerful village elites. A public agitation in Nalloor village (Thillai block) assumed confrontational dimensions when the women in the village (led by the SHG leaders) forcibly entered the homes of 15 affluent families in order to break the panchayat-financed taps that these families had installed inside their homes. Their action had followed a long period of petitioning that had yielded no results. The women were infuriated by the registration of cases against six women (all SHG members) by the local police station and its refusal to take cognisance of the appropriation of public resources by the wealthy families that had provoked their action. The women were equally incensed at the vituperative abuse of the SHGs by a village male co-resident, who had demanded to know 'why women took the lead in the agitation when men were present'. When a crowd of 150-strong SHG women surrounded the police station, threatening to launch an indefinite public agitation (including the stopping of buses), the inspector registered a case against the man who had abused the women and dropped the case against the SHG members.

The SHG women's frequent interactions with state institutions and their presence in public spaces were regarded as challenges to the dominant norms of feminine propriety in the region of study. When the SHGs in Prakasam village spent Rs 5,000 to set up a big stage and conduct a public event in the village, the men boycotted the event en masse stating that they would not attend an event in which 'women sit on chairs'. Snide remarks and jokes about the reversal of gender roles with SHG women being 'men in saris' and 'men being good enough only to wash dishes and cook meals' were reported. During the formation of the earliest SHGs in Prakasam village, the village administrative officer had chastised men for permitting the women to 'roam freely', and it was rumoured that women would boycott agricultural work with the advent of SHGs. The men reportedly commented that women strode out of the village on SHG work 'as if they were walking over the heads of men'. However, the women reported that the frequency and severity of these attacks had diminished in the face of continuous official support for SHGs and the women's unwillingness to tolerate criticism of their SHGs by unsympathetic outsiders.

The official support to SHGs appeared to have signalled that collective organising by women (even if only for the limited purpose of saving and borrowing money) mattered to the state and should be respected by rural communities. The exhibitions organised by the local administration to showcase enterprises financed by SGSY loans and celebrate the emergence of 'female entrepreneurs' provoked the women to frantically organise adequate and sometimes costly proof of enterprise activity (discussed in Chapter 6). And yet, these exhibitions also served to publicly demonstrate the official endorsement that the SHGs commanded. Commenting on an exhibition at the BDO, the president of Annai Janaki SHG (MaThi-SC) said, 'Women were swarming the BDO for a whole week. To see so many women managing the stalls filled us with pride! It made the men wonder at us with envy.' *It did not matter that the SHGs did not actually own or operate the enterprises on display* when the exhibition served as a powerful means to convey a sense of what women could achieve and suggested that women had stormed the corridors of governmental power at local levels.

It appeared that state involvement in SHG promotion and financing was popularly interpreted as tacit support for an agenda of gender equality. The disgruntled husband of an SHG member in Prakasam village informed me that the state government had made the 'big mistake' of publicly declaring that 'women are equal to men' through its support for women's SHGs and all-women police stations. He added that men often discussed in private conversations with each other that the SHGs should be dismantled since they had taught women to use the 'language of law' at home and spawned the idea that women have power too. He said, 'Women tell their husbands that "even the government says we have equal rights".' It was widely believed that the presence of a woman chief minister (Dr Jayalalithaa) during the term of the AIADMK (2001–6) had paved the way for official support for the SHG phenomenon. This perception was reflected in a comment that I heard frequently, that women's meetings (SHG meetings) were being held because a woman was in power.[9]

At a public event organised as part of a state-sponsored adult literacy programme in Thillai town, a male participant remarked that men need their own SHGs to build unity, strengthen their bargaining power and counter the perceived public successes of women's SHGs. That several men in the audience appreciated and applauded this comment bespoke a widespread perception that women's social status and power as a collective had grown since the advent of SHGs. As both my fieldwork in Tamil Nadu and the secondary literature from other parts of the country that I discussed in this section suggest, this was an outcome, not so much of women's ability to generate capital or manage their 'micro-banks', but of the visible presence of diverse state actors in SHG promotion and financing and the network of contacts that the women had developed with them.

Conclusion

The proliferation of opportunities for engagement with state institutions and actors provided women valuable insights into the messiness and internal contradictions of the state, also giving them the means to work this dissonance to their advantage. The disparate, discontinuous and fragmentary sightings of the state (Corbridge *et al.* 2005; Gupta 2006) by SHG women shaped the way they constructed the state. It enabled the women to see state institutions as constituted by different fractions that they could appeal to as allies or rally against as adversaries. Not infrequently, the women appealed to one actor to mitigate the excesses of another, such as appealing to an upright bank manager to counter a corrupt block official or using their contacts in the block office to curb bank managers raring to inspect the women's group enterprises. The women members of SHGs cultivated a dense network of ties with state actors that they strategically drew upon to advance their interests in diverse contexts, as individuals and as collectives. As both my fieldwork and reports on SHGs from other states indicate, the interests that the women sought to advance included the right to meaningfully participate in the local panchayat meetings, to press their demands upon the grama sabha, to seek justice and relief for aggrieved individuals in specific instances of domestic violence and marital abuse, to challenge harassment and violence against women in public spaces, to challenge the widespread social sanction for male alcoholism, to make their voice heard with regard to the allocation of state-provided development resources for their village and to challenge local elites who appropriated public resources.

It was not uncommon for the women to appeal to higher-level state functionaries to reign in and check lower-level bureaucrats and local village leaders, indignant at women's growing confidence in inhabiting public spaces. The widespread perception that the SHGs enjoyed state endorsement and backing enabled their constituency of rural poor women to gain spaces for manoeuvre and defy household and community-level patriarchies in ways that were recognised as transgressive by men and local community leaders. Even while SHG-banking brought the women into conflict with bank personnel and officials of the BDO on numerous occasions, the women eschewed a position of thoroughgoing opposition to the state given the valuable, survival-oriented resources it offered and, equally importantly, their experience-derived recognition of what feminist scholars have reiterated in multiple contexts – that the state can be a valuable ally and intermediary, a 'powerful agency for change and arbitration' (Sangari 2007) for women who negotiate multiple patriarchies embedded within family/kin relationships and at broader community levels (Rai 2008).

Rai (2008) reminds us that the position of 'against the state' is untenable for women as civil society (or political society) is as deeply masculinist as state relations and institutions. The case studies discussed in this chapter suggest that, besides *learning about the state* in ways that enabled them to more successfully wrest development resources from the state, women learn that their collusive participation in state-sponsored projects of female entrepreneurship is necessary to sustain statist narratives of empowerment and poverty alleviation. By seeing from close quarters the desperate quest (of multiple governmental actors) for legitimacy through association with women's microfinance SHGs, the women catch glimpses of the state as vulnerable. Simultaneously, they learn that the 'fluidity' and 'dispersal' of power within the state implies that different state fractions can be both oppressors and allies in women's struggles for other forms of justice and claims to rights and well-being (Rai 2008). If political society is a 'site of negotiation and contestation opened up by the activities of governmental agencies aimed at population groups' (Chatterjee 2004: 74), the SHG phenomenon opens up spaces within political society for women to emerge as the principal actors negotiating with the state for development resources, besides contesting the oppressive practices and inequitable relations of gender and caste, striving thereby to democratise political society.

Notes

1 I met the president and secretary of several SHGs of Velpatti village (name changed) at one of the block-level SHG meetings conducted at the block office. Their story about the 'exemplary' bank manager and his antipathy to corruption was quite striking.

2 This was discussed in Chapter 1 in the section titled 'Contours of SHG promotion in Thillai block (Tamil Nadu)'.

3 The point made here is that the women were willing to monitor institutions that supplied vital services to rural communities if their intervention could improve their overall quality and functioning. However, when they felt unduly burdened with managing government schemes that had little use or purpose and sought merely to use their labour without devolving any powers to them, they resisted, as discussed in the case of the sanitary complex in Chapter 6.

4 This was discussed in Chapter 1 in the section titled 'Contours of SHG promotion in Thillai block (Tamil Nadu)'.

5 The advocates of the opposition party (the DMK) somewhat weakly attempted to counter this by clarifying the relative expenditures of the central and state governments (ratio of 75:25) on the scheme. They sought (unsuccessfully) to argue that the greater expenditure from the

central government, with which the opposition DMK was in alliance, invalidated any claims the state government could make with respect to the swift implementation of the scheme.

6 Meetings of the grama sabha include all adult voters in the area of the village panchayat.

7 The first police station to be staffed only by women was introduced in Chennai in 1992, to create an institutional environment that encourages women victims of abuse and violence to seek redress. Currently, there are 199 such women-only police stations in Tamil Nadu (Selvaraj 2014).

8 Sanyal (2009) distinguishes 'normative' actions or those that sanction men's behaviour and challenge conventional social practices from 'pragmatic' actions or those that promote community resources and infrastructure.

9 The sentiment was expressed thus: 'A woman's rule and hence women's *Sangams*' (*Pombala rajiyam, Pombala sangam*). The men half jokingly commented that women had got 'uppity' since a woman was in power and that when Dr Karunanidhi of the rival DMK returned to power, he would send them all packing home.

Conclusion

> In India, leaders in the southern state of Andhra Pradesh, which accounts for about a third of the country's microloans, have accused lenders of impoverishing customers. Stories proliferated in the local news media about women who had amassed debts of $1,000 or more as loan officers cajoled them into borrowing more than they could afford and then browbeat them to repay.
>
> From a report that appeared in the *New York Times* (Bajaj 2011)

> These MFIs are the new-age moneylenders, who loot the savings of the poor. . . . Why are you giving loans to the MFIs under priority sector lending? You are giving them loans at 10 per cent and allow them to charge 26 per cent. You are encouraging money-lending.
>
> Ms Brinda Karat, member of Parliament, at a press conference in Mumbai on 1 November 2011 reporting on a discussion with the governor of the RBI
>
> (*The Hindu* 2011)

Microfinance programmes have been in the eye of a storm recently. Influential sections of the global media such as the *New York Times* (2011) have reported over-lending or the unbridled flow of finance capital from MFIs and commercial banks to low-income households, the resultant spiralling indebtedness of borrowers (both in India and in other parts of the world) and coercive and abusive loan recovery strategies deployed by lenders, even culminating in suicides in some instances. The ensuing crisis throws into question the 'eradicating poverty through profits' (Prahalad 2005) edifice on which microfinance rests, besides alerting us to the violent and exploitative forms that ongoing processes of capital accumulation may assume under neo-liberal capitalism (Harvey 2003: 145; Sassen 2010). In India, murmurs of discontent started as early as 2006 when the Indian media reported the suicides of microfinance borrowers in the coastal districts of Andhra Pradesh. Poor households were reportedly inundated with loans from a burgeoning microfinance industry (for-profit MFIs in this case) that subsequently coerced the poor to repay, no matter the circumstances (Kumar 2006; Reddy 2006; Surya 2006). By the end of 2010, media representations of unaccountable, even tyrannical lenders and discontented and oppressed borrowers had become far more commonplace (Bajaj 2011; Buncombe 2011; Hornak 2011; Menon 2010).

In India, the national leaders of a prominent women's organisation, the All India Democratic Women's Association (AIDWA),[1] met the governor of the central bank of the country, the Reserve Bank of India (RBI), on 31 October 2011, to demand that microfinance lenders targeting poor women and subjecting them to 'harassment' and 'intimidation' be legally prosecuted and that the RBI withdraw the priority status it had conferred upon the 'new age moneylenders who loot the savings of the poor' (*The Hindu* 2011). Significantly, the AIDWA's memorandum submitted to the RBI in October 2011 is not a condemnation of microfinance per se, and counter-poses the SHGs (to the MFIs that were denounced) as an alternative, pro-women model of credit delivery that has not received the official support due to it (People's Democracy 2011). This nuanced response to the 'global' crisis of microfinance, which may be stated as 'Finance SHGs, Regulate MFIs', is an acknowledgement of the institutional spaces within the formal banking sector that the SHGs have opened up for rural poor households and the relative autonomy that SHGs, as grassroots collectives, enjoy vis-à-vis external actors such as MFI lenders. The SHG-banking model of microfinance has, by and large, remained relatively unscathed by the storm over the suicides, attributed to (some) growth-oriented MFIs in the country. Nonetheless, the intertwined trajectories of SHG-based microfinance and an emergent neo-liberal capitalism in India are manifest and have constituted the central theme of this book.

In the concluding chapter, I summarise and highlight the key arguments regarding microfinance, gender and neo-liberal governmentalities that this book has advanced. I also examine in some detail the efficacy of SHG-based microfinance as an instrument to 'reverse primitive accumulation', drawing on the evidence available from different parts of India, as well as the toll imposed on women by self-help projects that entail an incessant 'capitalisation of the self'. Towards the end of the chapter, I review some of the key debates, developments and issues of concern that have unfolded in the Indian microfinance sector since 2010 and discuss these issues in the light of the theoretical frameworks elaborated in the book. In particular, I discuss the rise of commercial microfinance and its implications for SHGs, the debates on the cost of credit (interest rates) and the terms of lending to the poor, demands by civil society actors such as organised women's groups in favour of state regulation of the sector and recent initiatives by NABARD ('SHG-2') to invigorate SHG-banking.

Governing 'at a distance'

At the start of this book, I foregrounded the paradoxical emergence and growth of SHG-banking in the face of the steady decline and erosion of the Indian state's commitment to the social banking agenda with the inception of neo-liberal economic and financial policies in the post-SAP years. The severe contraction of rural and agricultural lending is, in fact, used by Mihir Shah (2008) to counter Chatterjee's (2008a) assertion that governmental provisioning and welfarist measures have endured and even expanded during the 1990s and the 2000s in order to stem the ongoing dispossession of marginalised communities and classes in India. In this book, I have proposed that the rise of SHGs signals not so much the expansion of welfarism, but the emergence of new technologies of rule that provide people institutionalised spaces to participate in the delivery of public services as organised groups of citizens or 'end users', enhancing thereby the *efficacy* of delivery mechanisms at the grassroots. Hence, the proliferation of SHGs, even as the overall quantum of rural financial flows to agriculture or to designated weaker sections, may have diminished since the 1990s.

In this book, I have shown how SHG-banking, as a technology of rule in an emergent neo-liberal India, aims to create 'rational economic' women (Karim 2011; Rankin 2001) who efficiently participate in the new self-regulating markets for microfinance that it spawns (Weber 2002), advancing thereby the agenda of rural financial deepening at the grassroots (Von Pischke 2003). Simultaneously, it coopts the 'denizens' of political society within civil society forms of associational activities and makes their claims upon state-mediated entitlements contingent on their self-fashioning, in particular, prescribed ways. In doing so, it strives to achieve what Chatterjee (2012: 317) describes as a 'steady widening and deepening of the web of governmental power in India' by giving rural women of marginal households and communities a 'strategic' and 'moral' stake in the processes of governmental power (Chatterjee 2008b: 93). By autonomising and responsibilising women's grassroots collectives and inducing a capitalisation of the self (Rose 1999), the SHG phenomenon in India aims to constitute women as diligent savers and disciplined borrowers who willingly monitor the financial decisions and actions of themselves and their peer group members.

In order to better understand the remarkable ascendance of SHG-banking since its inception as a NABARD-pioneered experimental project in the early 1990s, I discussed how the state steers a multitude of actors (both formally distanced from the state and state actors) to provide and seek access to bank credit through processes of 'translation' that construct consonant and allied interests (Miller and Rose 1990) between the personal projects of diverse institutions and the financial inclusion goals of women's SHGs. The processes of translation are also central to the recruitment of 'interpretive communities' (Mosse 2004) or supporting actors who come to be invested in the policy idea of microfinance delivery to rural poor households via all-women's grassroots collectives. I showed how SHG promotion and financing have taken root and flourished through the responsibilising of these diverse supporting actors (promoter agencies, financing banks, the SHG collectives and their members), sought to be governed through their freedoms (Rose 1999).

Through SHG-banking, commercial banks were divested of direct responsibility for the decisions and behaviour of numerous individual borrowers, dealing instead with the peer groups who took it on themselves to 'weed out' undesirable borrowers and enforce on-time loan repayment. The banks' 'autonomous' quest for competitive behaviour, portfolio quality and performance enhancement was thus aligned with the agenda of SHG-banking, discursively constituted in ways that demarcated it from the ethos of the erstwhile social banking era. Charged with the responsibility of implementing the SGSY scheme inaugurated in April 1999, the rural development administration at the block and village levels was recruited for the tasks of SHG promotion in order that there may be a sufficiently large number of groups across the country capable of absorbing the financial assistance made available through the (target-driven) scheme. State policies have directed and steered development NGOs to 'autonomously' choose SHG promotion vis-à-vis other priority areas of developmental action. The state has used financial incentives to direct promoter NGOs towards ensuring that the SHGs on their watch forge successful financial linkages with commercial banks. At the level of the SHG, its women members are steered towards choosing appropriate modes of self-governed financial behaviour through group-level practices that allow for a greater degree of decisional autonomy than is commonly found among the village-level peer groups in the MFI model of microfinance delivery to the poor.

The authoritative norms and calculations informing group transactional practices (relating to the generation, the distribution and the repayment of capital as well as the management of 'microbanks') activated and harnessed women's self-steering capacities and self-regulating mechanisms (Miller and Rose 1990) towards the end of accumulating and responsibly managing group capital. Promoter agencies and financing banks endeavoured to shape women's values, judgements and decisions so that they may prioritise a financial rationality and fashion themselves as fiscally disciplined, creditworthy actors. Insofar as the generation of capital was concerned, the secondary literature on SHGs from other parts of the country and my field study in Tamil Nadu suggest that the livelihood conditions of the village economy and the terms of lending in the local moneylending markets shaped women's decisions regarding acceptable and appropriate terms of saving and borrowing capital. The prevalence of heterogeneous financial practices (with respect to group savings, the interest rates, repayment duration and enforcement) among groups in the same village and promoted by the same agency underscores the scope for group-level decision-making in SHG transactions, as my field study in Tamil Nadu demonstrates. And yet, the women's calculations, judgements and actions with regard to the generation of capital were undoubtedly governed from a distance, making them the bearers of a regulated autonomy (Rose 1996). The cases discussed in Chapter 2 suggest that the women were mindful of the collective mandate of their SHGs (as lenders) to generate adequate finance and ensure its efficient and rapid repayment sans delay or interruption, of promoters' directives and stipulations towards this end and of the imperative of cultivating financial linkages with commercial banks.

The SHGs' autonomous decisions and actions regarding the distribution of the groups' corpus (as intra-group loans) were governed by their judgements and calculations on how to optimally invest scarce resources by assessing and minimising the risks posed by the prospective borrowers of SHG funds. The SHGs constituted themselves as 'calculative spaces' through incessant calculations that included self and peer assessments of a member's creditworthiness and of the 'membership worthiness' of particular individuals. These assessments were, in turn, shaped by the perceived financial solvency and asset ownership of a woman's household, the stability of the livelihoods that sustained the household economy and the reliability of adult male income earners. My fieldwork in Tamil Nadu and the literature on SHGs from other parts of India suggest that the household economic status of the women and their household and kin-based social relationships mediated women's loan access within the SHGs. When (poorer) women sought loans that were seen as incommensurate with their repayment capacities, my fieldwork showed that group leaders pursued loan-rationing strategies such as the delay or the outright denial of loans, seeking to dissuade them from staking equal claim to credit on par with their better-off peer group members.

Resisting governmentalities: dissenting counter-conducts

As I have shown in the book (Chapters 2–4), the constitution of SHGs as micro-banks that intermediate financially between savers and borrowers was not given a priori, but took place over a period of time through routinised calculations, judgements, decisions and actions. Through these recursive practices that reflected a 'regulated autonomy', the SHGs constituted themselves as *lender-collectives* whose interests and imperatives could diverge from those of their *individual member-borrowers*. The collective's interest in ensuring the rapid generation of capital conflicted with the individual-member/borrowers' requirement of long-duration loans at lower interest rates repaid with a degree of flexibility, allowing for household or livelihood-related crises. The collective's interest in securing the prudent distribution of its micro-capital through loans to borrowers perceived as financially viable played out in ways that conflicted with the financial requirements of individual (usually poorer) women. Its attempts to safeguard the group's financial health entailed the eviction of individual members in distress, who made delayed or irregular repayment of loans or ceased to make savings. The efforts of the group as a collective, and a rational economic actor in the making, to manage its capital resources judiciously and prudently by eliminating any extraneous expenditure of funds conflicted with a few individuals' (the leaders') need to be compensated for their labour, skill and services.

These multiple and competing interests rendered the judgements, calculations and actions that constituted SHGs as micro-banks vulnerable to dispute and contestation. And thus, the question of how SHG-based microfinance may contribute to a 'steady widening and deepening of the web of governmental power in India' (Chatterjee 2008b: 93) is incompletely understood without appreciating the simultaneous resistance and challenge to (some elements of) neoliberal governmental rationalities mounted by the women sought to be governed. Several instances, drawn from my fieldwork in Tamil Nadu and the literature from other states, show that women refused to dis-embed or abstract the calculus of decision-making from local socio-economic environments or village livelihood contexts or to conform to a financial rationality in all contexts. SHGs have chosen transactional practices that mitigate the disciplinary dynamics of microfinance, accepting the trade-off by way of a slower pace of capital generation. They have refused to raise interest rates despite promoter instructions to do so (in some cases) and have distributed among members interest incomes and/or the entire financial corpus periodically, notwithstanding the warning (issued by banks, the BDO or NGOs) that they eschew any practice that diminishes the quantum of group capital. SHGs have charged diminishing interest rates even during delayed loan repayment so as to spare their members additional economic strain and, in many cases reported across the country, permitted flexible (or 'balloon') repayment of internal loans. Occasionally, they have decided to not rotate group savings as internal loans to each other, defying the logic of unceasing capital rotation and braving the disapproval of promoter/financing agencies in the specific instances discussed in the book.

The SHGs' distribution of micro-capital (as intra-group loans) opened up spaces for their women members to debate and fight over the ways in which household asset ownership and gendered power dynamics mediated individual members' credit entitlements.

As my fieldwork has shown, the deployment of 'repayment skill' (*kattum thiramai*) to apportion credit brought to the fore class-related tensions within the SHGs and instigated multiple charged and fraught discussions around the legitimacy of claims – what made some claims more legitimate than others when the quantum of savings was uniform and unvarying? In the course of the routine weekly meetings held to transact SHG business, the women challenged the ways in which the class- and gender-based determinants of rural poverty and vulnerability (of unstable incomes, uncertain livelihoods, landlessness, alcoholic, 'vagabond' husbands, high dependency ratios in women-headed households) were continuously invoked and inscribed in the discussions that preceded the sanction of loans. Women from poorer households and 'push-out' women contested the 'capacity' discourse and its implication that they were unfit for large-sized loans or for group membership. They repudiated the calculations, judgements and evaluations that regulated, governed and ultimately diminished or nullified the legitimacy of their claims in their respective SHGs.

Conflicts also erupted whenever the leaders challenged the expectation (of co-members and of promoter agencies) that they perform free services. The management of micro-banks demanded exacting skills and competencies of formal literacy, numeracy and account keeping and some respite from the daily imperatives of wage labour. Besides the skills required and the investment of time, the absence of the periodic financial supervision of group accounts by the promoter agencies charged with the task contributed to the disproportionate autonomising and responsibilising of the group leaders. While the members of SHGs sought a greater regulation of their leaders' discretionary actions, of their autonomy as it were, the promoter agencies lacked the wherewithal to provide this oversight in a systematic fashion. Resisting the regulation of their autonomy, the leaders foregrounded instead the extent of their responsibilities, the burdens they imposed and the risks and costs they entailed. Their strategies might also be seen as resistance to the logic of rapid capital accumulation and its propensity to both invisibilise and disregard the labour and efforts of (some) women on behalf of the collective.

While the social relations and hierarchies of gender and social class informed the processual dynamics by which the SHGs constituted themselves as micro-banks, the outcomes were varied in terms of specific battles won or lost. The women of poorer households, who were disadvantaged in terms of loan access within the SHGs, nevertheless successfully defended the equal distribution of group revenue or interest incomes, despite contending claims by their better-off peer, as discussed in Chapter 4. Both my fieldwork and other studies have drawn attention to how societal power hierarchies, including those of household economic status, formal literacy skills and proximity to local power structures, have assigned group leadership positions to relatively privileged women. However, group members, backed by promoter and financing agencies and sometimes their male kin, effectively curtailed, on occasion, the autonomous actions of group leaders and, in diverse ways, sought to monitor and counter the latter's claims upon the groups' financial resources.

Caste-related dynamics were particularly visible when the SHGs sought bank loans. Large-scale studies of the bank linkage programme in Andhra Pradesh found that groups comprising women of the scheduled castes and tribes have not secured bank loans on par with those consisting of the socially dominant castes (APMAS 2007; Reddy 2005). A micro-study of SHGs in Mahabubnagar district (Andhra Pradesh) highlighted the intermediary role of male kin and community members in securing bank loans and the relative disadvantage of SHG women belonging to the oppressed castes, whose male kin lacked the know-how and the self-confidence to negotiate bank bureaucracy (Rao 2008). My field study in Tamil Nadu found that the cautionary strategies of risk-averse bank personnel constituted women of the scheduled castes as potential defaulters and portfolio risks to a greater extent than women of the OBCs. Yet this did not manifest as outright exclusion from bank loans in the fieldwork villages. The anti-poverty mandate of the SGSY scheme and its prioritisation of marginalised social groups generally served to protect the access of SC women to the SGSY loans. Despite the reluctance of the bank to finance the SC women's SHGs in Nalloor village (Thillai block), the requirement to simultaneously manage two distinct loan schemes led to the sanction of the linkage loans to the SC-only SHGs as well (described in Chapter 5). Besides being contingent on specific contexts, the outcomes in terms of access (or not) to specific bank loans were also determined by the women's unceasing endeavours to secure the loans.

When seeking bank loans, the women pressed their claims even when they did not adhere to the conditions and the professed objectives and formal rules of the schemes through which they availed resources. The women in one of the SC-only SHGs of Nalloor village coaxed, beseeched and argued with the bank manager to obtain the linkage loan, although the repayment record of their internal loans was judged inadequate. In another instance in Nalloor, the women contested the presumed right of bank managers to judge their internal accounts and declare them inadequate, arguing that group decisions to accommodate a borrower's delayed repayment should not concern external actors. Apart from my study in Tamil Nadu which found a fudging of SHG account books in order to create the impression of disciplined loan repayment in preparation for bank appraisal and grading of group accounts, a report from Assam also found that the groups maintained 'attractive' records that showed higher figures for repayment and internal loans than was actually the case (APMAS 2009a). Despite their rejection of the enterprise-management clause of the SGSY scheme, the SHG women who applied for these loans (in my fieldwork villages in Thillai block) strove to realise what they perceived as their rightful entitlement to the financial assistance. In several instances, women acted in ways that blurred the boundaries between the poverty orientation of the SGSY and the market-friendly logic of the linkage scheme, staking claim to development resources, not only as credit-worthy borrowers but, equally and when deemed necessary, as needy, impoverished beneficiaries.

The women also blurred the boundaries between the direct linkage and subsidy-bearing scheme by responding to the loan repayment imperative of both schemes in similar ways, as my fieldwork in Tamil Nadu found. While the women vigorously defended their right to permit flexibility and latitude with respect to the repayment schedules of their internal loans, they recognised that the disciplinary dynamics that accompanied bank loans were of a different kind altogether. Resorting to punitive disciplinary mechanisms, the women bent over backwards to repay all bank loans at considerable costs to themselves. Studies from other parts of India (such as Andhra Pradesh and Rajasthan) have also pointed to the SHGs' prioritisation of the repayment of bank loans vis-à-vis internal or group loans, the transfer of group savings to settle bank loans either by the financing bank directly or the women themselves and the sound commercial operation that SHG-banking offered, from the financing banks' point of view (APMAS 2007; APMAS and CMF 2006). It appears that, by and large, banking with SHGs has offered the advantage of a new, hyper-disciplined and feminised clientele to commercial banks operating in a performance-oriented and portfolio-conscious reform environment.[2]

Negotiations on a political terrain

In Chapter 7, I discussed how the presence of multiple institutional actors in SHG promotion and financing made it possible for the women to appeal to one actor to help mitigate the perceived excesses of another, to invoke higher-level officials of the BDO against 'overly corrupt' juniors, to alert sympathetic and 'honest' bank officials to the rent-seeking proclivities of the BDO, to request officials of the BDO to curb zealous bank managers, raring to inspect women's enterprises, or to consolidate ties with the financing bank, in order to disengage from promoter NGOs. My account of women's negotiations with multiple actors, of how they sought the protection and patronage of one promotional actor, denounced another, deserted a third and sought temporary alliances to move a specific loan, speaks to the high-cost, effortful, risk-fraught nature of women's engagement with state institutions. Chatterjee (2004) argues that the claims of people in political society are a constant political negotiation, and their entitlements, even when recognised by the state, never quite become rights. In the case of the SHGs, the entitlements of their women members to state developmental resources, *even if officially legitimised*, were relentlessly negotiated by the women on an 'uncertain political terrain'.

As I showed, these political negotiations were shaped by the unequal 'partnerships' that were forged between rural women of marginal social status and more powerful actors, given particular policy and institutional contexts (for instance, a legacy of poor loan repayment of pre-SHG-era loan schemes in the villages of study in Tamil Nadu and other states marked the bank–SHG relationships in particular ways). The negotiations were also shaped by the endeavours of commercial banks, the BDO and promoter NGOs to 'enterprise' themselves or to fulfil their diverse 'practical interests' (Mosse 2004), rendering the women members of SHGs vulnerable to their institutional imperatives and ambitions. The emergence of women's SHGs as potential vote banks or a rallying point for political parties, prior to local or state-level elections, in several states such as Andhra Pradesh, Karnataka, Rajasthan and Odisha (EDA and APMAS 2006; Pattenden 2010) has also shaped these negotiations, with the women offering their support for particular candidates or their collective presence at election meetings and rallies in exchange for the quick sanction of loans or other gifts of material resources. Finally, these conflict-ridden negotiations have also reflected the women's struggles to stake claim to entitlements even as they refused, in some critical respects, to govern their selves in keeping with the imperatives of policymakers or the 'centres of calculation'.

If SHG-based microcredit sought to govern from a distance by making citizenship conditional upon conduct (Rose 1999), we see that the outcomes were uneven and partial, involving as they did conflict, collaboration, collusion and outright subversion. In the many instances discussed in this book, the individual woman member or the SHG collective challenged the group-imposed norms or policy-determined regulations that sought to shape the ways they 'capitalised the self' and make their credit entitlements contingent upon disciplined financial intermediation or the assumption of entrepreneurial subjectivities. The making of SHGs as micro-banks that were permitted a regulated autonomy shaped women's subjectivities (as 'the women who take more' and those 'who take less', as 'leaders' and 'members', as 'push-out' women, as 'disciplined borrowers', as 'the needy poor') in ways that brought them into conflict with each other and with the collective as they strove to expand spaces of manoeuvre within the SHGs. Neither pre-given nor existing a priori (Mohanty 1991; Sharma 2010), women's emergent identities and interests, generated in and through their negotiations with peer group members and with financing banks and promoter agencies, were central to how they claimed resources from their self-managed collectives and from the state.

Reversing primitive accumulation

If women of rural poor households are able to stake successful claims to state resources through their SHGs, does this point to an effective 'reversal of primitive accumulation' on the ground? In their response to Chatterjee (2008a), John and Deshpande (2008) wonder if Chatterjee does not perhaps equate the policy *intention* (of reversal) and actual *outcomes* and whether the palliative measures offered by the operation and spread of governmental schemes are reversing dispossession and pauperisation on the ground, as Chatterjee appears to suggest. While I have argued that the state's imperative to protect the 'dangerous classes' (Chatterjee 2008a) from utter destitution or the *intention* (of reversal) accounts, in part, for the emergence of SHG-banking in India and its anchoring to a (pre-liberalisation) agenda of extending banking services and anti-poverty schemes to those denied access, I find no evidence of countervailing processes effective or powerful enough to admit discussion of an actual reversal. In other words, both my fieldwork in Tamil Nadu and the available evidence from other parts of India (discussed later) do not permit a case for *outcomes* that match policy intentions.

The weight of the evidence available suggests that SHGs have provided their women members a (limited) safety net (Karides 2010; Weber 2002) that buttresses or shores up the poverty-coping strategies of their households, even though microfinance access may not have mitigated income insecurity by expanding private entrepreneurship and effectively absorbing surplus labour in rural economies (Weber 2002). In the study villages in Tamil Nadu, the women valued their SHG membership for the economic and non-economic resources they provided; the relinquishment of membership was never experienced without regret or dismay. Internal or group-sourced loans were entirely untied with regard to possible end-uses and could be (and were) used for household survival-oriented purposes that the microfinance literature identifies as 'consumption-smoothing' or making good temporary shortfalls in food and current consumption needs (discussed in Chapter 6). It mattered little to the women that their loans (whether group or bank-sourced) were not commonly used to finance new micro-enterprise or business activities. In the fieldwork villages in Tamil Nadu, a significant pathway by which the women used bank loans to strengthen their poverty coping strategies such as building up the asset base of their households and redeeming long-term debt was the *unintended* outcome of subversion of the SGSY scheme, rather than its stated goal of fostering women's management of collectively owned enterprises. In this case, the women converted state support for micro-enterprise development to a form of government transfer or welfare provisioning through their (labour-, cost- and effort-intensive) appropriation of the SGSY-provided financial assistance, strengthening thereby the safety-net component of SHG-based microfinance.

A study of 34 SHGs in Karnataka (Chitradurga district) and 35 in Tamil Nadu (Kancheepuram district) also points to the consumption-smoothing purpose that the groups served through the internal and bank loans they made available to their members (Gadenne and Vasudevan 2007). The women acknowledged that the biggest benefit from their groups was the assistance in filling gaps in household expenditure and, in particular, the provision of emergency funds for unexpected and urgent expenses. Of the members who had faced an emergency, such as an accident or a death in the family, since joining the groups (about 40% of all members), 80% had received a loan on time from the groups' savings. In contrast, only 38% of the women attested that their incomes had increased after joining the SHGs (ibid.). Interviews with 293 women in 83 SHGs in three districts of Andhra Pradesh (Kurnool, Mahabubnagar, Ananthapur) also testify to benefits most closely associated with the safety-net function of SHG-based microfinance. When compared to 157 non-members in the same set of villages, the households of the women in the sample SHGs appear to have enjoyed greater access to basic necessities that included food, nutrition, water, fuel, electricity, housing, education and health. The study noted a reduction in the percentage of members pledging assets with moneylenders and in the seasonal migration (for work) of member households, as compared to non-members (Murthy *et al.* 2005).

Data from a large-scale survey conducted in eight districts of Andhra Pradesh that covered 5,753 households in 601 revenue villages was used to examine the economic and non-economic impacts of SHGs formed through the District Poverty Initiatives Project and the Rural Poverty Reduction Project (RPRP).[3] While the programmes aimed to increase income and assets for the participants (SHG members), no significant difference was found between treated and control areas for these variables. On the other hand, the study established an economically and statistically significant programme impact on mean per capita spending for participants, but not for those who failed to join the SHGs. The study concluded that, at the time of the survey, the programme's main economic impact had taken place through credit-mediated consumption smoothing, rather than income enhancement or the accumulation of assets over time (Deininger and Liu 2013).

The findings of the SHG studies in India do not appear to be isolated or exceptional cases. Interestingly, the poverty-reduction claims advanced by the global microfinance industry have evolved and changed in the face of a growing body of research (from several parts of the world) showing inconsistent evidence of the enhancement of incomes through 'promotional' lending (Hulme and Mosley

1996) or lending exclusively oriented to financing micro-enterprises in the hope of mitigating income poverty. The literature has established that the pre-existing poverty levels of borrowers, their life circumstances and macro-policy environments mediate the relationships between access to micro-loans, the successful management of viable businesses and income enhancement (Hulme and Mosley 1996). By way of response to these findings, the representations of microfinance as a poverty-alleviation strategy have been tempered and re-engineered; this is best exemplified by the changing representation of microfinance between the World Bank's *World Development Report 1990: Poverty*, and the *WDR 2000–01: Attacking Poverty* (Kalpana 2005).

In the *WDR (1990)*, microfinance found place in the chapter titled 'Promoting economic opportunities for the poor'. Increasing the access of the poor to credit was identified as a strategy to increase their participation in growth processes, along with increasing access to land, infrastructure and technology. The report concluded that micro-enterprise lending has exercised considerable impact on the income levels of the poor (World Bank 1990). In contrast, the commissioned study on microfinance for the *WDR (2000–01)* focused on the impact of microfinance on *non-income* dimensions of poverty and the use of microfinance services to reduce vulnerability, mitigate risks and build and diversify assets that may be drawn upon in times of need (Sebstad and Cohen 2000). *The WDR 2000–01* highlighted the use of micro-loans to redeem debt, meet household expenses in the period following a crisis, enable consumption-smoothing and serve as a household-level money-management strategy (World Bank 2001). The World Bank's framework for attacking poverty, as elucidated in the *WDR (2000–01)*, emphasised action on three interrelated fronts: empowerment, security and opportunity. It is interesting to note that microfinance was discussed in the section on 'security' as one of the policy responses for improving risk management alongside health insurance, old-age assistance, unemployment insurance and others (World Bank 2001).

The rigours of 'capitalising the self'

While SHG women valued the safety-net-type governmental provisioning that microfinance access had made available, it was equally the case that sustained SHG participation entailed costs that could not be easily discounted. The rigours of 'capitalising the self' and the unceasing activity that it necessitated, or the active citizenship (Rose 1999) it demanded, had exacting repercussions for the women. The women members of those SHGs (in my fieldwork villages in Thillai block) that sought the quick repayment of loans over short duration enforced with great stringency strove to constitute themselves as the ruthless, unsparing monitors of time-bound repayment by restraining their bodily hungers and wants, disciplining children and risking angry words and arguments with husbands to save sufficient cash. To constantly work on their capital generation and loan repayment capacities was exhausting for women, particularly for those in difficult household circumstances, depleting as it did their personal energies and financial resources. The dissolution of the group corpus that took place periodically was deemed both *desirable* from the point of view of making available lump sums of cash to SHG members and *necessary* from that of allowing women a period of respite and the option of rejoining membership, should they desire it. It was widely acknowledged that all women could not submit themselves to the self- and peer disciplining that SHG participation warranted. The women who dropped out of SHGs speculated if they would ever be able to (re)-join SHGs and sometimes they declared it impossible (as discussed in Chapter 3).

Anti-poverty as well as other development interventions that rely on and instrumentally use women's participation to enhance the efficacy of their delivery mechanisms has been critiqued for assuming that women's resources (of labour, time and effort) are infinitely elastic and may be appropriated and harnessed towards the end of meeting project goals, disregarding the physical and psychological toll they may take on women (Molyneux 2002; Moser 1993: 69–73). A study of selected SHGs in Chitradurga district (Karnataka) and Periyar[4] district (Tamil Nadu) found that, given the subsistence nature of the livelihoods that sustained the households of the women, the savings money was generated through a reduction of expenditure on essentials and not from surplus domestic resources (Puhazhendi and Jayaraman 1999). The SHG women members taking up non-farm and animal husbandry activities had increased after the formation of the groups. The percentage of those taking up more than one income-generating activity had increased from 30% in the pre-group formation to 53% in the post-group formation phase. While the study approvingly notes that the women had taken up additional economic activities earning double the net annual incomes they formerly did, it does not make the women's additional labour effort and associated implications an area of enquiry.

A study involving a sample of 64 SHGs sponsored by the NGO MYRADA in Holalkere taluk of Karnataka district has investigated some of these issues more closely (Krishna 2000). The study found that 40% of members in groups aged three years and 33% in groups aged five years were doing extra work in order to be able to manage their saving commitment and loan repayment. The coping strategies of women for handling the work put off while undertaking either SHG-related or income-generating activities included a lengthening of the working day (number of hours of work) as the most important strategy and delegation of work to other women and girls within the household as the second most significant coping strategy (Krishna 2000). In the SHGs organised by the NGO Swayam Shikshan Prayog in two districts of Maharashtra (Latur and Osmanabad), the women were able to allot some outdoor tasks such as fetching water and feeding cattle to their sons when they were away on SHG-related work. Even when husbands and sons had engaged in cooking chores in the absence of their women kin in nuclear families in a few cases, the main support in SHG member households was provided by other female members (Parthasarathy 2005).

The preoccupation with the much-celebrated repayment rates of SHGs, and microfinance more generally, has been criticised for camouflaging the difficulties that women might encounter in delivering these repayment rates. Garikipati's (2008) study involving 397 group members from 27 SHGs in two villages of Mahabubnagar district (Andhra Pradesh) finds that the 100% repayment rates in the groups surveyed were sustained in the face of adverse impacts on intra-household gender relations and women's loss of control over allocation of their work time. When women's SHG loans were invested in family-owned enterprises and land purchases or used as working capital in family farms (as opposed to being invested in their own enterprise or other earning activities), they were seen as having little control over the incomes and assets generated. Even though the women's loans had helped their households diversify and improve incomes, the women's lack of effective authority over family assets resulted in their inability to direct the ensuing income streams to discharge the loans. Consequently, the women, who had worked on family farms or within their households before obtaining SHG loans, had begun to work as wage labourers primarily to repay the loans and, in some cases, had pledged their labour for very low wages, compelled by the need to make repayments. Interviews with the women indicated that they resented withdrawing their labour from working on their own assets and performing wage labour instead, considered socially inferior in the study region (Garikipati 2008).

SHGs as political safety nets

Theoretical analyses that situate the rise of microfinance with respect to the global advance of neo-liberalism have underscored the *political* safety net that microfinance offers by dampening or containing resistance at local levels to the unfettered operation of markets (Weber 2002). In Weber's formulation, microfinance, as part of the policy response to popular resistance against self-regulating markets, may be seen as disciplining the politics of the 'second movement' (Polanyi 1957), which aims to re-embed the economy within social and political control. Along similar lines, analysts also point to the rhetoric of 'self-reliance' and self-sufficiency (Fernando 2006) that accompany the emergence of microfinance-based development paradigms and provide legitimacy for the withdrawal of the state from discharging its social and developmental obligations. As this book has argued, SHG-based microfinance, rather than legitimating the disappearance of the state, has brought to the fore a new constituency of actors who make renewed demands on the state for developmental resources. These actors do not limit their demands (of the state) to low-cost bank credit or subsidy-bearing financial assistance from banks and the rural development administration. As discussed in Chapter 7, they manipulate the 'fluidity' and 'dispersal' of power within the state and seek allies and activate ties and contacts that assist in their endeavours to democratise political society.

Contrary to Weber's (2002) expectation, the collective mobilising that SHGs make possible may also bring within the purview of critical scrutiny the unfettered operation of markets and the capital accumulation strategies of private capital, however unsuccessfully. In Thillai block (Tamil Nadu), the women members of SHGs used the platform provided by the SHGs to bring to the attention of state representatives their anger and despair at the deplorable working conditions that prevailed in the lower rungs of the informal sector in which they were employed. During the monthly block-level meetings (held to discuss the routine management and smooth functioning of SHGs and the repayment of bank loans) organised by promoter NGOs and attended by government representatives, the women raised issues relating to the unsanitary work environment of the leather-processing industries in the region, the pitiably low wages offered by the smaller shoe companies, the Rs 10-a-day wage that home-based beedi work earned and the verbal abuse and sexual exploitation of women workers (of the subordinate castes) in the construction sector by the (mostly dominant caste) site supervisors, despite the evident inability of either NGO staff or the government officials in attendance to meaningfully respond to the range of issues they raised.

Refusing to confine their concerns to the self-employment-oriented micro-enterprise activities that were deemed the exclusive business of the SHGs, the women – agricultural daily wagers, construction and brick kiln workers, beedi workers and shoe company employees – persistently drew attention to *all the sites in which they laboured.* Urging the state to legislate effectively in order to increase the monetary returns to their labour in the informal sector and to restructure their everyday work lives and attenuate its oppressive dimensions, the women demanded, in effect, a 're-embedding of the economy within social and political control' (Polanyi 1957 in Weber 2002) and sought to hold the state to account for its evident disinterest in doing so. The demand to 're-embed the economy within social and political control' has also been asserted with respect to the microfinance sector in India, albeit in a different context and by other actors. I discuss this at length in the following two sections.

Growth of commercial microfinance: SHGs under attack?

Over the past decade and a half, there has been a rapid upscaling of for-profit or commercial microfinance in India via growth-oriented MFIs that have secured prominent financiers, including India's ICICI bank, multi-national banks such as the ABN Amro, HSBC, Standard Chartered and private venture capital funds. In the 1990s, microfinance wholesalers such as the Friends of Women's World Banking and Small Industries Development Bank of India began bulk lending to MFIs, besides undertaking the capacity building of these organisations. Subsequently, private commercial banks followed by public sector banks began to lend to MFIs, whose near-perfect repayment rates greatly enhanced their appeal in the eyes of the formal banking sector (Ghate 2006: 115–123). Commercial banks such as the ICICI innovated on-lending models that used MFIs to expand their retail operations in rural hinterlands without incurring the expenses of establishing infrastructure and even launched programmes to create new MFIs in 'under-served' areas so as to cover the rural financial markets in their entirety (Ananth 2004). By 2010, MFIs had a client outreach of 26.7 billion, loan portfolio of Rs 183.44 billion, 18% growth in clients and 56% growth in loan portfolio over the previous year, according to the *Microfinance India State of the Sector Report 2010*. A poll of 50 investment banking firms and companies identified microfinance as the top-ranking destination for financial sector investments in the country (Srinivasan 2010).

The growing commercialisation of the microfinance sector in India has worried researchers who point out that the rise of a new class of profit-oriented microfinance promoters and the predominance of investor interests in the management and governance of MFIs does not bode well for the sector's responsiveness towards the poor clients it ostensibly serves (Nair 2010). The lending and repayment practices of MFIs first came under the radar following news reports in April 2006 of the suicides of borrowers of Grameen-replicator MFIs in Andhra Pradesh. The media reported loan collection strategies that included making women stand in the sun until co-members paid up, demanding physical collateral such as house title deeds of borrowers and charging 'non-transparent' interest rates, often inflated through hidden costs (Kumar 2006; Reddy 2006; Surya 2006). Commenting on the ensuing crisis in the sector, the *Microfinance in India State of the Sector Report, 2006* (Ghate 2006), acknowledged that the MFIs' policy of 100% repayment and zero tolerance of default had carried high costs in terms of client dissatisfaction. It cautioned the MFIs to not overlook the dangers of over-financing households in the 'rush to grow' or the imperative to increase scale of outreach and attain financial self-sufficiency.

As an outcome of the crisis, Sa-dhan, the national association of MFIs, adopted a voluntary code of conduct that included charging reasonable and transparent interest rates and the eschewal of intimidation tactics by MFI staff (Ghate 2006). Though the code of conduct was adopted by all MFIs after the 2006 crisis, the *Microfinance India State of the Sector Report 2009* (Srinivasan 2009) points out that very few had clearly communicated the terms of lending (interest rates and loan structures) to their clients, who remained uninformed about the actual price of their loans. Besides the terms of lending and repayment strategies, allegations of over-lending to the same set of households have dogged the sector. Some (not all) parts of the country have seen a concentration of multiple microfinance lenders and fierce competition for 'client acquisition'. The *State of the Sector Report 2009* notes that this trend has been particularly visible in the states of Andhra Pradesh, Karnataka and Tamil Nadu. In Andhra Pradesh, where this concentration was most pronounced, both SHG and MFI lending for 2008–9 had together covered more than 20 million microfinance clients in a state with 16 million households. Statistically, more than 125% of all households in the state had been provided microfinance loans. Assuming that only poor families (that numbered about 2.52 million) had been targeted, each family had been targeted eight times with microfinance (Srinivasan 2009).

The growth of the for-profit microfinance sector cannot possibly leave the SHG-bank linkage model of microfinance delivery untouched. Field reports suggest that the SHGs (whether as collectives or their individual members) also borrow from MFIs owing to their inability to easily access bank loans and the banks' preference to lend to MFIs rather than lend directly to SHGs or SHG federations (Reddy 2010). Besides qualifying for priority-sector lending, loans to MFIs further lowered banks' costs and risks, as compared to lending to SHGs. For instance, a loan of Rs 100 million to one MFI was more economical from the financing bank's point of view than loans of Rs 0.2 million each to 500 SHGs (Rajshekhar 2010). The bias of banks towards MFIs is reported to be more acute in some states than in others. In Karnataka, for instance, NABARD data indicates that the banks lent Rs 26 billion to MFIs and no more than Rs 10 billion to SHGs in 2009–10 (Arun 2010). Where women are borrowers of both SHGs and MFIs, the pressures to make weekly payment to MFIs and their coercive tactics have resulted in SHGs defaulting on loans to banks, unable to repay both loans simultaneously (Reddy 2010). Field reports indicate that the MFIs have even split established SHGs to form the Joint Liability Groups more suited to receive MFI loans (Reddy 2010) and, in states such as Odisha, blocked the access of women's SHGs to bank loans via anti-poverty schemes (AIDWA 2010). Aloysius Fernandez, a pioneer of the SHG-bank linkage project in India, has alleged that for-profit MFIs have systematically destroyed the institutions of the poor – the SHGs in particular – in their drive to commercialise microfinance (Fernandez 2009).

While microfinance can be a (partial and limited) governmental resource aiming to mitigate the consequences of primitive accumulation, it is evident that it can just as well be an instrument of immiserisation and expropriation. Much it would seem depends on the organisational arrangements for the delivery of credit to the poor (whether top-down or democratic and amenable to control by the poor), the social relationships between financial service providers and end users and the ability of the latter to control the terms of savings, credit and other microfinance services on offer. The discussion in this section indicates that sustained ethnographic study will provide a deeper understanding than we have at present of the new risks and dangers that emerge when SHGs confront corporate lenders, of the ways in which the women appear to be negotiating these and of the ensuing transformation of the gendered political economy of financial services provision in India.

Disciplining microfinance

News reports of the excesses committed by MFIs and MFI-induced suicides in both 2006 and 2010 have provoked divergent reactions from state governments, India's vibrant civil society movements, especially women's organisations that have organised protests and led several delegations to state actors in charge of financial policymaking, such as the Finance Ministry, the RBI and NABARD and these central government actors themselves. In 2010, following news reports of the suicides, the state government of Andhra Pradesh introduced the Andhra Pradesh Microfinance Institutions (Regulation of Money Lending) Ordinance that sought to limit the freedoms of MFIs. It required MFIs to register themselves, to conduct meetings with borrowers in prominent public places like the panchayat office, to display their effective interest rates openly, to not impose any cost on borrowers apart from the interest rate, to calculate interest rates on a diminishing basis, to change their loan recovery from a weekly to a monthly basis and so on (GoAP n.d.). Political rivalry between key players at the state level, the Telugu Desam Party and the Congress, and electoral considerations with the local (panchayat and municipal) elections due to take place a year after the crisis were perceived to have paved the way for the ordinance. The Congress government in power in Andhra Pradesh was reported to have introduced the ordinance in some haste, under attack from the TDP that sought to appeal to rural constituencies by claiming that it had created the SHGs, whereas the Congress had created the MFIs. If the state government acted quickly, partly driven by anxiety to not appear weak, the ordinance was welcomed by sections of the state-level bureaucracy that had been at loggerheads with the MFIs for several years (Rajshekhar 2010).

The explosive growth of multiple financial service providers targeting the 'bottom of the pyramid' has also alarmed a section of civil society actors, which seized the opportunity, provided by the tabling of a Bill on Microfinance in the Indian Parliament by the finance minister on 20 March 2007, to express their concerns. The Micro Financial Sector (Development and Regulation) Bill, 2007, aimed to secure the 'promotion, development and orderly growth of the microfinance sector in rural and urban areas' and 'regulation of the micro finance organisations not being regulated by any law for the time being' (PRS n.d.).[5] Speakers at a joint national convention on the bill held on 15 May 2007, and attended by over 2,000 women representing SHG federations in 13 states, strongly reprimanded the central government for its perceived unwillingness to effectively regulate commercial microfinance in the country[6] (AIDWA 2007a). In a memorandum submitted in June 2007 to the Parliamentary Standing Committee on the Microfinance Bill, the AIDWA, a national women's organisation, demanded that the state proactively monitor the loan collection strategies of MFIs and enforce a ceiling on their interest rates with a view to protecting the interests of poor women who seek microfinance from commercial lenders (AIDWA 2007b).

The women's organisations in India, which have opposed for-profit MFIs, regard their activities as part of the unfettered operation of market forces in the microfinance sector. Asking why for-profit MFIs that borrow funds at 10%–14% interest rates from the banking sector should be allowed to charge rates as high as 35%–40% when they lend to the rural poor, the AIDWA insisted that the RBI cap the interest charged (by the MFIs) at a rate only marginally higher than prevailing bank interest rates so that 'microfinance is not a profit making activity based on the savings of poor and labouring women' (AIDWA 2010). The argument of the commercial microfinance sector (both globally and in India) that higher-end interest rates are warranted by the small size of transactions and the high costs associated with making large numbers of small loans to dispersed population groups cuts no ice with the women's organisations that seek to regulate its operation. Significantly, they have contrasted the costs at which the poor access microfinance from commercial lenders vis-à-vis the housing loans and personal loans (targeted generally to the urban middle classes) offered by the formal financial sector at 9% and 12%–13% interest rates, respectively (AIDWA 2010). Through their vigorous interventions, organised women's groups and some NGOs in India have raised issues that resonate with the concerns that Rob Aitken (2010) has articulated vis-à-vis MFIs that charge their borrowers interest rates that are significantly higher than the rates at which other clientele borrow from the formal financial sector. Consequently, he argues, the agenda of financial inclusion of the poor is simultaneously an entrenchment of a 'two-tier' system of credit wherein marginal groups are marked out for high-cost credit.

In October 2010, the RBI, during a meeting of its board of directors, formed a subcommittee of its board (under the chairmanship of Y.H. Malegam) to study and report on issues and concerns in the microfinance sector, which included examining the practices with respect to 'interest rates, lending and loan recovery so as to identify trends that impinge on borrowers' interests'. The Malegam Committee Report recommended the creation of a separate category of NBFC-MFIs, stipulated that their individual loans not exceed Rs 25,000 and prescribed interest rates of 24% for all personal loans they made and a 'margin cap' of 10%–12% for MFIs, depending on the size of their outstanding loan portfolios. Among several other recommendations, the committee also advised that no more than two MFIs serve the same client and that the pricing of the loan have only three components, namely a processing fee, interest charge and insurance premium (*RBI* 2011b). It has been argued that some of the committee's recommendations display a bias towards larger MFI lenders with 'deep pockets' as compared to the smaller and emerging MFIs and do not really hurt the interests of the large non-banking financial companies (NBFCs) with substantial stakes in the microfinance sector (Nair 2011). Nonetheless, it is apparent that India's histories of state intervention in rural credit markets or its 'path dependencies' (Harriss 2011), competitive electoral politics at regional and state levels and the vibrancy of its civil society movements have been reflected in efforts, however effective, to discipline microfinance, which seeks to discipline the poor.

The demand to reduce interest rates in microfinance lending has been raised with respect to the SHG sector as well. In July 2004, the Andhra Pradesh government introduced the *Pavala vaddi*, an interest subsidy scheme that required banks to make loans at 3% annual interest rates to SHGs through the linkage scheme. Banks received a subsidy from the state government that covered the difference between their rate of lending to the SHGs and the specified rate (of 3%). Being back-ended, the subsidy was passed on and the amount remitted to the SHGs' account after they completed on-time repayment of the loan.[7] State government-level initiatives to operationalise interest subsidies through the SHG-bank linkage programme have been welcomed by women's organisations from the point of view of strengthening the pro-poor dimensions of SHG-based microfinance. In its memorandum submitted to the RBI in October 2011, the AIDWA pointed out that interest rates charged by banks on SHG lending had been left to their discretion and appealed to the RBI to ensure that all SHGs country-wide be extended bank loans at 4% annual rates (People's Democracy 2011).

The interventions by state governments and organised women's groups have focused policy attention on the cost of credit and have countered, in some ways, the autonomising of the banking sector with respect to the terms of lending under the bank linkage scheme.[8] These efforts may be seen as repudiating the development rationalities that have sought to dissociate the SHG-bank linkage scheme from erstwhile poverty-lending schemes, which have often included interest subsidies or concessional interest rates as key components. In these attempts to anchor the direct linkage scheme more firmly to anti-poverty mandates, we see (as argued earlier in the book) the 'uneven articulation' (Ong 2006) of particular policy contexts and political histories by neo-liberal technologies of governing (such as microfinance).

The 'decline' of SHG-banking and revival attempts

Besides the growth of commercial microfinance and its implications for SHGs, other recent developments in SHG-banking have provoked a sense of disquiet among financial policymakers. The most significant of these developments has been a marked slowdown in the annual growth in bank loans to SHGs at an all-India level.

The *Microfinance India: State of the Sector Report 2013* observes that the annual growth rates for the key indicators of physical and financial progress of the SHG-bank linkage programme since 2010 indicate a picture of stagnation and decline (Nair and Tankha 2014: 6–7). The number of SHGs receiving bank loans during the year increased by 26% per annum between 2006 and 2010, while it declined by 8.4% per annum between 2010 and 2013. The amount of bank loans disbursed to SHGs during the year increased by 34% per annum during 2006–10, as compared to an increase of 12.5% in 2010–13 (ibid.). The impression of stagnation and decline is further reinforced by the progress of the SHG-bank linkage programme for the four-year period of 2010–14, after factoring in NABARD's most recent data available till the end of March 2014. The *Inclusive Finance India Report 2014* points to a major deceleration in the growth rate of the number of SHGs receiving loans during the year and the number with loans outstanding for 2010–14, as compared to 2006–10 (Nair and Tankha 2015: 80–82).

Several reasons have been offered by way of explaining the poor performance of the SHG-bank linkage programme in recent years. They range from 'bank fatigue' in lending to SHGs given the small size of SHG loans, the cumbersome procedures and reporting requirements, the possible saturation of the SHG-bank linkage programme in South India and the absence of institutional arrangements, on the part of state governments (barring a few), to proactively foster SHG-bank linkages that do not automatically develop on their own (Tankha 2012: 41–43). It appears that the MFI sector crisis of 2010 adversely impacted bank lending not only to MFIs but also to SHGs. The number of bank loans disbursed to SHGs during 2010–11 rose only by 0.7% over the previous year, as compared to annual increases of 26% during 2006–10. As SHG members can be borrowers of MFIs as well, the banks have been apprehensive (especially in a few states like Andhra Pradesh and Tamil Nadu) that SHG borrowers might use bank loans to repay MFI-sourced debt (ibid.).

The slowdown of the SHG-bank linkage programme apart, a rise in the non-performing assets (NPAs) on bank loans to SHGs has triggered alarm bells within the banking sector. While banks have experienced close to 100% loan recovery from their SHG portfolio for a long period since the inception of the linkage scheme, more recently, the situation appears to be changing. NABARD (2013) observes that NPAs, which were 2.9% of total bank loan outstanding to SHGs during 2009–10, had reached 7.1% by the end of March 2013. The overall NPAs on bank loans to SHGs rose from Rs 22.3 billion in the end of March 2012 to Rs 27.9 billion in the end of March 2013, accounting for an increase of 26% over the year (NABARD 2013). NABARD-sponsored studies on this phenomenon (of rising NPAs) in the states of Uttar Pradesh and Odisha[9] have found that group formation appeared to be solely oriented towards seeking and securing subsidy assistance from government, that the SHGs formed through the SGSY scheme were barely functioning (no regular meetings or internal savings and no reports of transactions) and that neither the banks nor the promoter agencies were involved in monitoring the groups, providing training or any form of capacity-building assistance (NABARD 2013).

Taking cognisance of these developments as well as field reports that women were often members of multiple SHGs and that bankers, especially at the branch level in many parts of the country, were reluctant to finance SHGs or approve repeat loans, NABARD responded by revisiting the linkage programme and prescribing modifications. This took the form of 'SHG-2', introduced through a NABARD circular issued to all commercial banks, cooperatives and RRBs on 27 March 2012 (NABARD 2012). The guidelines of SHG-2 advised banks to create a suitable framework by which group members had the option of making voluntary savings above the mandated minimum of their groups. When lending to SHGs, the banks were advised to adopt a cash credit or overdraft system with loan limit ranging from three to five years, thus reducing the need for repeat documentation and providing the groups additional loanable funds with greater flexibility. Banks were permitted to sanction loans beyond a multiple of four times the SHGs' corpus, when approving repeat cycles of cash credit to the groups.[10] To render banks confident about lending to the groups, SHG-2 recommended the use of 'self-rating' tools by which group members are educated on how to assess their own strengths and weaknesses. Banks were also advised to identify and engage the members of well-functioning SHGs or promoter NGOs to provide continuing support, financial audit and mentorship to the groups that required them (NABARD 2012).

It appears, then, that via SHG-2, NABARD is seeking to tighten quality control measures within the SHG sector. Since the capacities of those whose business it is to 'conduct the conduct' of SHG members have proved, thus far, to be limited and far too weak in relation to the task at hand, the SHGs' capacities for self-governance (self-rating) are sought to be tapped and strengthened. Simultaneously, SHG-2 aims to marshal the resources required to oversee the groups' efficient functioning, repayment discipline, accounts maintenance and other parameters of financial performance. It is hoped that these resources might be acquired, in a cost-effective manner, by mobilising locally available skills and resource persons. On the whole, SHG-2 seeks to motivate banks to intensify financial linkages with SHGs by shoring up 'risk-mitigation' (NABARD 2012) mechanisms through the self-rating tools and the external audits of the SHGs. Should SHG-2 succeed in putting in place more effective audits of SHGs and their internal lending and borrowing practices, it remains to be seen what this enhanced oversight will mean in terms of respecting the SHG-level decisions that the women are seen to take with respect to their transactional practices (that may well differ between groups promoted by the same agency and in the same village) and the differing priorities these decisions embody.[11]

Will the 'equilibrium' hold? charting the future of neo-liberal India

In December 2014, the union cabinet minister for women and child development Maneka Gandhi made an unexpected and somewhat startling public statement about SHGs. She expressed her distaste for SHGs, which, she claimed, humiliated women by making them approach banks for loans as group members, rather than as individuals. The minister also referred to the organisational revamping of the Rashtriya Mahila Kosh that would not make loans to SHGs anymore, but would instead provide loans to individual women after training them and building their entrepreneurial skills (Venugopal 2014). Ms Gandhi's statements provoked criticism from women's activists associated with the SHG programme in Karnataka (Aji 2014) and M. Karunanidhi, president of the DMK and former chief minister of Tamil Nadu, who expressed concern over the move to 'scrap' women's SHGs (*The Hindu* 2014). Ms Gandhi's pronouncements have not since been reflected in any policy change initiated by the RBI or NABARD with respect to SHGs. Given the high visibility of SHGs and of SHG-banking in several parts of the country, it is difficult to imagine how this programme might suddenly be scuttled. On the contrary, all the visible signs indicate that even if SHG-banking has faced complex challenges in recent years, it remains a key component of strategies aiming to 'reverse the effects of primitive accumulation' at the level of both the central government and various state governments.

Some of the large-scale, multilateral, donor-funded anti-poverty initiatives of several state governments contain microfinance and livelihood promotion components, all of which are operationalised through women's SHGs. A few prominent cases in point are the anti-poverty initiatives of Bihar, Odisha, Andhra Pradesh, Telangana and Tamil Nadu. Financially supported by the World Bank from October 2007 to October 2016, the Bihar Rural Livelihoods Project or *Jeevika* (as it is locally known) aims to improve rural livelihoods and enhance the social and economic empowerment of the rural poor by developing their organisations, assisting them to negotiate services from public and private sector agencies and promoting the development of microfinance and agribusiness sectors. The core strategy of Jeevika is to 'build vibrant and bankable women's community institutions in the form of SHGs, who through member savings, internal loaning and regular repayment become self sustaining organisations' (Jeevika n.d.).

The government of Odisha launched a rural livelihoods project, the Targeted Rural Initiatives for Poverty Termination and Infrastructure, which received financial support from the World Bank from March 2009 to June 2015. Implemented in 38 poverty-intensive blocks of 10 coastal districts of Odisha, the project aimed to enhance the socio-economic status of the rural poor, especially women and disadvantaged groups, through building and strengthening sustainable economic organisations of the poor (such as SHGs and their federations), enabling women's groups to play a more vocal role in local decision-making, helping them access financial services from public and private financial institutions and increasing the incomes of SHG members by enhancing rural livelihoods and developing market linkages (World Bank 2016 n.d.). In Andhra Pradesh, the two principal poverty-alleviation projects supported by the World Bank in the 2000s, namely the Andhra Pradesh District Poverty Initiatives Project (APDPIP) and the Andhra Pradesh Rural Poverty Reduction Project (APRPRP), have had substantial microfinance and SHG promotion components. The APRPRP, initially operational in 16 districts of Andhra Pradesh, was extended to all the rural areas of the state and renamed *Indira Kranthi Patham* (IKP) in 2005.[12] Implemented by the Society for Elimination of Rural Poverty (SERP), set up by the government of Andhra Pradesh in 2000, the IKP is currently operational in all districts in the states of Telangana and Andhra Pradesh and aims to reduce poverty levels through social mobilisation of the rural poor and improvement of their livelihoods (SERP n.d.).

In Tamil Nadu, the Tamil Nadu Corporation for the Development of Women (TNCDW), the nodal agency that implements the state government's Mahalir Thittam, was transferred from the administrative control of the Social Welfare Department to the Department of Rural Development and Panchayati Raj in July 2006. The new institutional location of the TNCDW acknowledges the pivotal role of the rural development administration in executing the SHG-targeted SGSY scheme, thereby re-embedding SHGs within the state government's anti-poverty and livelihood-promotion interventions. As with the other states discussed here, a World Bank–financed and state government–implemented empowerment and poverty-alleviation programme, namely the *Pudhu Vaazhvu* (translated as 'New Life'), seeks to build on the state government's SHG programme. Covering 70 backward administrative blocks in 15 districts when it was launched in August 2006, the Pudhu Vaazhvu Project (PVP), extended until September 2016, is currently implemented in 120 blocks in 26 districts of the state (PVP n.d.).

When it was introduced, the primary objective of the PVP was to reach governmental resources to the 'unreached poor', that is the poorest of poor households, the destitute, widows, the most vulnerable social groups and the disabled. The scheme drew its rationale from the perceived need to bridge the gaps in the existing poverty-reduction initiatives of the state government (GOTN 2007).[13] The gaps in Mahalir Thittam were identified as being the inadequate coverage of SHGs in the state and the inability of the SHGs to 'graduate' to micro-enterprises and make sustainable livelihood improvements. Consequently, the project emphasised forming women's SHGs among the 'excluded poor', financing and promoting SHG members' livelihood initiatives and strengthening Panchayat Level Federations (PLFs) of the groups. A Village Poverty Reduction Committee (VPRC), the primary community-based organisation that implements and monitors the projects at village levels, is assigned a minimum corpus fund (of Rs 600,000) to assist the SHGs in the panchayat initiate economic activities (ibid. 5–7).

It is evident that the World Bank–financed PVP has created a new set of institutional actors in the microfinance landscape in Tamil Nadu. In the project blocks, the SHGs have to contend with project staff, the VPRCs formed and fostered by the project and the PLFs, vested with the function of liaising between the SHGs and external agencies. The PLFs have been empowered to act as financial intermediaries that source project funds as well as financial assistance from NABARD and commercial banks and make these available to their constituent SHGs. A question that emerges in this context is whether the apportioning of bank-sourced and other loanable resources through these federations, constituted by SHGs of the socially oppressed and the dominant castes, will reflect and re-constitute caste hierarchies and discriminations and if this may not further erode the 'pro-poor' and the pro-poorest orientation that the PVP seeks to impart to the SHG programme in the state. The project also claims to have addressed the inconsistent quality of support that SHGs receive by creating over 3,000 SHG trainers belonging to local communities (GOTN 2009: 160). In Chapter 4, I had described the great difficulties the SHGs faced in accessing the social intermediation services that promoter agencies were required to provide, despite the presence of multiple agencies often competing with each other to seek association with women's SHGs. It remains to be seen how the community trainers identified by Pudhu Vaazhvu might fill the void in support services that SHG women face and if they do so effectively enough to mitigate the hostilities and suspicions between group members and leaders that have flourished in the absence of external support.

At the national level, the National Rural Livelihoods Mission (NRLM) formally launched on 3 June 2011, with the goal of reaching 70 million rural poor households across 600 districts, 6,000 blocks and 600,000 villages, (re)-constitutes SHGs as central components of a national agenda of livelihoods promotion and rural poverty reduction.[14] Drawing on the Report of the Committee on Credit-Related Issues under the SGSY (chaired by R. Radhakrishna), the central government restructured the SGSY as the NRLM. The committee criticised the scheme's singular, exclusive focus on self-employment as a means of poverty reduction and pointed out that this approach would miss a large proportion of poor households (GOI 2009). Building on this conceptual shift, the NRLM acknowledges that multiple livelihoods currently sustain households living below the poverty line and proposes a comprehensive package of support to the entire portfolio of livelihoods of the targeted populations that include agriculture, livestock, fisheries and forest produce, besides micro-enterprises.

The NRLM aims to bring a woman from each identified rural poor household under the SHG network, which is promoted as a key feature of the universal social mobilisation strategy the Mission espouses (GOI n.d. 3). Rather than expecting the SHGs to choose from a predetermined list of income-generation activities (the SGSY approach), the NRLM anticipates that SHGs will draw up household investment plans (that may include both livelihood and other essential needs) that are aggregated to form SHG-level investment plans. Financial assistance that enables households to smooth consumption and finance food and health-related needs are accommodated by the NRLM by way of support to the goal of vulnerability reduction (ibid.). Evidently then, the NRLM aims to strengthen the safety-net function of SHG-based microfinance so that it might effectively address the goals of risk mitigation and vulnerability reduction that the dominant microfinance discourse has espoused in recent years. The NRLM, as well as the anti-poverty interventions of the state governments briefly discussed here, also seeks to supplement the financial and other resources provided to the SHGs so that they may assist the income-generation endeavours of their members, thereby making a dent in the income-poverty of rural households as well.

It is hardly surprising then that the provision of microfinance to rural households has come to be regarded by India's policymakers as a key developmental tool targeted to the dangerous classes (Chatterjee 2008a) in the hope that it will combat 'left wing extremism' in 'Naxal-affected' districts in the country. In his budget speech delivered to Parliament on 16 March 2012, the then finance minister Pranab Mukherjee announced that subsidised credit at concessional interest rates would be provided (via women's SHGs) on priority basis to 150 economically backward districts in the country, including all those affected by left wing extremism (Budget 2012–13). This resolve was reiterated by NABARD, which plans to accelerate the formation of women's SHGs and intensify bank lending to the groups over a five-year period (2013–17) in the targeted 150 districts (NABARD 2013: 5). In the budget speech delivered to the 16th (and current) Lok Sabha on 10 July 2014, Finance Minister Arun Jaitley announced that bank lending at low interest (annual 4% rates) to women's SHGs, already in place in 150 backward districts, would be extended to a 100 more (Livemint 2014).

It appears therefore that the agenda of responsibilising rural women via microfinance for the alleviation of household poverty of low-income and land-poor communities and classes is here to stay. As I have argued in this book, the SHG women and their households are subject to a statist agenda of financial governance that seeks to bring them in line with mainstream financial practices and constitutes them as disciplined neo-liberal subjects in particular ways. Nonetheless, the women resist those elements of neo-liberal governmental rationalities that conflict with the survival imperatives of their households. The question, therefore, of what forms of counter-mobilisations, subversions and challenges will emerge at microfinance project interfaces cannot be known in advance and opens up multiple and fascinating lines of enquiry. What new strategies will women devise to wrest development resources from the state, even while they may (or may not) fully or partially reform their conduct and fashion themselves in keeping with policy expectations? What other claims upon the state (besides microcredit) will women SHG members advance? Will women's struggles 'in and against the state' (Rai 2008: 56) as they play out in the evolving terrain of SHG-based microfinance challenge entrenched patriarchies or perhaps even halt neo-liberal advances in social policies? Corbridge *et al.* (2011) ask whether the 'tenuous equilibrium' that Chatterjee (2008a) describes between the full-fledged sway of capital, on the one hand, and governmental efforts to temper and contain it, on the other, can be sustained in neo-liberal India or if it will be replaced by a volatile and violent disequilibrium in the years to come. Perhaps one of the many ways to seek answers to this might be to attend closely to the new sites opened up by development interventions that solicit the participation of women living in poverty and harness their collective energies and to bear witness to the multiple contestations they generate.

Notes

1 AIDWA was founded in 1981 as a national-level mass organisation committed to achieving democracy, equality and women's emancipation. It has an organisational presence in 22 states in India and a current membership of more than 9 million. Two-thirds of its strength is derived from poor rural and urban women. The AIDWA has frequently intervened in policy debates on microfinance (aidwaonline.org).

2 This was certainly the case for a period of nearly two decades starting from the inception of SHG-banking (early 1990s). More recent developments (since 2010) indicate that defaults on bank loans to SHGs have been on the increase. This is discussed subsequently.

3 The DPIP was studied in Adilabad, Anantapur and Srikakulam districts, while the RPRP was studied in Kadapa, Nalgonda, Nellore, Visakhapatnam and Warangal districts. The eight districts covered all the macro-regions of Andhra Pradesh.
4 This was renamed Erode district in 1996.
5 The bill lapsed when the term of the 14th Lok Sabha expired in 2009. A Micro Finance Institutions (Development and Regulations) Bill, which was introduced in June 2011 in Parliament, was re-drafted and laid in the Rajya Sabha on 13 February 2014 and presented to the Lok Sabha on 17 February 2014 (India Microfinance n.d.).
6 Some of the participating organisations included AIDWA, Bharat Gyan Vigyan Samiti, MALAR federation of SHGs (Tamil Nadu), AVARD (Bihar), Procheshta (Assam), Nirantar, Center for Women's Development Studies, Joint Women's Programme and the Young Women's Christian Association.
7 Concessional interest rates are also extended to women's SHGs active in 150 designated 'economically backward' districts in the country. The National Rural Livelihoods Mission (NRLM) mandates that women's SHGs in these districts avail bank loans at effective interest rates of 4% (NRLM 2013–14).
8 This was discussed at length in Chapter 1.
9 The Uttar Pradesh (UP) study covered a representative sample of high and low NPA districts within all the major regions of the state. The four districts included in the UP study were Hamirpur, Hardoi, Gorakhpur and Bareilly. The Odisha study included one district (Jajpur). The majority of the groups surveyed in these regions were formed as part of the SGSY scheme.
10 The banks were also advised to permit those SHG members, who may require larger loans to initiate or expand enterprise activities, to form Joint Liability Groups (JLGs) within the SHGs.
11 This was discussed at length in Chapter 2.
12 The World Bank supported the APDPIP from August 2000 to December 2006 and the APRPRP from May 2003 to September 2011. During the project period, the APRPRP claims to have reached 11.3 million households in (the then unbifurcated) Andhra Pradesh by forming one million SHGs. Details on both the projects are available in the World Bank (2015).
13 All details regarding the vision and strategy of the project are taken from the Project Implementation Plan of Vazhndhu Kaatuvom (the older name of the Pudhu Vaazvhu scheme) (GOTN 2007).
14 The Mission set up support units at the national, state, district and sub-district levels. State Rural Livelihood Missions at the state levels monitor the implementation of all NRLM activities in the states.

Annexure

SHG-wise data by village

Table A.1 SHGs in Karisal village, 2005–6

Serial number	*SHG name*	*Age (in years)*	*Caste composition*	*Promoter agency*	*Direct linkage loan (Rs)*	*SGSY loan-cum-subsidy (Rs)*
1	Pavalam	6.4	SC	INGO	–	100,000
2	Pushpam	6.5	15 SC and 4 OBC	INGO	–	200,000
3	Alamelu	6.5	SC	INGO	–	100,000
4	Annai Meenakshi	6.2	11 SC and 9 OBC	INGO	–	150,000
5	Jeyam	5.3	SC	INGO	–	200,000
6	Vennila	3.3	OBC	INGO	–	–
7	Tamarai	3.3	OBC	INGO	–	–
8	Sembaruthi	3.2	OBC	INGO	–	–
9	Vanavil	3	SC	BDO	–	–
10	Mullai	3	SC	BDO	–	–

Source: Fieldwork by author.

Table A.2 SHGs in Prakasam village, 2005–6

Serial number	*SHG name*	*Age (in years)*	*Caste composition*	*Promoter agency*	*Direct linkage loan (Rs)*	*SGSY loan-cum-subsidy (Rs)*
1	Roja	4.6	SC	Mahalir Thittam	–	100,000
2	Vaigai	4.4	SC	Mahalir Thittam	–	100,000
3	Ponni	4.4	SC	Mahalir Thittam	–	–
4	Ganga	3.4	OBC	Mahalir Thittam	–	100,000
5	Kaveri	4.8	OBC	Mahalir Thittam	–	100,000
6	Annai Parasakthi	3.1	SC	Mahalir Thittam	–	100,000
7	Annai Janaki	3.1	SC	Mahalir Thittam	–	100,000
8	Thangam	3.3	SC	BDO	–	–

Source: Fieldwork by author.

Table A.3 SHGs in Nalloor village, 2005–6

Serial number	*SHG name*	*Age (in years)*	*Caste composition*	*Promoter agency*	*Direct linkage loan (Rs)*	*SGSY loan-cum-subsidy (Rs)*
1	Magudam	7.2	SC	Bank	40,000	–
2	Bharathi	4.5	SC	Bank	80,000	–
3	Annai Indira	4.4	SC	Bank	110,000	–
4	Ilam Pirai	4.3	SC	Bank	150,000	–
5	Mangalam	4.3	OBC	Bank	200,000	300,000*
6	Nelmani	3.8	OBC	Bank	200,000	300,000*
7	Then-Koodu	3.8	OBC	Bank	200,000	50,000
8	Vetri Magalir	3.7	OBC	Bank	200,000	–
9	Tazampoo	3.4	OBC	Bank	200,000	50,000

* The loan was sanctioned but not disbursed to Mangalam SHG and Nelmani SHG during the period of the study.

Source: Fieldwork by author.

Bibliography

Adams, Dale W. and Robert C. Vogel. 1986. 'Rural Financial Markets in Low-Income Countries: Recent Controversies and Lessons', *World Development*, 14 (4): 477–487.

Agnihotri, Indu and Vina Mazumdar. 1995. 'Changing Terms of Political Discourse: Women's Movement in India, 1970s–1990s', *Economic and Political Weekly*, 30 (29): 1869–1878.

Aitken, Rob. 2010. 'Ambiguous Incorporations: Microfinance and Global Governmentality', *Global Networks*, 10 (2): 223–243.

Aji, Sowmya. 2014. 'Activists Condemn Maneka Gandhi's Move to Scrap Women's Self Help Groups Scheme', *The Economic Times*, 12 December.

All India Democratic Women's Association (AIDWA). 2007a. 'On Joint National Convention on Micro-Finance Bill', 15 May, http://aidwaonline.org/issues_of_concern/joint-national-convention-micro-finance-bill (accessed on 20 December 2015).

———. 2007b. 'Memorandum to Parliamentary Standing Committee on Micro Finance Sector (Development and Regulation) Bill', 31 July, http://aidwaonline.org/issues_of_concern/memorandum-parliamentary-standing-committee-micro-finance-sector-development-and-r (accessed on 20 December 2015).

———. 2010. 'Memorandum on Regulation of Micro Finance Institutions', 22 October, http://aidwaonline.org/issues_of_concern/memorandum-regulation micro finance institutions (accessed on 20 December 2015).

Anand, Jaya S. 2002. 'Self-Help Groups in Empowering Women: Case Study of Selected SHGs and NHGs', *Discussion Paper No. 38*, Kerala Research Programme on Local Level Development, Thiruvananthapuram: Centre for Development Studies.

Ananth, Bindu. 2004. 'Financing Micro Finance – The ICICI Bank Partnership Model', *Working Paper Series, Social Initiatives Group*, Mumbai: ICICI.

Andhra Pradesh Mahila Abhivruddhi Samiti (APMAS). 2007. *Self Help Group-Bank Linkage Programme: A Recurrent Study in Andhra Pradesh*. Hyderabad: APMAS.

———. 2009a. 'Quality and Sustainability of SHGs in Assam', Sponsored by NABARD, Hyderabad: APMAS.

———. 2009b. 'Suggestions for National Rural Livelihood Mission: A Review of SGSY', Prepared by National Network of Resource Organisations (NNRO), Hyderabad: APMAS.

Andhra Pradesh Mahila Abhivruddhi Samiti (Mahila Abhivruddhi Society, Andhra Pradesh) and Centre for Micro Finance (CMF). 2006. *Quality Issues in the Microfinance Sector in Rajasthan*. Hyderabad: APMAS and Jaipur: CMF.

Arun, M.A. 2010. 'Banks Drive Self Help Groups into Microfinance Debt Trap', *Deccan Herald*, 18 December.

Bajaj, Vikas. 2011. 'Microlenders, Honored with Nobel, Are Struggling', *The New York Times*, 6 January.

Banerjee, N. and Joyanti Sen. 2003. *The Swarnajayanti Gram Swarozgar Yojana: A Policy in Working*. Kolkata: Sachetana, http://www.idrc.ca/uploads/user-S/11138471151Swarnajayanti__Gram_Swarozgar_Yojana.pdf (accessed on 20 December 2015).

Batliwala, Srilatha and Deepa Dhanraj. 2007. 'Gender Myths That Instrumentalize Women: A View from the Indian Frontline', in Andrea Cornwall, Elizabeth Harrison and Ann Whitehead (eds.), *Feminisms in Development: Contradictions, Contestations and Challenges*, pp. 21–34, London and New York: Zed Books.

Bhende, M.J. 1986. 'Credit Markets in Rural South India', *Economic and Political Weekly*, 21 (39): A119–A124.

Budget. 2012–13. 'Speech of Pranab Mukherjee, Minister of Finance', 16 March 2012, http://indiabudget.nic.in/ub2012-13/bs/bs.pdf (accessed on 20 December 2015).

Buncombe, Andrew. 2011. 'Suicides and Pressure Tactics Tarnish Image of Micro-Finance Lending', *The Independent*, Sunday, 23 October.

Burchell, G. 1996. 'Liberal Government and Techniques of the Self', in Andrew Barry, Thomas Osborne and Nikolas Rose (eds.), *Foucault and Political Reason: Liberalism, Neo-Liberalism and Rationalities of Government*, pp. 19–36, Chicago: The University of Chicago Press.

Byres, T.J. 1998. 'Introduction: Development Planning and the Interventionist State versus Liberalisation and the Neo-Liberal State, India 1989–1996', in Terence J. Byres (ed.), *The State, Development Planning and Liberalisation in India*, pp. 1–35, New Delhi: Oxford University Press.

Chakravarti, Uma. 2008. 'Beyond the Mantra of Empowerment: Time to Return to Poverty, Violence and Struggle', *IDS Bulletin*, 39 (6): 10–17.

Chatterjee, Partha. 1998. 'Development Planning and the Indian State', in Terence J. Byres (ed.), *The State, Development Planning and Liberalisation in India*, pp. 82–103, New Delhi: Oxford University Press.

———. 2004. *Politics of the Governed: Reflections on Popular Politics in Most of the World*. New Delhi: Permanent Black.

———. 2008a. 'Democracy and Economic Transformation in India', *Economic and Political Weekly*, 43 (16): 53–62.

———. 2008b. 'Classes, Capital and Indian Democracy', *Economic and Political Weekly*, 43 (46): 89–93.

———. 2012. 'The Debate over Political Society', in Ajay Gudavarthy (ed.), *Re-Framing Democracy and Agency in India: Interrogating Political Society*, pp. 305–322, London; New York; New Delhi: Anthem Press.

Chaudhuri, S. 2006. 'What Difference Does a Constitutional Amendment Make? The 1994 Panchayati Raj Act and the Attempt to Revitalize Rural Local Government in India', in Pranab Bardhan and Dilip Mookherjee (eds.), *Decentralization and Local Governance in Developing Countries: A Comparative Perspective*, pp. 153–202, Cambridge, Massachusetts: MIT Press.

Cheston, S. and L. Kuhn. 2002. 'Empowering Women through Microfinance', Paper Commissioned by the *Micro Credit Summit Campaign + 5*, New York, 10–13 November. Published by UNIFEM, http://www.seepnetwork.org/filebin/pdf/gender/71_Empowering_Women_Through_Microfinance.pdf (accessed on 20 December 2015).

Chintala, G.R. and Gyanendra Mani. 2009. 'Is Convergence of SHGs and SGSY Approaches of Lending a Necessary Condition for the Growth of Microfinance Sector in India?' *The Microfinance Review, Journal of the Centre for Microfinance Research*, January–June, 1 (1): 121–130.

Consultative Group to Assist the Poorest (CGAP). 2003. *CGAP Phase III Strategy 2003–2008*. Washington, DC: The World Bank, http://pdf.usaid.gov/pdf_docs/Pnacs770.pdf (accessed on 20 December 2015).

———. 2004. 'Helping to Improve Donor Effectiveness in Microfinance', *Donor Brief No. 19*, June, Washington, DC: The World Bank, http://www.cgap.org/sites/default/files/CGAP-Donor-Brief-The-Role-of-Governments-in-Microfinance-Jun-2004.pdf (accessed on 20 December 2015).

———. 2007. 'Sustainability of Self-Help Groups in India: Two Analyses', *Occasional Paper No. 12*. August, https://www.cgap.org/sites/default/files/CGAP-Occasional-Paper-Sustainability-of-Self-Help-Groups-in-India-Two-Analyses-Aug-2007.pdf (accessed on 20 December 2015).

———. n.d. 'About CGAP', http://www.cgap.org/about (accessed on 20 December 2015).

Cooke, Bill and Uma Kothari. 2001. 'The Case for Participation as Tyranny', in Bill Cooke and Uma Kothari (eds.), *Participation: The New Tyranny*, pp. 1–15, London: Zed Books.

Corbridge, Stuart. 2007. 'The (Im)possibility of Development Studies', *Economy and Society*, 36 (2): 179–211.

Corbridge, Stuart, J. Harriss, S. Ruparelia and S. Reddy. 2011. 'Introduction: India's Transforming Political Economy', in Sanjay Ruparelia, Sanjay Reddy, John Harriss and Stuart Corbridge (eds.), *Understanding India's New Political Economy: A Great Transformation?*, pp. 1–16, London and New York: Routledge.

Corbridge, Stuart, Glyn Williams, Manoj Srivastava and Rene Veron. 2005. *Seeing the State: Governance and Governmentality in India*. Cambridge, UK: Cambridge University Press.

Cruikshank, B. 1999. *The Will to Empower: Democratic Citizens and Other Subjects*. Ithaca and London: Cornell University Press.

Dadhich, C.L. 2001. 'Micro Finance – A Panacea for Poverty Alleviation: A Case Study of Oriental Grameen Project in India', *Indian Journal of Agricultural Economics*, 56 (3): 419–426.

Dasgupta, Rajaram. 2001. 'An Informal Journey through Self-Help Groups', *Indian Journal of Agricultural Economics*, 56 (3): 370–386.

———. 2009. 'SGSY: Need for a Paradigm Shift', *Economic and Political Weekly*, 44 (43): 21–23.

Deininger, Klaus and Yanyan Liu. 2013. 'Economic and Social Impacts of an Innovative Self-Help Group Model in India', *World Development*, 43: 149–163.

Devika, J. and Binitha V. Thampi. 2007. 'Between "Empowerment" and "Liberation": The Kudumbashree Initiative in Kerala', *Indian Journal of Gender Studies*, 14 (1): 33–60.

Dreze, J. 1990. 'Poverty in India and the IRDP Delusion', *Economic and Political Weekly*, 29 September, A-95–A-103.

Dwivedi, A. 2007. *Examining Literacy and Power within Self Help Groups: A Quantitative Study*. Special Inputs: Jaya Sharma and Soma K. Parthasarathy. New Delhi: Nirantar.

EDA. 2005. *The Maturing of Indian Microfinance: Findings and Policy Implications from a National Study*. Gurgaon, India: EDA Rural Systems Private Ltd.

EDA and APMAS. 2006. *Self-Help Groups in India: A Study of the Lights and Shades*. Gurgaon and Hyderabad: EDA Rural Systems Private Ltd. and Andhra Pradesh Mahila Abhivruddhi Society.

EPW Editorial. 2000. 'Bank Credit: Eroding Priority', *Economic and Political Weekly*, 18 November, 35 (47): 4071–4072.

EPW Research Foundation (EPWRF). 2005. 'Metamorphic Changes in the Financial System', Special Statistics – 38, *Economic and Political Weekly*, 19 March, 40 (12): 1264–1266.

Fernandez, Aloysius P. 2000. 'Is Micro Credit Heading towards a Macro Mess?' *Sa-Dhan Newsletter*, Special Issue on Policy and Regulatory Issues in Micro-Finance, 1 (1): March.

———. 2002. *Impact of Self Help Groups (Group Processes) on the Social/Empowerment Status of Women Members in South India*. Mumbai: NABARD.

———. 2009. 'Is Microfinance Leading to a Macro Mess?' Paper 55, MYRADA Rural Management Systems Series, http://myrada.org/myrada/rms55 (accessed on 20 December 2015).

Fernando, Jude L. 2006. 'Introduction: Microcredit and Empowerment of Women: Blurring the Boundary between Development and Capitalism', in Jude L. Fernando (ed.), *Microfinance: Perils and Prospects*, pp. 1–42, London and New York: Routledge.

Foucault, Michel. 1993. 'About the Beginning of the Hermeneutics of the Self: Two Lectures at Dartmouth', ed. Mark Blasius, *Political Theory*, 21 (2): 198–227.

Gadenne, Lucie and Veena Vasudevan. 2007. 'How Do Women in Mature SHGs Save and Invest Their Money? Evidence from Self Help Groups in India', *Centre for Microfinance Working Paper Series*, Chennai: Institute for Financial Management and Research (IFMR).

Garikipati, S. 2008. 'The Impact of Lending to Women on Household Vulnerability and Women's Empowerment: Evidence from India', *World Development*, 36 (12): 2620–2642.

Ghate, Prabhu. 2006. *Microfinance in India: A State of the Sector Report, 2006*. New Delhi: Microfinance India.

Ghate, Prabhu, Evelinda Ballon and Virginia Manalo. 1996. 'Poverty Alleviation and Enterprise Development: The Need for a Differentiated Approach', *Journal of International Development*, 8 (2): 163–178.

Gonzalez-Vega, C. 2003. 'Deepening Rural Financial Markets: Macroeconomic, Policy and Political Dimensions', Lead Paper Presented at Conference on *Paving the Way Forward: An International Conference on Best Practices in Rural Finance*, Washington, DC, 2–4 June, http://citeseerx.ist.psu.edu/viewdoc/download?doi=10.1.1.519.8636&rep=rep1&type=pdf (accessed on 20 December 2015).

Government of Andhra Pradesh (GoAP). n.d. 'The Andhra Pradesh Micro Finance Institutions (Regulation of Money Lending) Rules 2010 – Orders – Issued', *G.O. Ms. No. 35*, http://apmfi.cgg.gov.in/downloads/2010PR_MS356.PDF (accessed on 20 December 2015).

Government of India (GOI). 2001a. *Annual Report 2000–2001*. Department of Women and Child Development, New Delhi: Ministry of Human Resource Development.

———. 2001b. *Report of the Working Group on Rural Poverty Alleviation Programmes for the Tenth Five Year Plan 2002–2007*. TFYP WG Report, No. 81/2001, Planning Commission, New Delhi: Ministry of Rural Development.

———. 2009. *Report of the Committee on Credit-Related Issues under the SGSY*. Department of Rural Development, Ministry of Rural Development.

———. n.d. 1. *National Rural Livelihoods Mission: Mission Document*. New Delhi: Ministry of Rural Development.

———. n.d. 2. *SwarnJayanti Gram Swarozgar Yojana Guidelines*. New Delhi: Ministry of Rural Development.

———. n.d. 3. *National Rural Livelihoods Mission: Framework for Implementation*. New Delhi: Ministry of Rural Development, http://rural.nic.in/sites/downloads/latest/NRLM_23122010.pdf (accessed on 20 December 2015).

Government of Orissa. 2008. 'Project Implementation Plan', Targeted Rural Initiatives for Poverty Termination and Infrastructure (TRIPTI),

Orissa Poverty Reduction Mission, Panchayati Raj Department, SIRD Campus, Bhubaneswar, Orissa.

Government of Tamil Nadu (GOTN). 2004. 'Speech of Thiru. C. Ponnaiyan, Minister for Finance and Food Presenting the Budget for 2004–2005 to the Legislative Assembly on 11th February 2004', *Budget 2004–2005*, Tamil Nadu Legislative Assembly, http://www.assembly.tn.gov.in/archive/Budget/2004-2005/Budget%20Speech%202004-05.htm (accessed on 20 December 2015).

———. 2006. 'Governor's Address in the Legislative Assembly on 24th May 2006', http://www.tnrd.gov.in/Announcement_pdf/governor_addr_May2006.pdf (accessed on 20 December 2015).

———. 2007. 'Project Implementation Plan', *Vazhndhu Kaatuvom – Tamil Nadu Empowerment and Poverty Reduction Project*, Department of Rural Development and Panchayat Raj, http://tnrd.gov.in/externallyaidedprojects/Vazhndhukattuvom/project%20implementation%20plan/chapter_draft.pdf (accessed on 20 December 2015).

———. 2009. 'Policy Note 2009–2010', Rural Development and Panchayat Raj Department, http://www.tnrd.gov.in/policynotes/policy_notes_2009_2010_en.pdf (accessed on 20 December 2015).

———. 2010. 'Policy Note 2010–2011', Rural Development and Panchayat Raj Department, http://www.tnrd.gov.in/policynotes/pr_eng_2010-2011.pdf (accessed on 20 December 2015).

———. n.d. 'Renovation of Integrated Sanitary Complex for Women', *Schemes: State Schemes*, Rural Development and Panchayat Raj Department, http://www.tnrd.gov.in/schemes/st_riscw.html (accessed on 20 December 2015).

Guerin, Isabelle, Santhosh Kumar and Isabelle Agier. 2013. 'Women's Empowerment: Power to Act or Power over Other Women? Lessons from Indian Microfinance', *Oxford Development Studies*, 41 (Supplement): S76–S94.

Guijt, I. and M.K. Shah. 1999. 'Waking Up to Power, Conflict and Process', in Irene Guijt and M.K. Shah (eds.), *The Myth of Community: Gender Issues in Participatory Development*, pp. 1–23, New Delhi: Vistaar Publications.

Gupta, Akhil. 2006. 'Blurred Boundaries: The Discourse of Corruption', in Aradhana Sharma and Akhil Gupta (eds.), *The Anthropology of the State: A Reader*, pp. 211–242, Malden, Massachusetts; Oxford, UK; Victoria, Australia: Blackwell Publishing Ltd.

Gupta, Akhil and Aradhana Sharma. 2006. 'Globalization and Postcolonial States', *Current Anthropology*, 47 (2): 277–307.

Gupta, Akhil and K. Sivaramakrishnan. 2011. 'Introduction: The State in India after Liberalization', in Akhil Gupta and K. Sivaramakrishnan (eds.), *The State in India after Liberalization: Interdisciplinary Perspectives*, pp. 1–27, London and New York: Routledge.

Harper, Malcolm. 2002a. 'Self-Help Groups and Grameen Bank Groups: What Are the Differences?', in Thomas Fisher and M.S. Sriram (eds.), *Beyond Micro-Credit: Putting Development Back into Micro-Finance*, pp. 169–198, New Delhi: Vistaar Publications; Oxford, UK: Oxfam; and London: New Economics Foundation.

———. 2002b. *Promotion of Self Help Groups under the SHG Bank Linkage Program in India*. Mumbai: Micro Credit Innovations Department, NABARD.

Harriss, John. 2011. 'How Far Have India's Economic Reforms Been "Guided by Compassion and Justice"? Social Policy in the Neoliberal Era', in Sanjay Ruparelia, Sanjay Reddy, John Harriss and Stuart Corbridge (eds.), *Understanding India's New Political Economy: A Great Transformation?*, pp. 127–139, London and New York: Routledge.

Harvey, David. 2003. *The New Imperialism*. Oxford: Oxford University Press.

The Hindu. 2005. 'Your Victory Is My Victory, Jayalalithaa Tells SHG Members', Friday, 26 August, Online Edition, http://www.thehindu.com/2005/08/26/stories/2005082604990400.htm (accessed on 20 December 2015).

———. 2011. 'MFIs New-Age Moneylenders, Says Brinda Karat', 1 November, Mumbai.

———. 2014. 'Karunanidhi Opposes Move to Scrap Women SHGs', 17 December, Chennai.

Holvoet, Nathalie. 2005. 'The Impact of Microfinance on Decision-Making Agency: Evidence from South India', *Development and Change*, 36 (1): 75–102.

Hornak, Leo. 2011. 'Why the Dream of Microfinance Is Turning Sour', *The Independent*, Sunday, 23 October.

Hulme, David and Paul Mosley. 1996. *Finance against Poverty: Volume 1*. London and New York: Routledge.

IFAD. n.d. 'Completion Evaluation', *India: Tamil Nadu Women's Development Project*, http://www.ifad.org/evaluation/public_html/eksyst/doc/prj/region/pi/india/r240ince.htm (accessed on 20 December 2015).

India Microfinance. n.d. 'Microfinance Institutions (Development and Regulations) Bill – 2012', http://indiamicrofinance.com/microfinance-bill-2012-2013-2014-pdf.html (accessed on 20 December 2015).

Jackson, Cecile. 1996. 'Rescuing Gender from the Poverty Trap', *World Development*, 24 (3): 489–504.

———. 1997. 'Actor Orientation and Gender Relations at a Participatory Project Interface', in Anne Marie Goetz (ed.), *Getting Institutions Right for Women in Development*, pp. 161–175, London and New York: Zed Books.

Jeevika. n.d. 'Highlights', *Programmes: Institution and Capacity Building*, Bihar Rural Livelihoods Promotion Society, State Rural Livelihoods

Mission (SRLM), Bihar, http://223.30.251.85:8090/web/brlp/home;jsessionid=E0BEE76A1EE6082E84A94C8F33F0E994 (accessed on 20 December 2015).

John, Mary E. 1996. 'Gender and Development in India, 1970s–1990s: Some Reflections on the Constitutive Role of Contexts', *Economic and Political Weekly*, 31 (47): 3071–3077.

John, Mary E. and Satish Deshpande. 2008. 'Theorising the Present: Problems and Possibilities', *Economic and Political Weekly*, 43 (46): 83–86.

Johnson, Susan and Ben Rogaly. 1997. *Microfinance and Poverty Reduction*. Oxford: Oxfam (UK and Ireland); and London: ACTIONAID.

Jones, H., M. Williams, Y. Thorat and A. Thorat. 2003. 'Attitudes of Rural Branch Managers in Madhya Pradesh, India, toward Their Role as Providers of Financial Services to the Poor', *Journal of Microfinance*, 5 (2): 140–167.

Joshi, Anuradha and Mick Moore. 2004. 'Institutionalized Co-Production: Unorthodox Public Service Delivery in Challenging Environments', *Journal of Development Studies*, 40 (4): 31–49.

Kabeer, Naila. 1995. *Reversed Realities: Gender Hierarchies in Development Thought*. New Delhi: Kali for Women.

———. 2005. 'Is Microfinance a "Magic Bullet" for Women's Empowerment?' *Economic and Political Weekly*, 40 (44–45): 4709–4718.

Kabeer, Naila and Ranjani K. Murthy. 1996. 'Compensating for Institutional Exclusion? Lessons from Indian Government and Non-Government Credit Interventions for the Poor', *IDS Discussion Paper 356*, Brighton, UK: Institute of Development Studies.

Kalpana, K. 2005. 'Shifting Trajectories in Microfinance Discourse', *Economic and Political Weekly*, 40 (51): 5400–5409.

———. 2008. 'The Vulnerability of "Self-Help": Women and Microfinance in South India', *IDS Working Paper 303*, Brighton, UK: Institute of Development Studies.

Karides, Marina. 2010. 'Theorizing the Rise of Microenterprise Development in Caribbean Context', *Journal of World Systems Research*, 16 (2): 192–216.

Karim, Lamia. 2011. *Microfinance and Its Discontents: Women in Debt in Bangladesh*. Minneapolis: University of Minnesota Press.

Knowledge@Wharton. 2006. 'ICICI's K.V. Kamath Shapes a Business Plan in Rural India's Uncertain Financial Terrain', 26 July, Wharton: University of Pennsylvania, http://knowledge.wharton.upenn.edu/article/icicis-k-v-kamath-shapes-a-business-plan-in-rural-indias-uncertain-financial-terrain/ (accessed on 20 December 2015).

Kohli, Renu. 1997. 'Directed Credit and Financial Reform', *Economic and Political Weekly*, 32 (42): 2667–2676.

Krishna, Mamata. 2000. 'Documenting the Experiences of MYRADA's Self Help Groups in Holalkere Taluk, Chitradurga District', Paper Presented at the Asian Regional Conference Jointly Organized by INASIA and CDF on *The Potential and Limitations of Economic Initiatives in Grassroots Development – Current Issues and Asian Experiences*, BRAC Centre for Development Management, Rajendrapur, Bangladesh, 27–30 November.

Kropp, E.W. and B.S. Suran. 2002. *Linking Banks and (Financial) Self Help Groups in India – An Assessment.* Mumbai: Micro Credit Innovations Department, NABARD.

Kudva, Neema. 2005. 'Strong States, Strong NGOs', in Raka Ray and Mary Fainsod Katzenstein (eds.), *Social Movements in India: Poverty, Power and Politics*, pp. 233–265, Lanham, Maryland: Rowman and Littlefield Publishers.

Kumar, S. Nagesh. 2006. 'The Makings of a Debt Trap in Andhra Pradesh', *The Hindu*, 20 April.

Lemke, Thomas. 2001. '"The Birth of Bio-Politics": Michel Foucault's Lecture at the College de France on Neo-Liberal Governmentality', *Economy and Society*, 30 (2): 190–207.

Livemint. 2014. 'Union Budget 2014: Finance Minister Arun Jaitley's Full Speech', 10 July 2014, http://www.livemint.com/Politics/n2CKOUxRPwNprqgu2StUlL/Union-Budget-2014-Finance-minister-Arun-Jaitley-full-speech.html (accessed on 20 December 2015).

Mahalir, Thittam. n.d. *Mahalir Thittam Kuzhu Kaiyedu (Mahalir Thittam Group Handbook).* Chennai: Tamil Nadu Women's Development Corporation.

Malhotra, Rakesh. 2000. 'SwarnJayanti Gram Swarozgar Yojana: Improvisation in Anti-Poverty Programmes', in Sawalia Bihari Verma and Dinesh Kumar Verma (eds.), *Strategy for Promoting Rural Infrastructure*, Jaipur: Pointer Publishers.

Marr, Ana. 2003. 'A Challenge to the Orthodoxy Concerning Microfinance and Poverty Reduction', *Journal of Microfinance*, 5 (2): 7–42.

Mathur, Kuldeep. 1996. 'Designing Poverty Alleviation Programmes: International Agencies and Indian Politics', in Kuldeep Mathur (ed.), *Development Policy and Administration, Volume 1, Readings in Indian Government and Politics Series*, pp. 178–199, New Delhi; Thousand Oaks: Sage Publications.

Mayoux, Linda. 1989. 'Income Generation for Women in India: Problems and Prospects', *Development Policy Review*, 7 (1): 5 28.

———. 1998. 'Microfinance Programmes and Women's Empowerment: Approaches, Issues and Ways Forward', *DPP Working Paper No. 41*, Milton Keynes: The Open University.

———. 2002. 'Women's Empowerment or Feminisation of Debt? Towards a New Agenda in African Microfinance', Report Based on a *One World Action Conference*, London, March 2002, https://static1.squarespace.com/static/536c4ee8e4b0b60bc6ca7c74/t/543810e2e4b06169c234b37d/1412960482860/49.Womens+Empowerment+or+Feminisation+of+Debt.pdf (accessed on 20 December 2015).

Menon, Parvathi. 2010. 'Need to Regulate Microfinance Institutions: AIDWA', *The Hindu*, 12 November, Kanpur.

The Microcredit Summit. 1997. 'The Microcredit Summit Report', http://www.microcreditsummit.org/uploads/resource/document/1997_summit_report_full_42681.pdf (accessed on 9 April 2016).

Microcredit Summit Campaign. n.d. 'Women Clients Reached', *Mapping Pathways Out of Poverty: The State of the Microcredit Summit Campaign Report 2015*, http://stateofthecampaign.org/2015/12/15/2015-report-women-clients-reached/ (accessed on 20 December 2015).

Miller, Peter and Nikolas Rose. 1990. 'Governing Economic Life', *Economy and Society*, 19 (1): 1–31.

Mishra, I. 2000. 'Experience Sharing on the Performance of Rashtriya Mahila Kosh,' in Kishanjit Basu and Krishan Jindal (eds.), *Microfinance: Emerging Challenges*, pp. 325–334, New Delhi: Tata McGraw-Hill Publishing Company Limited.

Mohanty, Chandra T. 1991. 'Under Western Eyes: Feminist Scholarship and Colonial Discourses', in Chandra Talpade Mohanty, Ann Russo and Lourdes Torres (eds.), *Third World Women and the Politics of Feminism*, pp. 51–80, Bloomington: Indiana University Press.

Molyneux, Maxine. 2002. 'Gender and the Silences of Social Capital: Lessons from Latin America', *Development and Change*, 33 (2): 167–188.

Mooij, Jos and Mahendra S. Dev. 2002. 'Social Sector Priorities: An Analysis of Budgets and Expenditures in India in the 1990s', *IDS Working Paper 164*, Brighton, UK: Institute of Development Studies.

Morduch, Jonathan. 2000. 'The Microfinance Schism', *World Development*, 28 (4): 617–629.

Moser, Caroline O.N. 1993. *Gender Planning and Development: Theory, Practice and Training*. London and New York: Routledge.

Mosse, David. 2004. 'Is Good Policy Unimplementable? Reflections on the Ethnography of Aid Policy and Practice', *Development and Change*, 35 (4): 639–671.

Mujumdar, N. A. 1999. Reviving Rural Credit, *Economic and Political Weekly*, 34 (25): 1577–1579.

Murari, S. 2006. 'Tamil Nadu Women SHGs in Eye of a Storm', *Deccan Herald*, Saturday, 29 April.

Murray, Jessica and Richard Rosenberg. 2006. 'Community-Managed Loan Funds: Which Ones Work?', *Small Enterprise Development*, 17 (3): 13–27.

Murthy, Ranjani K., K. Raju and A. Kamath with Research Team. 2005. 'Towards Women's Empowerment and Poverty Reduction: Lessons from the Andhra Pradesh South Asia Poverty Alleviation Programme', in Neera Burra, Joy Deshmukh-Ranadive and Ranjani K. Murthy (eds.), *Micro-Credit, Poverty and Empowerment: Linking the Triad*, pp. 61–115, New Delhi; London; Thousand Oaks: Sage Publications.

Nair, Tara S. 2010. 'Commercial Microfinance and Social Responsibility: A Critique', *Economic and Political Weekly*, 45 (31): 32–37.

———. 2011. 'Microfinance: Lessons from a Crisis', *Economic and Political Weekly*, 46 (6): 23–26.

Nair, Tara S. and Ajay Tankha. 2014. *Microfinance India: State of the Sector Report 2013*. New Delhi: Sage Publications.

———. 2015. *Inclusive Finance India Report 2014*. New Delhi: Oxford University Press.

Narayana, D. 2000. 'Banking Sector Reforms and the Emerging Inequalities in Commercial Credit Deployment in India', *CDS Working Paper No. 300*, Thiruvananthapuram: Centre for Development Studies.

National Bank for Agriculture and Rural Development. 1992. *Guidelines for the Pilot Project for Linking Banks with Self Help Groups*, Circular dated 26 February, Development Policy Department, NABARD.

———. 1996. 'Project of Linking Self Help Groups with Banks', Circular dated 1 October, Development Policy Department, NABARD, www.sa-dhan.net/Adls/Microfinance/Circulars/ProjectoflinkingSHGs.doc (accessed on 20 December 2015).

———. 1999. 'Microfinance Scenario in the Country', *Task Force on Supportive Policy and Regulatory Framework for Microfinance, Report*, Mumbai: National Bank for Agriculture and Rural Development.

———. 2005. *Annual Report 2004–2005*. Mumbai: National Bank for Agriculture and Rural Development.

———. 2006. *Progress of SHG Bank Linkage in India 2005–06*. Mumbai: National Bank for Agriculture and Rural Development.

———. 2007. *Annual Report 2006–2007*. Mumbai: National Bank for Agriculture and Rural Development.

———. 2012. 'Revisiting the SHG Bank Linkage Programme', 27 March. Circular No: 65(A)/MCID-04/2011-12. Micro Credit Innovations Department. Mumbai: National Bank for Agriculture and Rural Development.

———. 2013. *Status of Microfinance in India 2012–2013*. Micro Credit Innovations Department. Mumbai: National Bank for Agriculture and Rural Development.

———. 2014. *Status of Microfinance in India 2013–2014*. Micro Credit Innovations Department. Mumbai: National Bank for Agriculture and Rural Development.

———. n.d. 1. *Banking with Self Help Groups: How and Why? A Handbook for Branch Level Bankers*. Mumbai: National Bank for Agriculture and Rural Development.

———. n.d. 2. *A Handbook on Forming Self Help Groups*. Mumbai: National Bank for Agriculture and Rural Development.

Nobelprize.org. 'The Nobel Peace Prize for 2006', http://www.nobelprize.org/nobel_prizes/peace/laureates/2006/press.html (accessed on 20 December 2015).

Ong, Aihwa. 2006. *Neoliberalism as Exception: Mutations in Citizenship and Sovereignty*. Durham and London: Duke University Press.

Outlook. 2007. 'The SHG Revolution: What Next?' Full Text of the Silver Jubilee Lecture at the *Society for the Promotion of Wastelands Development*, New Delhi, 5 May 2007, by the Minister of State for Commerce and Industry, Shri Jairam Ramesh, http://www.outlookindia.com/article/The-SHG-Revolution-What-Next/234592.

Pagura, Maria and Marie Kirsten. 2006. 'Formal-Informal Financial Linkages: Lessons from Developing Countries', *Small Enterprise Development*, 17 (1): 16–29.

Parthasarathy, S.K. 2005. 'Awareness, Access, Agency: Experiences of Swayam Shikshan Prayog in Microfinance and Women's Empowerment', in Neera Burra, Joy Deshmukh-Ranadive and Ranjani K. Murthy (eds.), *Micro-Credit, Poverty and Empowerment: Linking the Triad*, pp. 200–244, New Delhi; London; Thousand Oaks: Sage Publications.

Pathak, D.C and S.K. Pant. 2008. 'Microfinance: A Case Study of Jaunpur District', in Daniel Lazar and P. Palanichamy (eds.), *Microfinance and Poverty Eradication: Indian and Global Experiences*, pp. 469–491, New Delhi: New Century Publications.

Pattenden, J. 2010. 'A Neoliberalisation of Civil Society? Self-Help Groups and the Labouring Class Poor in Rural South India', *Journal of Peasant Studies*, 37 (3): 485–512.

People's Democracy. 2011. 'AIDWA's Appeal to RBI', VXXXV, No. 45, 6 November, archives.peoplesdemocracy.in/2011/1106_pd/11062011_15.html (accessed on 20 December 2015).

Pitt, Mark M. and Shahidur R. Khandker. 1998. 'The Impact of Group-Based Credit Programs on Poor Households in Bangladesh: Does the Gender of Participants Matter?', *Journal of Political Economy*,106 (5): 958–996.

Polanyi, Karl. 1957. *The Great Transformation: The Political and Economic Origins of Our Time*. Boston: Beacon Press.

Poonacha, V. 1996. 'Gendered Step: Review of Two Decades of Women's Movement and Women's Studies', *Economic and Political Weekly*, 29 (13): 725–728.

Prahalad, C.K. 2005. *The Fortune at the Bottom of the Pyramid: Eradicating Poverty through Profits*. Upper Saddle River, New Jersey: Prentice Hall.

Premchander, Smita with V. Prameela, M. Chidambaranathan and L. Jeyaseelan. 2009. *Multiple Meanings of Money: How Women See Microfinance*. New Delhi: Sage Publications.

Pringle, Rosemary and Sophie Watson. 1992. '"Women's Interests" and the Post-Structuralist State', in Michele Barrett and Anne Phillips (eds.), *Destabilizing Theory: Contemporary Feminist Debates*, pp. 53–73, Stanford, California: Stanford University Press.

PRS. n.d. 'Legislative Brief: The Micro Financial Sector (Development and Regulation) Bill', 2007, PRS Legislative Research, http://www.prsindia.org/uploads/media/1182418292/legis1182421756_Legislative_Brief_Micro_Finance_Bill_2007.pdf (accessed on 20 December 2015).

Pudhu Vaazvhu Project (PVP). n.d. 'Project Coverage', An Empowerment and Poverty Reduction Initiative of Government of Tamil Nadu, Rural Development and Panchayat Raj Department, http://www.pudhu vaazhvu.org/project-coverage.html (accessed on 20 December 2015).

Puhazhendi, V. and K.C. Badatya. 2002. *SHG-Bank Linkage Programme for Rural Poor: An Impact Assessment*. Mumbai: NABARD.

Puhazhendi, V. and B. Jayaraman. 1999. 'Increasing Women's Participation and Employment Generation among Rural Poor: An Approach through Informal Groups', *Indian Journal of Agricultural Economics*, 54 (3): 287–295.

Pulley, Robert V. 1989. 'Making the Poor Creditworthy: A Case Study of the Integrated Rural Development Program in India', *WDP 58, World Bank Discussion Papers*, Washington, DC: The World Bank.

Rahman, Aminur. 1999. 'Micro-Credit Initiatives for Equitable and Sustainable Development: Who Pays?', *World Development*, 27 (1): 67–82.

Rai, Shirin M. 2008. *The Gender Politics of Development*. New Delhi: Zubaan and London and New York: Zed Books.

Rajagopalan, Shashi. 2005. 'Micro-Credit and Women's Empowerment: The Lokadrusti Case', in Neera Burra, Joy Deshmukh-Ranadive and Ranjani K. Murthy (eds.), *Micro-Credit, Poverty and Empowerment: Linking the Triad*, pp. 200–244, New Delhi; Thousand Oaks; London: Sage Publications.

Rajasekhar, D. 2004. *Effects and Ramifications of Bank Interest Rates on SHG Members: A Study in Grama Vikas Project Area*. Decentralisation and Development Unit, Bangalore: Institute for Social and Economic Change.

Rajshekhar, M. 2010. 'Microfinance: What's Wrong with It', *The Economic Times*, 11 November.

Ramachandran, Vimala. 1996. *Critical Consciousness, Credit and Productive Assets: Key to Sustainable Livelihood*. New Delhi: UNICEF and Hyderabad: Commissioner Rural Development, Government of Andhra Pradesh, www.eruindia.org/files/Critical Consciousness-Credit-and Pro ductive-Assets1996.pdf (accessed on 20 December 2015).

Ramachandran, V. K. and Madhura Swaminathan. 2002. 'Rural Banking and Landless Labour Households: Institutional Reform and Rural Credit Markets in India', *Journal of Agrarian Change* 2(4): 502–544.

Rankin, K.N. 2001. 'Governing Development: Neoliberalism, Microcredit and Rational Economic Woman', *Economy and Society*, 30 (1): 18–37.

Rao, Smriti. 2008. 'Reforms with a Female Face: Gender, Liberalization and Economic Policy in Andhra Pradesh, India', *World Development*, 36 (7): 1213–1232.

Razavi, Shahra. 1997. 'Fitting Gender into Development Institutions', *World Development*, 25 (7): 1111–1125.

Razavi, Shahra and Carol Miller. 1995. 'From WID to GAD, Conceptual Shifts in the Women and Development Discourse', *Occasional Paper 1*,

United Nations Research Institute for Social Development, United Nations Development Programme.

Reddy, C.S. 2005. *A Study on SHG-Bank Linkage in Andhra Pradesh*. Hyderabad: Mahila Abhivruddhi Society (APMAS).

———. 2010. 'Will the Indian SHG Movement Withstand Competition from MFIs?', *CGAP, Advancing Financial Inclusion to Improve the Lives of the Poor*, http://www.cgap.org/blog/will-indian-shg-movement-withstand-competition-mfis (accessed on 20 December 2015).

Reddy, Ravi. 2006. 'MFI Suicides: 60 Suicide Cases Reported', *The Hindu*, 17 April.

Reserve Bank of India Bulletin. 1994. 'Banking with the Poor', Keynote address by Dr C. Rangarajan, Governor, RBI, at the Indian National Workshop for Bankers, Organised by the Foundation for Development Cooperation Limited, Australia, and Indian Banks' Association at Bombay on 31 January 1994 reported in the *RBI Bulletin*, February, Mumbai: Reserve Bank of India.

———. 1997. 'Role of Non-Governmental Organisations in Rural Credit Delivery System', Inaugural address by Dr C. Rangarajan, Governor, RBI, at the 35th Excom Meeting of APRACA at Bangalore on 28 October 1996 reported in the *RBI Bulletin*, January, Mumbai: Reserve Bank of India.

Reserve Bank of India. 2000. 'Micro Credit', 18 February, RPCD.No.PL.BC.62/04.09.01/99-2000, http://rbi.org.in/scripts/NotificationUser.aspx?Id=127&Mode=0 (accessed on 20 December 2015).

———. 2009. 'Master Circular on Micro Credit', 1 July, RBI/2009-10/40, http://rbidocs.rbi.org.in/rdocs/notification/PDFs/40MCMC010709_F.pdf (accessed on 20 December 2015).

———. 2011a. 'Master Circular on Priority Sector Lending – Special Programmes – SGSY', 1 July, RBI/2011-12/88, http://rbi.org.in/scripts/BS_ViewMasCirculardetails.aspx?Id=6557&Mode=0 (accessed on 20 December 2015).

———. 2011b. *Report of the Sub-Committee of the Central Board of Directors of Reserve Bank of India to Study Issues and Concerns in the MFI Sector*. Mumbai: Reserve Bank of India.

———. 2013. 'Master Circular – Priority Sector Lending – Targets and Classification', RBI/2013-14/107, 1 July, http://rbidocs.rbi.org.in/rdocs/notification/PDFs/107010713PSLFL.pdf (accessed on 20 December 2015).

Robinson, Marguerite S. 2001. *The Microfinance Revolution: Sustainable Finance for the Poor*. Washington, DC, and New York: The World Bank and Open Society Institute.

Rose, Nikolas. 1996. 'Governing "Advanced" Liberal Democracies', in A. Barry, T. Osborne and N. Rose (eds.), *Foucault and Political Reason: Liberalism, Neo-Liberalism and Rationalities of Government*, pp. 37–64, Chicago: The University of Chicago Press.

———. 1999. *The Powers of Freedom: Reframing Political Thought*. Cambridge: Cambridge University Press.

———. 2000. 'Government and Control', *British Journal of Criminology*, 40: 321–339.

Rose, N. and Peter Miller. 1992. 'Political Power beyond the State: Problematics of Government', *British Journal of Sociology*, 43 (2): 172–205.

Rutherford, Stuart. 2000. *The Poor and Their Money*. New Delhi: Oxford University Press.

Sangari, Kumkum. 2007. 'Shaping Pressures and Symbolic Horizons: The Women's Movement in India', in Neloufer De Mel and Selvy Thiruchandran (eds.), *At the Cutting Edge: Essays in Honour of Kumari Jayawardena*, pp. 36–67, New Delhi: Women Unlimited.

Sanyal, Paromita. 2009. 'From Credit to Collective Action: The Role of Microfinance in Promoting Women's Social Capital and Normative Influence', *American Sociological Review*, 74, August: 529–550.

Sarap, Kailas. 1991. *Interlinked Agrarian Markets in Rural India*. New Delhi: Sage Publications.

Sassen, Saskia. 2010. 'A Savage Sorting of Winners and Losers: Contemporary Versions of Primitive Accumulation', *Globalizations*, 7 (1–2): 23–50.

Satish, P. 2001. 'Institutional Alternatives for the Promotion of Microfinance Self Help Groups in India', *Journal of Microfinance*, 3 (2): 49–74.

Scott, James.1990. *Domination and the Arts of Resistance: Hidden Transcripts*. New Haven, Connecticut: Yale University Press.

Sebstad, Jennefer and Monique Cohen. 2000. *Microfinance, Risk Management and Poverty*. Washington, DC: AIMS.

Selvaraj, A. 2014. 'Tamil Nadu Tops Nation in All Woman Police Stations', *The Times of India*, 17 August.

Seth, Mira. 2001. *Women and Development: The Indian Experience*. New Delhi; Thousand Oaks; London: Sage Publications.

Shah, Mihir. 2008. 'Structures of Power in Indian Society: A Response', *Economic and Political Weekly*, 43 (46): 78–83.

Shahjahan, K.M. 1999. 'Priority Sector Bank Lending: How Useful?', *Economic and Political Weekly*, 34 (51): 3572–3574.

Sharma, Aradhana. 2010. *Paradoxes of Empowerment, Development, Gender and Governance in Neoliberal India*. New Delhi: Zubaan.

Sheokand, S.M. 2000. 'Reorienting Banking with the Poor: The SHG-Bank Linkage Way', in Kishanjit Basu and Krishan Jindal (eds.), *Microfinance: Emerging Challenges*, pp. 75–89, New Delhi: Tata McGraw-Hill Publishing Limited.

Shramshakti. 1988. *Report of the National Commission on Self-Employed Women and Women in the Informal Sector*. New Delhi: The Commission.

Shylendra, H.S. and K. Bhirdikar. 2005. ' "Good Governance" and Poverty Alleviation Programmes: A Critical Analysis of SwarnaJayanti Gram Swarozgar Yojana (SGSY)', *International Journal of Rural* Management, 1 (2): 203–221.

Sinha, S. 2000. 'Poverty Reduction through Microfinance', *The Economic Times*, 21 August.

Society for Elimination of Rural Poverty (SERP). n.d. 'About SERP', Indira Kranthi Patham, http://www.serp.ap.gov.in/SHGOLD/aboutus.jsp (accessed on 20 December 2015).

Srinivasan, N. 2009. *Microfinance India State of the Sector Report 2009*. Access Development Services, New Delhi: Sage Publications.

———. 2010. *Microfinance India State of the Sector Report 2010*. Access Development Services, New Delhi: Sage Publications.

Sriram, M.S. and R.S. Upadhyayula. 2004. 'The Transformation of the Microfinance Sector in India: Experiences, Options and Future', *Journal of Microfinance*, 6 (2): 89–112.

Sundar, Aparna and Nandini Sundar. 2012. 'The Habits of the Political Heart: Recovering Politics from Governmentality', in Ajay Gudavarthy (ed.), *Re-Framing Democracy and Agency in India*, pp. 269–288, London, New York and Delhi: Anthem Press.

Surya, D. 2006. 'Did Small Loans Lead to 7 Suicides?' *The Economic Times*, 17 March.

Swain, R.B. and Fen Yang Wallentin. 2009. 'Does Microfinance Empower Women? Evidence from Self-Help Groups in India', *International Journal of Applied Economics*, 23 (5): 541–546.

Swaminathan, Mathura. 1991. 'Segmentation, Collateral Undervaluation and the Rate of Interest in Agrarian Credit Markets: Some Evidence from Two Villages in South India', *Cambridge Journal of Economics*, 15 (2): 161–178.

Tankha, Ajay. 2002. 'Self Help Groups as Financial Intermediaries in India: Cost of Promotion, Sustainability and Impact', A Study Prepared for ICCO and Cordaid, the Netherlands, http://www.sa-dhan.net/Adls/Microfinance/PerspectiveMicrofinance/Self-helpGroupsasFinancial.pdf (accessed on 20 December 2015).

———. 2012. *Banking on Self-Help Groups: Twenty Years On*. New Delhi: Sage Publications and Access Development Services.

Tiwari, P. and S.M. Fahad. n.d. *Concept Paper: Microfinance Institutions in India*. Mumbai: Housing Development Finance Corporation, http://www.gdrc.org/icm/conceptpaper-india.html (accessed on 20 December 2015).

Van Stuijvenberg, Pieter A. 1996. 'Structural Adjustment in India – What about Poverty Alleviation?', in C.H. Hanumantha Rao and Hans Linnemann (eds.), *Economic Reforms and Poverty Alleviation in India*, pp. 31–89, New Delhi: Sage Publications.

Vasavi, A.R. and Catherine P. Kingfisher. 2003. 'Poor Women as Economic Agents', *Indian Journal of Gender Studies*, 10 (1): 1–24.

Venugopal, V. 2014. 'No More Credit Funds to Women Self Help Groups, Will Skill Them and Lend Directly: Government', *The Economic Times*, 11 December.

Von Pischke, J.D. 2003. 'The Evolution of Institutional Issues in Rural Finance: Outreach, Risk Management and Sustainability', Paper Presented at Conference on *Paving the Way Forward: An International*

Conference on Best Practices in Rural Finance, Washington, DC, 2–4 June.

Wallerstein, Immanuel. 2004. *World-Systems Analysis: An Introduction*. Durham and London: Duke University Press.

Weber, Heloise. 2002. 'The Imposition of a Global Development Architecture: The Example of Microcredit', *Review of International Studies*, 28 (3): 537–555.

Wenner, Mark D. 1995. 'Group Credit: A Means to Improve Information Transfer and Loan Repayment Performance', *Journal of Development Studies*, 32 (2): 263–281.

World Bank. 1990. *World Development Report 1990: Poverty*. New York: Oxford University Press.

———. 1991. *Gender and Poverty in India: A World Bank Country Study*. Washington, DC: The World Bank.

———. 2001. *World Development Report 2000/2001: Attacking Poverty*. New York: Oxford University Press.

———. 2015. *India – Andhra Pradesh District Poverty Initiatives Project; and Andhra Pradesh Rural Poverty Reduction Project*. Washington, DC: World Bank Group.

———. 2016. 'India – Orissa Rural Livelihoods Project', Washington D.C: World Bank Group, http://documents.worldbank.org/curated/en/2016/03/26047618/india-orissa-rural-livelihoods-project (accessed on 9 April 2016).

Yunus, Muhammad. 2005. 'Eliminating Poverty through Market-Based Social Entrepreneurship', *Global Urban Development Magazine*, 1 (1): 1–10.

Index